INTERNATIONAL MONEY AND FINANCE

The HarperCollins Series in Economics

Allen
Managerial Economics

Binger/Hoffman
Microeconomics with
Calculus

Bowles/Edwards
Understanding
Capitalism

Branson
Macroeconomic Theory
and Policy

**Browning/Browning
/Zupan**
Microeconomic Theory
and Applications

Burgess
The Economics of
Regulation

Byrns/Stone
Economics

Caniglia
Statistics for Economics

Canterbery
The Literate Economist:
A Brief History of
Economics

Carlton/Perloff
Modern Industrial
Organization

Caves/Frankel/Jones
World Trade and
Payments

Cooter/Ulen
Law and Economics

Ehrenberg/Smith
Modern Labor
Economics

Ekelund/Tollison
Economics

Fusfeld
The Age of the
Economist

Gordon
Macroeconomics

Gregory/Ruffin
Economics

Gregory
Essentials of Economics

Gregory/Stuart
Soviet and Post-Soviet
Economic Structure and
Performance

Hamermesh/Rees
The Economics of Work
and Pay

Hartwick/Olewiler
The Economics of
Natural Resource Use

Hogendorn
Economic Development

Hughes/Cain
American Economic
History

Hunt
History of Economic
Thought

Hunt
Property and Prophets

Husted/Melvin
International Economics

Kohler
Statistics for Business
and Economics

Krugman/Obstfeld
International
Economics: Theory and
Policy

Kwoka/White
The Antitrust
Revolution

Laidler
The Demand for Money

Lardaro
Applied Econometrics

**Lipsey/Courant/Purvis
/Steiner**
Economics

McCafferty
Macroeconomic Theory

McCarty
Dollars and Sense

Melvin
International Money and
Finance

Miller
Economics Today

Miller/Benjamin/North
The Economics of
Public Issues

Miller/Fishe
Microeconomics:
Price Theory in
Practice

Mills/Hamilton
Urban Economics

Mishkin
The Economics of
Money, Banking,
and Financial
Markets

Petersen
Business and
Government

Phelps
Health Economics

Ritter/Silber
Principles of Money,
Banking, and Financial
Markets

Ruffin/Gregory
Principles of
Economics

Ruffin
Intermediate
Microeconomics

Salvatore
Microeconomics

Sargent
Rational Expectations
and Inflation

Schotter
Microeconomics: A
Modern Approach

Studenmund
Using Econometrics

Tietenberg
Environmental and
Natural Resource
Economics

Tietenberg
Environmental
Economics and Policy

Zerbe/Dively
Benefit-Cost Analysis

INTERNATIONAL MONEY AND FINANCE

Fourth Edition

MICHAEL MELVIN

Arizona State University

HarperCollinsCollegePublishers

To My Family

Senior Acquisitions Editor: John Greenman
Project Coordination, Text and Cover Design: York Production Services
Electronic Production Manager: Christine Pearson
Printer and Binder: R.R. Donnelley & Sons Company
Cover Printer: The Lehigh Press, Inc.

International Money and Finance, 4/e

Library of Congress Cataloging-in-Publication Data

Melvin, Michael, 1948-
    International money and finance / Michael Melvin. — 4th ed.
        p.   cm.
    Includes index.
    ISBN 0-673-99207-1
    1. International finance.   I. Title.
HG3881. M443   1995
332'.042—dc20

                                                              94-17773
                                                                 CIP

9 8 7 6 5 4 3 2 1

Contents

3 Past and Present International Monetary Arrangements 45

4 Forward-Looking Market Instruments 73

5 Exchange Rates, Interest Rates, and Interest Parity 89

6 Foreign Exchange Risk and Forecasting 105

Preface

International finance is one of the growth areas of the finance and economics curricula. Today's financial marketplace is truly global. No student of economics or finance can fully understand current developments without some background in international finance. If after studying this text, a student can pick up *The Wall Street Journal* and understand the international financial news, along with its implications, then I feel that I have succeeded as a teacher. To this end, *International Money and Finance* offers a concise yet comprehensive overview of the subject. The basics of the foreign exchange market and the balance of payments are presented, along with accessible discussions of the most recent research findings related to exchange rate determination. Topics covered range from the nitty-gritty of financing international trade to intuitive discussions of overshooting exchange rates and currency substitution.

The first edition of *International Money and Finance* grew from my lecture notes used to teach undergraduate students. The notes, as well as the book, summarized the current literature in international finance, with only elementary math as a prerequisite. It was extremely gratifying to find that instructors at other institutions found the first three editions to be useful texts for undergraduate and MBA students. In fact, the adoption list ranged from the leading MBA schools in the country to small rural four-year colleges. The fact that the text proved successful with students of varying abilities and backgrounds was a feature that I strived to retain in preparing this fourth edition.

The fourth edition has been written in the same spirit as the first three—to provide a concise survey of international finance suitable for undergraduate and MBA classes.

ACKNOWLEDGMENTS

I am grateful to all who offered comments leading to the revision of *International Money and Finance.* They include countless former students and instructors at other institutions who provided informal comments on style and content. The third edition was reviewed by Mamadon K. Diallo of East Stroudsburg University, B.D. Elzas of Erasmus University, Judy L. Klein of Mary Baldwin College, Vibhas Madan of Drexel University, Kiminori Matsuyama of Northwestern University, Thomas Russell of Santa Clara University, Larry J. Sechrest of Sul Ross State University, Robert Sedgwich of Sheffield Hallam University, and Darrel Young of St. Edward's University. The second edition was formally reviewed by Carl Beidleman of Lehigh University, Glenn W. Boyle of Louisiana State University, David Ding of Memphis State University, Chen Jia-sheng of the University of Denver, Francis A. Lees of St. Johns University, and Chu-Ping Vijverberg of the University of Texas at Dallas. In addition, formal reviews of the first edition were provided by Robert Flood of Northwestern University, Samuel Katz of Georgetown University, Donald P. Stegall of California State University at Fresno, and Clas Wihlborg of the University of Southern California. While I could not incorporate all of their thoughtful suggestions, I appreciate their comments and have no doubt that the text has been much improved by their reviews.

I must also acknowledge the executive economics editor at HarperCollins. I cannot imagine an editor easier to work with than Jack Greenman. Finally, I welcome comments and criticism from users of the fourth edition of *International Money and Finance.* My hope is that the book will evolve over time to best suit your needs.

MICHAEL MELVIN

To the Student

WHY STUDY INTERNATIONAL FINANCE?

Why study the subject of international money and finance? One reason is that career goals are paramount to many people, and in this regard the topic of the text is related to a growth area in the labor market. This book provides a background in international finance for those who expect to obtain jobs created by international investment, international banking, and multinational business activity.

Other readers may have a more scholarly concern with "rounding out" their economic education by studying the international relationships between financial markets and institutions. Although a course in principles of economics is the only prerequisite assumed for this text, many students may have already taken intermediate macroeconomics, money and banking, or essentials of finance courses. But for those interested in international economic relationships, such courses may often lack a global orientation. The economic models and discussions of the typical money and banking course focus on the *closed economy,* closed in the sense that the interrelationships with the rest of the world are ignored. Here we study the institutions and analysis of an integrated world financial community, thus giving a better understanding of the world in which we live. We will learn that there are constraints as well as opportunities facing the business firm, government, and the individual investor that become apparent only in a worldwide setting.

FINANCE AND THE MULTINATIONAL FIRM

A *multinational firm* is a firm with operations that extend beyond its domestic national borders. Such firms have become increasingly sophisti-
cated in international financial dealings as international business poses
risk and return opportunities that are not present in purely domestic
business operations. A U.S. multinational firm may have accounts
payable and receivable that are denominated in U.S. dollars, Japanese
yen, British pounds, Mexican pesos, Canadian dollars, and German
marks. The financial managers of this firm face a different set of problems than the managers of a firm doing business strictly in dollars. It
may be true that "a dollar is a dollar," but the dollar value of yen, marks,
or pesos can and does change over time. As the dollar value of the yen
changes, the value of yen-denominated contracts will change when evaluated in terms of dollars.

Multinational finance responds to this new set of challenges with a
tool kit of techniques and market instruments used to maximize the return on the firm's investment subject to an acceptable level of risk.
Once we extend beyond the domestic economy, a rich variety of business opportunities exists that must be utilized with the appropriate financial arrangements. This book intends to cover many aspects of these
international financial transactions that the financial manager may encounter.

The financial side of international business differs from the study
of international trade commonly encountered in international economics courses. Courses in international trade study the determinants of the
pattern and volume of world trade—formally referred to as the theory
of *comparative advantage*. If country A produces and exports shoes in
exchange for country B's food, we say that A has a comparative advantage in shoes and B has a comparative advantage in food. Besides comparative advantage, such courses also examine the movement of factors
of production, labor, and capital goods between nations. Obviously,
these subjects are important and deserve careful study, but our purpose
is to study the monetary consequences of such trade. Although we will
not explicitly consider any theories of comparative advantage—such
theories are usually developed without referring to the use of money—
we will often consider the impact of monetary events on trade in real
goods and services. Our discussions range from the effects of the currency used in pricing international trade (Chapter 9) to financing trade
in the offshore banking industry (Chapter 13). We will find that monetary events can have real consequences for the volume and pattern of
international trade.

THE ACTORS

This course is not simply a study of abstract theories concerning the international consequences of changes in money supply or demand, prices, interest rates, or exchange rates. We also discuss the role and importance of the institutional and individual participants. Most people tend to think immediately of large commercial banks as holding the starring role in the international monetary scene. Because the foreign exchange market is a market where huge sums of national currencies are bought and sold through commercial banks, any text on international finance will include many examples and instances in which such banks play a major part. In fact, Chapter 1 begins with a discussion of the role of banks in the foreign exchange market.

Besides commercial banks, business firms play a key part in our discussion, since the goods and services they buy and sell internationally effect a need for financing such trade. The corporate treasurer of any multinational firm is well versed in foreign exchange trading and hedging and international investment opportunities. What is hedging? How are international investment opportunities related to domestic opportunities? These are subjects we address in Chapters 4 and 5.

Finally, we examine the role of government. Central banks, such as the Federal Reserve in the United States, are often important actors in our story. Besides their roles of buying, selling, lending, and borrowing internationally, they also act to restrict the freedom of the other actors. The policies of central governments and central banks are crucial to understanding the actual operation of the international monetary system, and each chapter will address the impact of government on the topic being described.

PLAN OF ATTACK

This book can be thought of in terms of three main sections. Chapters 1 through 8 identify the key institutions and relationships of the international monetary system. To aid our understanding of the relationships among prices, exchange rates, and interest rates, we will consider existing theories, as well as the current state of research that illuminates their validity. For those students who choose to proceed professionally in the field of international finance, the study of this text should provide both a good reference and a springboard to more advanced work—and ultimately employment.

Chapters 9 and 10 cover the next general area of the determinants of balance of payments and exchange rates. Government and industry de-

vote many resources in trying to forecast the balance of payments and exchange rates. The discussion in these chapters includes the most important recent developments. Although there is some disagreement among economists regarding the relative significance of competing theories, as far as possible in an intermediate-level presentation, the theories are evaluated in light of research evidence. Altogether, these chapters present a detailed summary of the current state of knowledge regarding the determinants of the balance of payments and exchange rates.

Chapters 11 through 13 are devoted to applied topics of interest to the international financial manager. Issues range from the "nuts and bolts" of financing imports and exports to the evaluation of risk in international lending to sovereign governments. The topics covered in these chapters are of practical interest to corporate treasurers and international bankers.

The concluding chapter is an analysis of macroeconomic issues in an open economy. This coverage of open-economy macroeconomics includes the determination of the equilibrium values of key macroeconomic variables and the effects of government monetary and fiscal policy on these variables.

At the beginning of this introduction we asked: Why study international money and finance? It is hoped that the brief preview provided here will have motivated you to answer this question. International finance is not a dull "ivory tower" subject to be tolerated or avoided if possible. Instead, it is a subject that involves dynamic real-world events. Since the material covered in this book is emphasized daily in the newspapers and other media, you will soon find that the pages in *International Money and Finance* seem to come to life. To this end, a daily reading of the *Wall Street Journal* or London *Financial Times* makes an excellent supplement for the text material. As you progress through the book, international financial news will become more and more meaningful and useful. For the many users of this text who do not go on to a career in international finance, the major lasting benefit of the lessons contained here will be the ability to understand the international financial news intelligently and effectively.

M.M.

chapter *1*

The Foreign Exchange Market

Foreign exchange trading refers to trading one country's money for that of another country. The need for such trade arises because of tourism, the buying and selling of goods internationally, or investment occurring across international boundaries. The kind of money specifically traded takes the form of bank deposits or bank transfers of deposits denominated in foreign currency. The *foreign exchange market,* as we usually think of it, refers to large commercial banks in financial centers, such as New York or London, that trade foreign-currency-denominated deposits with each other. Actual *bank notes* like dollar bills are relatively unimportant insofar as they rarely physically cross international borders. In general, only tourism or illegal activities would lead to the international movement of bank notes.

SPOT RATES

Figure 1.1 shows foreign *exchange rate* quotations for a particular day. An exchange rate is the price of one money in terms of another. In the figure we see that on Thursday, September 23, 1993, French francs were selling for $0.17487. Note that this exchange rate is quoted at a specific time, 3 P.M., since rates will change throughout the day as supply and demand for the currencies change. Notice also that these exchange rates are quotes based on large trades ($1 million or more), in what is essentially a wholesale market for money. The smaller the quantity of foreign exchange

1

purchased, the higher the price. For instance, if you were a U.S. importer buying wine from France at the dollar price of $10,000, your local bank would sell $10,000 worth of francs for more than $0.17487 per franc. Suppose the bank charges $0.200 per franc. You would then buy FF50,000 ($10,000/$0.200) to settle the account with the French exporter. An individual buying even smaller amounts of francs would pay a higher rate still.

In the example just considered, the U.S. importer found that $10,000 was equivalent in value to FF50,000. We calculated this by dividing the total dollar value of the purchase ($10,000) by the dollar price of 1 franc ($0.200). Note that the foreign exchange quotations also list quotes in terms of foreign currency units per dollar. In Figure 1.1 we see that on Thursday, September 23, the French franc sold for $0.17487. By looking farther to the right, we also see that on Thursday, the dollar was worth FF5.8279. It will always be true that, when we know the dollar price of the franc ($/FF), we can find the franc price of the dollar by taking the reciprocal (FF/$). Of course, this relationship works in the opposite direction as well. If the franc price of the dollar is FF5.8279, then the dollar price of the franc is found as the reciprocal (1/5.8279 = 0.17487). In the example of the U.S. wine importer, if the bank is selling francs for $0.200, then what is the implied franc price of the dollar? To find this we simply calculate the reciprocal: 1/0.200 = FF5.00. Had we initially been given the exchange rate quote in terms of francs per dollar, we could have found the franc equivalent of $10,000 by multiplying $10,000 by the franc price of 1 dollar: 10,000 × 5.00 = FF50,000. The importer buys this quantity of francs from the bank and actually pays for the wine with a check drawn on the bank (or a foreign associate of the bank).

Note that the exchange rate quotes in Figure 1.1 are selling rates. Banks bid to buy foreign exchange at lower rates, and the difference between selling and buying rates is called the *spread*. Table 1.1 lists the spreads at the close of business on Thursday, September 23, in London. We see that at the time the London market closed, the franc price a bank would pay for dollars was FF5.7250 per dollar. Dollars would be sold for francs by the bank at FF5.7300 per dollar. This spread of less than $1/10$ of 1 percent [(5.7300 − 5.7250)/5.7250 = 0.0009] is indicative of the normal spread in the market for major traded currencies. The existing

EXCHANGE RATES
Thursday, September 23, 1993
The New York foreign exchange selling rates below apply to trading among banks in amounts of $1 million and more, as quoted at 3 p.m. Eastern time by Bankers Trust Co., Telerate and other sources. Retail transactions provide fewer units of foreign currency per dollar.

Country	U.S. $ equiv.		Currency per U.S. $	
	Thurs.	Wed.	Thurs.	Wed.
Argentina (Peso)	1.01	1.01	.99	.99
Australia (Dollar)	.6543	.6555	1.5284	1.5256
Austria (Schilling)	.08648	.08727	11.56	11.46
Bahrain (Dinar)	2.6536	2.6536	.3769	.3769
Belgium (Franc)	.02855	.02871	35.03	34.83
Brazil (Cruzeiro real)	.0088067	.0089234	113.55	111.94
Britain (Pound)	1.5060	1.5178	.6640	.6588
30-Day Forward	1.5025	1.5142	.6656	.6604
90-Day Forward	1.4956	1.5074	.6686	.6634
180-Day Forward	1.4878	1.4995	.6721	.6669
Canada (Dollar)	.7561	.7580	1.3226	1.3193
30-Day Forward	.7552	.7571	1.3242	1.3209
90-Day Forward	.7530	.7550	1.3280	1.3245
180-Day Forward	.7498	.7517	1.3337	1.3303
Czech. Rep. (Koruna)				
Commercial rate	.0353357	.0356888	28.3000	28.0200
Chile (Peso)	.002516	.002523	397.49	396.42
China (Renminbi)	.174856	.174856	5.7190	5.7190
Colombia (Peso)	.001453	.001451	688.29	689.25
Denmark (Krone)	.1508	.1509	6.6315	6.6264
Ecuador (Sucre)				
Floating rate	.000525	.000525	1904.00	1904.00
Finland (Markka)	.17159	.17095	5.8279	5.8496
France (Franc)	.17487	.17632	5.7185	5.6715
30-Day Forward	.17425	.17568	5.7389	5.6921
90-Day Forward	.17309	.17449	5.7774	5.7310
180-Day Forward	.17184	.17330	5.8195	5.7705
Germany (Mark)	.6085	.6141	1.6435	1.6285
30-Day Forward	.6065	.6121	1.6487	1.6338
90-Day Forward	.6031	.6086	1.6580	1.6432
180-Day Forward	.5992	.6049	1.6685	1.6533
Greece (Drachma)	.004233	.004281	236.25	233.60
Hong Kong (Dollar)	.12921	.12925	7.7395	7.7370
Hungary (Forint)	.0109075	.0109878	91.6800	91.0100
India (Rupee)	.03212	.03212	31.13	31.13
Indonesia (Rupiah)	.0004757	.0004757	2102.21	2102.21
Ireland (Punt)	1.4217	1.4341	.7034	.6973
Israel (Shekel)	.3591	.3598	2.7846	2.7797
Italy (Lira)	.0006291	.0006344	1589.50	1576.32
Japan (Yen)	.009438	.009416	105.95	106.20
30-Day Forward	.009442	.009420	105.91	106.15
90-Day Forward	.009453	.009431	105.79	106.03
180-Day Forward	.009477	.009455	105.52	105.76
Jordan (Dinar)	1.4810	1.4810	.6752	.6752
Kuwait (Dinar)	3.3400	3.3400	.2994	.2994
Lebanon (Pound)	.000580	.000580	1724.50	1724.50
Malaysia (Ringgit)	.3917	.3922	2.5530	2.5496
Malta (Lira)	2.6560	2.6560	.3765	.3765
Mexico (Peso)				
Floating rate	.3219575	.3219575	3.1060	3.1060
Netherland (Guilder)	.5419	.5468	1.8453	1.8289
New Zealand (Dollar)	.5540	.5548	1.8051	1.8025
Norway (Krone)	.1396	.1408	7.1632	7.1035
Pakistan (Rupee)	.0336	.0336	29.78	29.78
Peru (New Sol)	.4919	.4955	2.03	2.02
Philippines (Peso)	.03592	.03593	27.83	27.83
Poland (Zloty)	.00005297	.00005304	18879.00	18854.00
Portugal (Escudo)	.005950	.006001	168.08	166.63
Saudi Arabia (Riyal)	.26665	.26665	3.7503	3.7503
Singapore (Dollar)	.6275	.6276	1.5935	1.5934
Slovak Rep. (Koruna)	.0310945	.0312891	32.1600	31.9600
South Africa (Rand)				
Commercial rate	.2917	.2919	3.4285	3.4253
Financial rate	.2191	.2155	4.5650	4.6400
South Korea (Won)	.0012362	.0012350	808.90	809.70
Spain (Peseta)	.007612	.007685	131.36	130.12
Sweden (Krona)	.1240	.1231	8.0614	8.1221
Switzerland (Franc)	.6979	.7036	1.4328	1.4213
30-Day Forward	.6970	.7026	1.4348	1.4233
90-Day Forward	.6954	.7009	1.4381	1.4267
180-Day Forward	.6938	.6994	1.4413	1.4298
Taiwan (Dollar)	.037538	.037594	26.64	26.60
Thailand (Baht)	.03975	.03975	25.16	25.16
Turkey (Lira)	.0000839	.0000841	11918.00	11891.00
United Arab (Dirham)	.2723	.2723	3.6725	3.6725
Uruguay (New Peso)				
Financial	.233863	.233863	4.28	4.28
Venezuela (Bolivar)				
Floating rate	.01046	.01047	95.64	95.54
SDR	1.41366	1.41204	.70738	.70820
ECU	1.16050	1.16920		

Special Drawing Rights (SDR) are based on exchange rates for the U.S., German, British, French and Japanese currencies. Source: International Monetary Fund.
European Currency Unit (ECU) is based on a basket of community currencies.

FIGURE 1.1 Foreign exchange rate quotations for September 23, 1993.
Source: The Wall Street Journal, September 24, 1993, p. C13. Reprinted by permission of the *The Wall Street Journal,* © 1993, Dow Jones and Company, Inc. All rights reserved worldwide.

spread in any currency will vary according to the individual currency trader, the currency being traded, and the trading bank's overall view of conditions in the foreign exchange market. The spread quoted will tend to increase for more thinly traded currencies (i.e., currencies that do not generate a large volume of trading) or when the bank perceives that the risks associated with trading in a currency at a particular time are rising.

Table 1.1   LONDON CLOSING SPREADS, SEPTEMBER 23, 1993

United Kingdom[a]	1,5055–1,5065
Ireland[a]	1.4200–1.4210
Canada	1.3230–1.3240
Netherlands	1.8460–1.8470
Belgium	34.90–35.00
Denmark	6.6400–6.6450
Germany	1.6445–1.6455
Portugal	167.60–167.70
Spain	131.15–131.25
Italy	1590.75–1591.25
Norway	7.1550–7.1600
France	5.7250–5.7300
Sweden	8.0550–8.0600
Japan	105.95–106.05
Austria	11.5575–11.5625
Switzerland	1.4340–1.4350

[a] Quotes for the United Kingdom and Ireland are in terms of U.S. dollars per British pound and Irish punt. All other quotes are domestic currency units per U.S. dollar.
Data are from the *Financial Times,* September 24, 1993, p. 36.

The large trading banks like Citibank or Bank of America stand ready to "make a market" in a currency by offering buy (bid) and sell (ask) rates on request. Actually, currency traders do not quote all the numbers indicated in Table 1.1. For instance, the table lists the spread on Canadian dollars as Can$1.3230 to Can$1.3240. In practice, this spread is quoted as Can$1.3230–40 or, in words, the Canadian dollar per U.S. dollar rate is one-thirty-two-thirty to forty. The listener then recognizes that the bank is willing to bid Can$1.3230 to buy U.S. dollars and will sell U.S. dollars at Can$1.3240.

Thus far, we have discussed trading French francs and Canadian dollars using the symbols FF and Can$, respectively. Table 1.2 lists the commonly used symbols for several currencies. Exchange rate quotations are generally available for all countries where currencies may be freely traded. In the cases where free markets are not permitted, the state typically conducts all foreign exchange trading at an official exchange rate, regardless of current market conditions.

Table 1.2 INTERNATIONAL CURRENCY SYMBOLS

Country	Currency	Symbol
Australia	Dollar	A$
Austria	Schilling	Sch
Belgium	Franc	BF
Canada	Dollar	Can$
Denmark	Krone	DKr
Finland	Markka	FM
France	Franc	FF
Germany	Deutsche mark	DM
Greece	Drachma	Dr
India	Rupee	Rs
Iran	Rial	RI
Italy	Lira	Lit
Japan	Yen	¥
Kuwait	Dinar	KD
Mexico	Peso	Ps
Netherlands	Guilder	FL
Norway	Krone	NKr
Saudi Arabia	Riyal	SR
Singapore	Dollar	S$
South Africa	Rand	R
Spain	Peseta	Pts
Sweden	Kronar	SKr
Switzerland	Franc	SF
United Kingdom	Pound	£
United States	Dollar	$

So far we have been discussing the buying and selling of foreign exchange to be delivered on the spot (actually, deposits traded in the foreign exchange market generally take two working days to clear); this is called the *spot market*. In our example of the U.S. wine importer, the importer wanted to buy $10,000 worth of francs for current payment. If the importer purchases the francs in the spot market today, in two days the bank will reduce the importer's checking account balance by $10,000 and wire the FF50,000 to be drawn on a French bank by the exporter (for relatively small transactions, the two-day delay may not be necessary).

In Chapter 4 we will consider the important issues that arise when the trade contract involves payment at a future date. First, however, we should consider in more detail the nature of the foreign exchange market.

ARBITRAGE

The foreign exchange market is a market where price information is readily available by telephone or computer networks. Since currencies are homogeneous goods (a dollar is a dollar regardless of where it is traded), it is very easy to compare prices in different markets. Exchange rates tend to be equal worldwide. If this were not so, there would be profit opportunities for simultaneously buying a currency in one market while selling in another. This activity, known as *arbitrage,* would raise the exchange rate in the market where it is too low, because this is the market in which you would buy, and the increased demand for the currency would result in a higher price. The market where the exchange rate is too high is one in which you sell, and this increased selling activity would result in a lower price. Arbitrage would continue until the exchange rates in different locales are so close that it is not worth the costs incurred from any further buying and selling. When this situation occurs, we say that the rates are "transaction costs close." Any remaining deviation between exchange rates will not cover the costs of additional arbitrage transactions, so the arbitrage activity ends.

For instance, suppose Citibank is quoting the German mark/U.S. dollar exchange rate as 1.6445–55 and Dresdner Bank in Frankfurt is quoting 1.6425–35. This means that Citibank will buy dollars for 1.6445 marks and will sell dollars for 1.6455 marks. Dresdner will buy dollars for 1.6425 marks and will sell dollars for 1.6435 marks. This presents an arbitrage opportunity. We could buy $10 million at Dresdner's ask price of 1.6435 and simultaneously sell $10 million to Citibank at their bid price of 1.6445 marks. This would earn a profit of DM0.0010 marks per dollar traded, or DM10,000 would be the total arbitrage profit.

If such a profit opportunity existed, the demand to buy dollars from Dresdner would cause them to raise their ask price above 1.6435, while the increased interest in selling dollars to Citibank at

their bid price of 1.6445 marks would cause them to lower their bid. In this way, arbitrage activity pushes the prices of different traders to levels where no arbitrage profits are earned. Suppose the prices moved to where Citibank is quoting the mark/dollar exchange rate at 1.6440–50 and Dresdner is quoting 1.6430–40. Now there is no arbitrage profit possible. The ask price at Dresdner of 1.6440 is equal to the bid price at Citibank. The difference between the bid and ask prices of each bank are equal to the spreads of DM0.001. In the wholesale banking foreign exchange market, the bid-ask spread is the only transaction cost. Therefore, when the quotes of two different banks differ by no more than the spread being quoted in the market by these banks, there is no arbitrage opportunity.

Arbitrage could involve more than two currencies. When we consider that the bulk of foreign exchange trading involves the U.S. dollar, we note the role of comparing dollar exchange rates for different currencies to determine if the implied third exchange rates are in line. Since banks quote foreign exchange rates with respect to the dollar (the dollar is said to be the "numeraire" of the system), such comparisons are readily made. For instance, if we know the dollar price of pounds ($/£) and the dollar price of marks ($/DM), we can infer the corresponding pound price of marks (£/DM). From now on we will explicitly write the units of our exchange rates to avoid the confusion that can easily arise. For instance, $/£ = $2.00 is the exchange rate in terms of dollars per pound.

To simplify the analysis of arbitrage involving three currencies, let's temporarily ignore the bid-ask spread and assume that we can either buy or sell at one price. Suppose that in London $/£ = $2.00, while in New York $/DM =$0.40. The corresponding *cross rate* is the £/DM rate. Simple algebra shows that, if $/£ = $2.00 and $/DM = 0.40, then £/DM = ($/DM)/($/£) = 0.40/2.00 = 0.2. If we observe a market where one of the three exchange rates—$/£, $/DM, £/DM—is out of line with the other two, there is an arbitrage opportunity. Suppose that in Frankfurt the exchange rate £/DM = 0.2, while in New York $/DM = 0.40 but in London $/£ = $1.90. Astute traders in the foreign exchange market would observe the discrepancy, and quick action would be rewarded. The trader could start with dollars and buy £1 million in London for $1.9 million since $/£ = $1.90. The pounds could be used to buy

marks at £/DM = 0.2, so that £1,000,000 = DM5,000,000. The DM5 million could then be used in New York to buy dollars at $/DM = $0.40, so that DM5,000,000 = $2,000,000. Thus the initial $1.9 million could be turned into $2 million with the *triangular arbitrage* action earning the trader $100,000 (costs associated with the transaction should be deducted to arrive at the true arbitrage profit).

As in the case of the two-currency arbitrage covered earlier, a valuable product of this arbitrage activity is the return of the exchange rates to internationally consistent levels. If the initial discrepancy was that the dollar price of pounds was too low in London, the selling of dollars for pounds in London by the arbitragers will make pounds more expensive, raising the price from $/£ = $1.90 back to $2.00. (Actually, the rate would not return to $2.00, because the activity in the other markets will tend to raise the pound price of marks and lower the dollar price of marks, so that a dollar price of pounds between $1.90 and $2.00 will allow a new equilibrium among the three currencies.)

Table 1.3 gives the cross rates for several currencies in New York on September 23, 1993. Effective arbitrage will ensure that by knowing any two exchange rates, we will be able to infer a third. For instance, we find that £/$ = 0.664 by looking across the U.S.$ row for the £ column, which happens to be the first column. To find the pound price of marks, we glance across the DM row for the £ column and notice that £/DM = 0.404; the implied cross rate for $/DM is determined by division: $/DM = (£/DM)/(£/$) = 0.404/0.664 = 0.608. We can look at the DM row and the $ column to see the cross rate of 0.608.

Table 1.3 FOREIGN EXCHANGE CROSS RATES, SEPTEMBER 23, 1993

	£	$	DM	¥
U.K pound (£)	1	1.505	2.473	159
U.S. dollar ($)	0.664	1	1.643	105
German mark (DM)	0.404	0.608	1	64
Japanese yen (¥)	0.006	0.009	0.015	1000

Note: Exchange rates are units of the currency listed in the top row per unit of the currency listed in the left-hand column.
Data are from Telerate.

Since there is active trading between the dollar or pound and many currencies, we can look to any two exchange rates involving dollars or pounds to infer the cross rates. So even if there is limited trading directly between, for instance, Belgian francs and yen, by using £/BF and £/¥ or $/BF and $/¥, we can find the implied BF/¥ rate. The depth of foreign exchange trading that involves dollars often makes it cheaper to go through dollars to get from some currency X to another currency Y when X and Y are not widely traded, since transaction costs are higher for lightly traded currencies. Thus, if a business firm in small country X wants to buy currency Y to pay for merchandise imports from small country Y, it may well be cheaper to sell X for dollars and then use dollars to buy Y rather than try to trade currency X for currency Y directly.

Although arbitrage will tend to equalize exchange rate quotes worldwide, we must remember that the different financial centers operate in different time zones. Therefore, it only makes sense to compare quotations at a time when the markets overlap. As Figure 1.2 indicates, we could not compare $/£ quotes in Chicago at 3 P.M. with London because the London market is closed by then. Figure 1.2 illustrates the 24-hour dimension of the foreign exchange market. We can determine the hours of major trading activity in each location by the country bars at the top of the figure. Time is measured as Greenwich Mean Time (GMT). The small clocks by each city indicate the local market time. For instance, the Singapore market may have active foreign exchange trading from 7:30 A.M. to 6:30 P.M. local time. The unshaded area of the clock indicates the local peak trading hours. The London market is active from 0830 (8:30 A.M., London time) to 1630 (4:30 P.M., London time). The New York market is active from 1300 (8:00 A.M., New York time) to 2000 (3:00 P.M., New York time). There is a 3 ½ hour overlap between the two markets. In a similar manner, we can determine the hours during which other trading centers are open simultaneously.

CENTRAL BANK INTERVENTION

Thus far we have not explicitly introduced government into the foreign exchange market, but of course, central banks and national treasuries play a large role in the market. Since the exchange rate is the price of one money in terms of another, changes in exchange rates will affect the prices of goods and services traded internation-

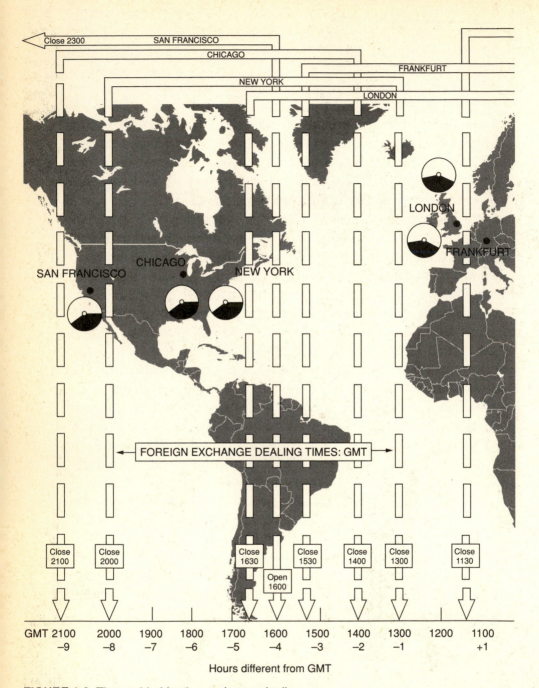

FIGURE 1.2 The world of foreign exchange dealing.
(*Source: Euromoney,* April 1979, p. 14.)

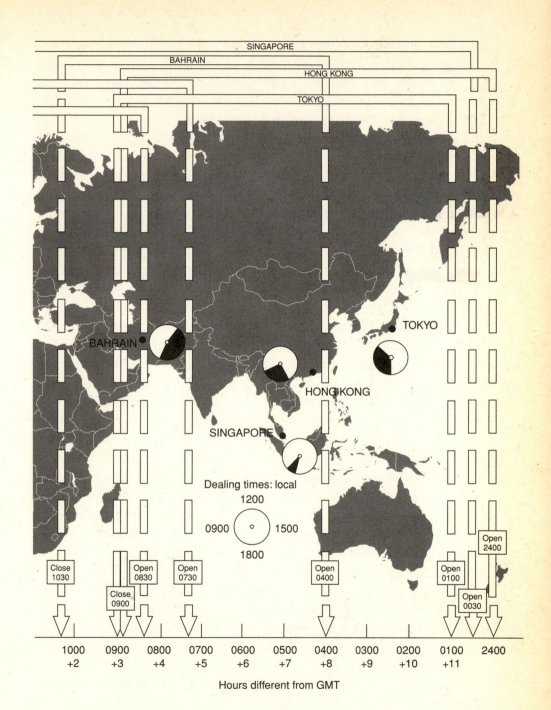

SINGAPORE

BAHRAIN

HONG KONG

TOKYO

BAHRAIN

TOKYO

HONG KONG

SINGAPORE

Dealing times: local

1200

0900 ⊙ 1500

1800

Close
1030

Close
0900

Open
0830

Open
0730

Open
0400

Open
0100

Open
2400

Open
0030

| 1000 | 0900 | 0800 | 0700 | 0600 | 0500 | 0400 | 0300 | 0200 | 0100 | 2400 |
| +2 | +3 | +4 | +5 | +6 | +7 | +8 | +9 | +10 | +11 | |

Hours different from GMT

ally and account for the official intervention in the foreign exchange market. Central banks such as the Federal Reserve in the United States buy and sell currencies to drive the value of their money to levels other than what the free market would establish. For instance, if the dollar per pound exchange rate is $/£ = $1.80, and then for some reason the pound begins to appreciate against the dollar, U.S. imports from England would become more expensive. This is clearly seen if we assume that the exchange rate has changed from $/£ = 1.80 to $/£ = 1.90. A product selling for £100 in England would find its dollar price in the United States changing from $180 to $190. To help stimulate U.K exports, the Bank of England may desire to halt the appreciation of the pound by selling pounds on the foreign exchange market. As the supply of pounds to the market increases, the price of pounds tends to fall, just as an increase in the supply of apples lowers the price of apples.

In the case of a depreciating domestic currency, central banks often sell foreign currencies in exchange for domestic currency to halt the depreciation. Because they often do not hold sufficient stocks of the desired foreign currencies, swap arrangements are used as an efficient way to borrow from foreign official institutions. The Federal Reserve has established line-of-swap arrangements with other institutions that may be drawn upon when the need arises. Table 1.4 indicates the magnitude of these arrangements. Any sizable central bank interventions in the foreign exchange market will involve either the Federal Reserve or a foreign central bank drawing currency balances from the swap facility, which are then replenished at a later date after the value of the currency has stabilized.

Official institutions appear in the foreign exchange markets for reasons other than intervening in the determination of exchange rates. In the course of the normal operations of government it is often necessary to use the foreign exchange market to facilitate the transfer of goods and services internationally. The role of the various central banks is to conduct foreign exchange operations for central governments.

One of the most notable foreign exchange events of recent years involved a coordinated intervention policy among the "Group of 5" (G5) countries—the United States, Japan, the former West Germany, France, and the United Kingdom—made in September 1985. Viewed by many as a response to large U.S. trade deficits, a joint policy aimed at reducing the dollar's foreign exchange value was announced on

Table 1.4 FEDERAL RESERVE RECIPROCAL CURRENCY ARRANGEMENTS
Millions of Dollars

Institution	Amount of facility
Austrian National Bank	250
National Bank of Belgium	1,000
Bank of Canada	2,000
National Bank of Denmark	250
Bank of England	3,000
Bank of France	2,000
German Federal Bank	6,000
Bank of Italy	3,000
Bank of Japan	5,000
Bank of Mexico	700
Netherlands Bank	500
Bank of Norway	250
Bank of Sweden	300
Swiss National Bank	4,000
Bank for international settlements	
Dollars against Swiss francs	600
Dollars against other authorized European currencies	1,250
Total	30,100

September 22, 1985. Since the early Reagan years had been a time when the U.S. Treasury followed a policy of free-market-determined exchange rates with no intervention, the G5 announcement was viewed as a major policy change. Even before any official sales of dollars, the dollar started to depreciate as market participants reacted to the announcement by selling dollars. Figure 1.3 displays the average value of the dollar relative to the other major currencies over the period from 1983 to 1985. The dollar had fallen in value starting in March 1985, but began to strengthen in September. Following the G5 announcement on September 22, the dollar fell rapidly, because of both private and official sales of dollars. The U.S. Treasury and Federal Reserve sold more than $3 billion during this period, and the central banks of France, Germany, Japan, and the United Kingdom combined sold approximately $5 billion.

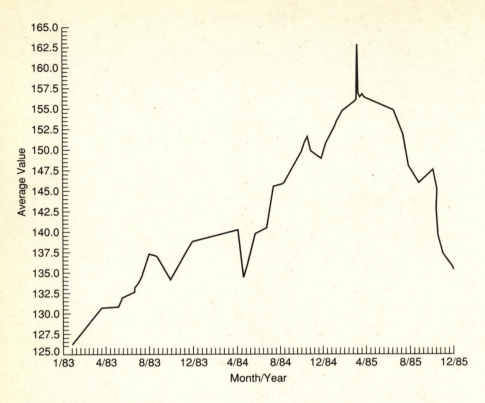

FIGURE 1.3 Average value of the dollar around G5 intervention. This is the index value of the dollar as computed by the IMF (International Money Fund) multilateral exchange rate model.
(*Source:* International Financial Statistics data bank.)

Central bank intervention is rarely as dramatic as the September 1985 action. Typically, the central bank's activities are not known because they are conducted in a secretive manner. While central banks have the ability to influence foreign exchange rates, this ability comes largely through making policy announcements to change private market behavior. The central banks command large resources, but when $1 trillion a day are traded in the foreign exchange market, it takes a huge commitment of central bank resources to change the direction of a currency by simply buying or selling without an accompanying policy signal to the financial community. The central bank is able to get maximum "bang per buck" by making its current policies known to the public. If private traders believe that the central bank is supporting a currency depreciation, they will be more reluctant to bet on an appreciation.

BLACK MARKETS AND PARALLEL MARKETS

So far, we have discussed the foreign exchange market as a market where currencies are bought and sold openly by individuals, business firms, and governments. For the major developed countries, this is an accurate description. However, developing countries generally do not permit free markets in foreign exchange and impose many restrictions on foreign currency transactions. These restrictions take many forms, such as government licensing requirements, limited amounts of foreign currency that may be purchased, a limited time following the receipt of foreign currency before it must be sold to the central bank, or even outright prohibitions of foreign currency use by private concerns.

As a result of government restrictions or legal prohibitions on foreign exchange transactions, illegal markets in foreign exchange develop to satisfy trader demand. These illegal markets are known as *black markets*. In many countries such illegal markets exist openly with little or no government enforcement of legal prohibitions. In other countries, foreign exchange laws are strictly enforced and lawbreakers receive harsh sentences when caught.

Often the government sets an official exchange rate that deviates widely from what the free market would establish. If the government will purchase foreign exchange only at the official rate but private citizens are willing to pay the market-determined rate, there will be a steady supply of foreign exchange to the black market. Obviously, government policy creates the black market. The demand arises because of legal restrictions on buying foreign exchange, and the supply exists because of government-mandated official exchange rates that offer less than the free market. Ironically, governments defend the need for foreign exchange restrictions based on conserving scarce foreign exchange for high-priority uses. But such restrictions work to reduce the amount of foreign exchange that flows to the government as traders turn to the black market instead.

In many countries facing economic hardship, the illegal markets have allowed normal economic activities to continue through a steady supply of foreign exchange. Some governments have unofficially acknowledged the benefits of a black market by allowing the market to exist openly. For instance, Guatemala had an artificially low official exchange rate of one quetzale per dollar for more than

three decades; however, a black market was allowed to flourish openly in front of the country's main post office where the exchange rate fluctuates daily with market conditions. In many Latin American countries, the post office is a center for black market trading since relatives living in the United States send millions of dollars in checks and money orders home. In Guatemala, the government allows such open activity, and foreign currency traders often call to people leaving the post office offering to buy dollars. This sort of government-tolerated alternative to the official exchange market is referred to as a *parallel market.*

Mexico has had a thriving parallel market during times of crisis when the official peso/dollar exchange rate has varied greatly from the market rate. For instance, in mid-August 1982, the Mexican government banned the sale of dollars by Mexican banks. Immediately, the parallel market responded. The official exchange rate was 69.5 pesos per dollar, but the rate on the street ranged from 120 to 150 as the parallel market demand increased with the ban on bank sales. Private currency trades between individuals were legal, so trading flourished at the Mexico City airport and other public places.

While many other anecdotes could be included, the point is that foreign exchange trading has a dimension beyond the open trading and single exchange rate that exist for the major developed countries. In developing countries, foreign exchange transactions are generally strictly regulated activities. In many countries, the official exchange rate has no relation to current economic reality, so we should expect black markets or parallel markets to flourish.

FOREIGN EXCHANGE TRADING VOLUME

The foreign exchange market is the largest financial market in the world. In April 1992, the Bank for International Settlements (BIS) conducted a survey of trading volume around the world and found that the average amount of currency traded each business day was $880 billion. The average size of individual trades reported by dealers in the United States was $6 million. In terms of individual currencies, the U.S. dollar is by far the most important currency, being involved in over 80 percent of all trades. Since foreign exchange trading involves pairs of currencies, it is useful to know which currency pairs dominate the market.

Table 1.5 reports the share of spot market activity taken by different currencies. The largest volume occurs in dollar/mark trading,

Table 1.5 THE SHARE OF FOREIGN EXCHANGE TRADING VOLUME BY CURRENCY PAIRS (SPOT TRANSACTIONS)

Currency pair	Percent of total
U.S. dollar/German mark	29.6
U.S. dollar/Japanese yen	15.7
U.S. dollar/U.K pound	8.5
U.S. dollar/Swiss franc	5.9
German mark/U.K. pound	4.9
German mark/Japanese yen	3.9
German mark/Swiss franc	2.9
U.S. dollar/Canadian dollar	2.0
U.S. dollar/Australian dollar	1.5
U.S. dollar/French franc	1.3
Other	23.8

Source: Bank for International Settlements, *Central Bank Survey of Foreign Exchange Market Activity in April 1992,* Basle, March 1993.

Table 1.6 FOREIGN EXCHANGE MARKET TRADING VOLUME IN DIFFERENT COUNTRIES (DAILY AVERAGES)

Country	Total volume (billions of dollars)
United Kingdom	369
United States	241
Japan	157
Singapore	87
Switzerland	79
Hong Kong	73
Germany	63
France	41
Australia	35

Source: Bank for International Settlements, *Central Bank Survey of Foreign Exchange Market Activity in April 1992,* Basle, March 1993.

accounting for 29.6 percent of the total. The next closest currency pair, the dollar/yen, involves roughly half as much spot trading as the dollar/mark. After these two currency pairs, the volume drops off dramatically.

In terms of the geographic pattern of foreign exchange trading, a small number of locations account for the great majority of trading. Table 1.6 reports the average daily volume of foreign exchange

trading in different countries. The United Kingdom, United States, and Japan account for over half of total world trading. The United Kingdom has long been the leader in foreign exchange trading. In 1992, it accounted for 27 percent of total world trading volume. While it is true that foreign exchange trading is a round-the-clock business with trading taking place somewhere in the world at any point in time, the peak activity occurs during the business hours in London, New York, and Tokyo.

SUMMARY

1. The foreign exchange market is a global market where foreign currency deposits are traded. Trading in actual currency notes is generally limited to tourism or illegal activities.
2. Arbitrage ensures that exchange rates are transaction costs close in all markets.
3. Central banks intervene in the foreign exchange market when they feel that exchange rates should be changed.
4. Black markets or parallel markets in foreign exchange arise because of government regulation of the foreign exchange market.
5. The dollar/mark currency pair dominates foreign exchange trading volume and the United Kingdom is the largest trading location.

EXERCISES

1. If in New York the German mark is selling for $0.5618 and the Japanese yen is selling for $0.0077, what is the cross rate between the mark and yen?
2. Suppose ¥1 = $0.0077 in London, $1 = DM2.00 in New York, and DM1 = ¥65 in Paris.
   a. If you begin by holding 10,000 yen, how could you make a profit from these exchange rates?
   b. Find the arbitrage profit per yen initially traded. (Ignore transaction costs.)
3. a. What is meant by "official intervention" in the foreign exchange market?
   b. What is the rationale behind this intervention?
   c. If the exchange rate changes from ¥/$ = 144.8 to ¥/$ = 141.65, and the Japanese government wants to keep the exchange rate fixed, then how does the Japanese government operate in the foreign exchange market? Illustrate by using a diagram.
   d. How might the credibility of central banks influence the future value of domestic currencies? Comment.
4. a. Compare and contrast black markets and parallel markets.
   b. Can you find real-world examples that would fit the description of these markets?

5. Suppose Mitsubishi Bank quotes the ¥/$ exchange rate as 110.30–.40 and Tokai Bank quotes 110.40–.50. Is there an arbitrage activity? If so, explain how you would profit from these quotes. If not, explain why not.

REFERENCES

Andrews, Michael, "Recent Trends in the U.S. Foreign Exchange Market," *Federal Reserve Bank of New York Quarterly Review,* Summer 1984, 38–47.

Gonnelli, Adam, *The Basics of Foreign Trade and Exchange,* Federal Reserve Bank of New York, 1993.

APPENDIX 1A: EXCHANGE RATE INDEXES

Suppose we want to consider the value of a currency. One measure is the bilateral exchange rate—say, the yen value of the dollar, or the lira value of the mark. However, if we are interested in knowing how a currency is performing globally, we need a broader measure of a currency's value against many other currencies. This is analogous to looking at a consumer price index to measure how prices in an economy are changing. We could look at the price of shoes or the price of a loaf of bread, but such single-good prices will not necessarily reflect the general inflationary situation—some prices may be rising while others are falling.

In the foreign exchange market, it is common to see a currency rising in value against one foreign money while it depreciates relative to another. As a result, exchange rate indexes are constructed to measure the average value of a currency relative to several other currencies. An *exchange rate index* is a weighted average of a currency's value relative to other currencies, where the weights are typically based on the importance of each currency to international trade. If we want to construct an exchange rate index for the United States, we would include those countries' currencies that are the major trading partners of the United States.

If half of U.S. trade was with Canada and the other half was with Mexico, then the trade-weighted dollar exchange rate index would be found by multiplying both the Canadian dollar/U.S. dol-

Appendix Table 1A.1 PERCENTAGE WEIGHTS ASSIGNED TO MAJOR CURRENCIES IN THREE U.S. DOLLAR EXCHANGE EXCHANGE RATE INDEXES

	Exchange rate index		
Country	BOG	IMF	FRBA
Germany	20.8	13.02	6.8
Japan	13.6	21.25	21.3
France	13.1	10.11	3.7
United Kingdom	11.9	5.06	6.9
Canada	9.1	20.28	28.8
Italy	9.0	7.47	3.3
Netherlands	8.3	3.24	3.0
Belgium	6.4	2.44	2.8
Sweden	4.2	2.73	1.2
Switzerland	3.6	1.69	1.5
Australia	—	4.86	2.0
Spain	—	2.44	1.3
South Korea	—	—	4.1
Denmark	—	1.40	—
All Other	—	4.01	18.0
Total	100.0	100.00	100.0

lar exchange rate and the Mexican peso/U.S. dollar exchange rate by ½ and summing the result. Table 1A.1 lists some popular exchange rate indexes and their weighting schemes. The indexes listed are the Federal Reserve Board's (BOG), the International Monetary Fund's multilateral exchange rate model (IMF), and the Federal Reserve Bank of Atlanta (FRBA).

Since the different indexes are constructed using different currencies, should we expect them to tell a different story? It is entirely possible for a currency to be appreciating against some currencies while it depreciates against others. Therefore, the exchange rate indexes will not all move identically, but they will all show the same general trends. Figure 1A.1 plots the movement of the various indexes from 1980 to 1992.

Figure 1A.1 indicates that the value of the dollar generally rose in the early 1980s and fell in the late 1980s—a conclusion we draw regardless of the exchange rate index used. Differences arise

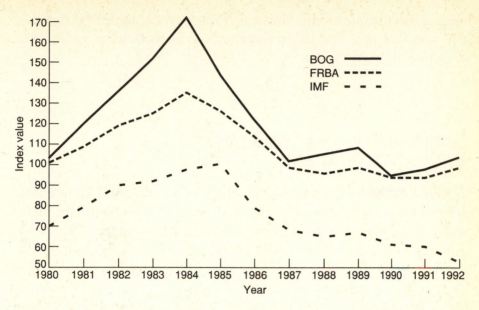

Figure 1A.1 The value of the dollar as measured by exchange rate indexes.

when we want to measure the amount of dollar appreciation or depreciation. From 1980 to 1984, the dollar rose in value by 40 percent according to the IMF index, or by 64 percent according to the BOG index. This suggests that, for discerning broad trends in the value of a currency, all indexes tell much the same story. Yet for shorter-term movements, where the magnitude of the change is important, there can be large differences across exchange rate indexes. Since different indexes assign a different importance to each foreign currency, this is not surprising. For instance, if we look at the weights in Table 1A.1, covering a period where the dollar appreciated rapidly against the German mark relative to other currencies, we would be led to use the BOG index and to record a rapid dollar appreciation relative to the FRBA index, which gives the mark a relatively low weight of 6.8.

Exchange rate indexes are commonly used tools of analysis in international economics. When changes in the average value of a currency are important, bilateral exchange rates (between only two currencies) are unsatisfactory. Neither economic theory nor practice gives a clear indication of which exchange rate index is best. In fact, for some questions, there is little to differentiate one index from another. In many cases, however, the best index to use will

depend on the question addressed. Typically, the preferred index is the one that best fits the researcher's prior beliefs regarding the conclusions to be drawn.

APPENDIX 1B: THE TOP FOREIGN EXCHANGE DEALERS

Foreign exchange trading is dominated by large commercial banks with worldwide operations. The market is very competitive, since each bank tries to maintain its share of the corporate business. *Euromoney* magazine provides some interesting insights into this market by supplying periodic surveys of the treasurers of the major multinational firms.

When asked to rank the factors that determined who got their foreign exchange business, the treasurers responded that the factors in Table 1B.1 were most important. The speed with which a bank executed transactions was ranked third. A second-place ranking was given to advice provided about the current state of the market. The most important factor was the firm's relationship with the bank. A bank that handles other banking needs of a firm is also likely to receive its foreign exchange business.

The significance of competitive quotes is indicated by the fact that treasurers often contact more than one bank to get several quotes before placing a deal. Another implication is that the market

TABLE 1B.1   RESPONSES OF TREASURERS WHO WERE ASKED TO RANK THE REASONS THEY CHOOSE BANK FOR FOREIGN EXCHANGE

1. Special relationship between bank and company
2. Bank's ability to analyze market conditions
3. Speed of execution
4. Competitiveness of quote only
5. Bank's ability to adapt to corporate needs
6. Relationships with traders
7. Efficiency of settlements

Rankings as reported in *Euromoney*, May 1990, p. 120.

Table 1B.2 THE TOP 20 FOREIGN EXCHANGE DEALERS

1993	1992	
1	1	**Citibank**
2	2	**Chemical**
3	13	**Deutsche Bank**
4	6	**JP Morgan**
5	*	**HSBC/Midland**[1]
6	15	**Swiss Bank Corporation**
7	3	**Barclays**
8	12	**Chase Manhattan**
9	7	**Union Bank of Switzerland**
10	16	**Royal Bank of Canada**
11	—	**ABN Amro**
12	4 =	**BankAmerica**
13	8	**NatWest**
14	17 =	**Goldman Sachs**
15	9	**Bankers Trust**
16	14	**First Chicago**
17	20	**Bank of Montreal**
18	19	**Standard Chartered**
19	—	**Banque Nationale de Paris**
20	—	**Morgan Stanley**

Notes: *Midland ranked joint 4th, Hongkong Bank ranked 10th.
[1]Includes Hongkong Bank and Midland.

Source: Euromoney, May 1993, p. 71.

will be dominated by the big banks, because only the giants have the global activity to allow competitive quotes on a large number of currencies. Table 1B.2 gives the rankings of the *Euromoney* survey. According to the rankings, Citibank receives more business than any other bank.

It appears that a smaller bank can "carve a niche" for itself by specializing in a minor currency. When the treasurers were asked to identify banks with expertise in a particular minor currency, they often named banks based in the particular region, as shown in Table 1B.3.

What makes Citibank the world's best foreign exchange dealer? There are many factors that have kept Citibank on top of the heap. An important factor is simply sheer size. Citibank holds

TABLE 1B.3 WHICH BANKS, WHICH CURRENCY?[a]
Corporate

Currency	Banks
Australian dollar, NZ dollar	Australia and New Zealand Banking Group, Westpac
Belgian franc	Generale, Banque Bruxelles Lambert
Canadian dollar	Royal Bank of Canada, Bank of Montreal
Dutch guilder	ABN Amro, Chemical
French franc	Banque Nationale de Paris, Credit Lyonnais
Irish pound	Allied Irish Bank, Bank of Ireland
Italian lira	Banca Commerciale Italiano, Citibank
Spanish peseta	Banco Bilbao Viscaya, Chemical
Singapore dollar	Standard Chartered, Citibank
Middle Eastern currencies	Citibank, Bank America
Latin American currencies	Citibank, Standard Chartered

[a]*Note:* Treasurers were asked to name banks they preferred for certain currencies. Banks scored on the number of mentions they received.
Source: Euromoney, May 1990, pp. 120–121.

the bank accounts for many corporations, giving it a natural advantage in foreign exchange trading.

Foreign exchange trading has emerged as an important center for bank profitability. Since each trade generates revenue for the bank, the volatile foreign exchange markets of recent years have often led to frenetic activity in the market with a commensurate revenue increase for the banks.

chapter 2

The Balance of Payments

We have all heard of the balance of payments. Unfortunately, common usage does not allow us to discuss *the* balance of payments because there are several ways to measure the balance, and the press often blurs the distinction among these various measures. In general, the *balance of payments* records a country's trade in goods, services, and financial assets with the rest of the world. Such trade is divided into useful categories that provide summaries of a nation's trade. A distinction is made between private (individuals and business firms) and official (government) transactions. Balance-of-payments data are reported quarterly for most developed countries. Figure 2.1 presents the balance of payments as reported by the U.S. Department of Commerce. This rather imposing document is of great use to economists, but it provides more detail than we need be concerned with here. To identify the popular summary measures of the balance of payments, we are only interested in broad definitions. We must be aware that although the several broad measures have their uses, they also have drawbacks, as will be pointed out in the following discussion.

The balance of payments is an accounting statement based on double-entry bookkeeping. Every transaction is entered on both sides of the balance sheet, as a credit and a debit. Credit entries are those entries that will bring foreign exchange into the country, whereas debit entries record items that would mean a loss of foreign exchange. In Figure 2.1, debit entries are recorded as a negative

Line	(Credits + : debits −)[1]	1960	1970	1980	1990	1992	Line
1	**Exports of goods, services, and income**	**30,556**	**68,387**	**344,440**	**688,806**	**730,460**	1
2	Merchandise, adjusted, excluding military[2]	19,650	42,469	224,250	389,303	440,138	2
3	Services[3]	6,290	14,171	47,584	148,302	179,710	3
4	Transfers under U.S. military agency sales contracts[4]	2,030	4,214	9,029	9,698	11,015	4
5	Travel	919	2,331	10,588	43,007	53,861	5
6	Passenger fares	175	544	2,591	15,298	17,353	6
7	Other transportation	1,607	3,125	11,618	21,954	22,773	7
8	Royalties and license fees[5]	837	2,331	7,085	17,069	20,238	8
9	Other private services[5]	570	1,294	6,276	40,608	53,601	9
10	U.S. Government miscellaneous services	153	332	398	668	869	10
11	Income receipts on U.S. assets abroad	4,616	11,748	72,606	151,201	110,612	11
12	Direct investment receipts	3,621	8,169	37,146	59,177	49,888	12
13	Other private receipts	646	2,671	32,898	81,512	53,687	13
14	U.S. Government receipts	349	907	2,562	10,512	7,038	14
15	**Imports of goods, services, and income**	**−23,670**	**−59,901**	**−333,774**	**−746,839**	**−763,965**	15
16	Merchandise, adjusted, excluding military[2]	−14,758	−39,866	−249,750	−498,336	−536,276	16
17	Services[3]	−7,674	−14,520	−41,491	−117,650	−123,299	17
18	Direct defense expenditures	−3,087	−4,855	−10,851	−17,531	−13,766	18
19	Travel	−1,750	−3,980	−10,397	−37,349	−39,872	19
20	Passenger fares	−513	−1,215	−3,607	−10,530	−10,943	20
21	Other transportation	−1,402	−2,843	−11,790	−23,401	−23,454	21
22	Royalties and license fees[5]	−74	−224	−724	−3,168	−4,986	22
23	Other private services[5]	−593	−827	−2,909	−23,753	−27,988	23
24	U.S.Government miscellaneous services	−254	−576	−1,214	−1,919	−2,290	24
25	Income payments on foreign assets in the United States	−1,238	−5,515	−42,532	−130,853	−104,391	25
26	Direct investment payments	−394	−875	−8,635	−2,970	−1,630	26
27	Other private payments	−511	−3,617	−21,214	−87,106	−61,582	27
28	U.S. Government payments	−332	−1,024	−12,684	−40,777	−41,179	28
29	**Unilateral transfers, net**	**−4,062**	**−6,156**	**−8,349**	**−33,827**	**−32,895**	29
30	U.S. Government grants[4]	−3,367	−4,449	−5,486	−17,434	−14,688	30
31	U.S. Government pensions and other transfers	−273	−611	−1,818	−2,934	−3,735	31
32	Private remittances and other transfers[5]	−423	−1,096	−1,044	−13,459	−14,473	32
33	**U.S. assets abroad, net (increase/ capital outflow(−))**	**−4,099**	**−9,337**	**−86,967**	**−44,132**	**−50,961**	33
34	U.S. official reserve assets, net[7]	2,145	2,481	−8,155	−2,158	3,901	34
35	Gold	1,703	787	–	–	–	35
36	Special drawing rights	–	−851	−16	−192	2,316	36
37	Reserve position in the International Monetary Fund	442	389	−1,667	731	−2,692	37
38	Foreign currencies	–	2,156	−6,472	−2,697	4,277	38
39	U.S.Government assets, other than official reserve assets, net	−1,100	−1,589	−5,162	2,307	−1,609	39
40	U.S. credits and other long-term						

FIGURE 2.1 U.S. International transactions (millions of dollars).
Note: Superscripts refer to detailed footnotes found in the original source.
(*Source: Survey of Current Business,* June 1993)

Line	(Credits + : debits −)	1960	1970	1980	1990	1992	Line
41	Repayments on U.S. credits and other long term assets,[8]	642	1,721	4,456	10,867	5,596	41
42	U.S. foreign currency holdings and U.S. short-term assets, net	−528	−16	242	−131	−65	42
43	U.S. private assets, net	−5,144	−10,229	−73,651	−44,280	−53,253	43
44	Direct investment	−2,940	−7,590	−19,222	−27,109	−34,791	44
45	Foreign securities	−663	−1,076	−3,568	−28,765	−47,961	45
46	U.S. claims on unaffiliated foreigners reported by U.S. nonbanking concerns	−394	−596	−4,023	−4,433	4,551	46
47	U.S. claims reported by U.S. banks, not included elsewhere	−1,148	−967	−46,838	16,027	24,948	47
48	**Foreign assets in the United States, net (increase/capital inflow (+))**	**2,294**	**6,359**	**58,112**	**105,173**	**129,579**	48
49	Foreign official assets in the United States, net	1,473	6,908	15,497	34,198	40,684	49
50	U.S. Government securities	655	9,439	11,895	30,243	22,403	50
51	U.S. Treasury securities[9]	655	9,411	9,708	29,576	18,454	51
52	Other[10]	–	28	2,187	667	3,949	52
53	Other U.S. Government liabilities[11]	215	−456	615	2,156	2,542	53
54	U.S. liabilities reported by U.S. banks, not included elsewhere	603	−2,075	−159	3,385	16,427	54
55	Other foreign official assets[12]	–	–	3,145	−1,586	−688	55
56	Other foreign assets in the United States, net	821	−550	42,615	70,975	88,895	56
57	Direct investment	315	1,464	16,918	48,014	2,378	57
58	U.S. Treasury securities	−364	81	2,645	−2,534	36,893	58
59	U.S. securities other than U.S. Treasury securities	282	2,189	5,457	1,592	30,274	59
60	U.S. liabilities to unaffiliated foreigners reported by U.S. nonbanking concerns	−90	2,014	6,852	7,533	741	60
61	U.S. liabilities reported by U.S. banks, not included elsewhere	678	−6,298	10,743	16,370	18,609	61
62	**Allocations of special drawing rights**	–	867	1,152	–	–	62
63	**Statistical discrepancy (sum of above items with sign reversed)**	**−1,019**	**−219**	**25,386**	**30,820**	**−12,218**	63
Memoranda:							
64	Balance on merchandise trade (lines 2 and 16)	4,892	2,603	−25,500	−109,033	−96,138	64
65	Balance on services (lines 3 and 17)	−1,385	−349	6,093	30,652	56,411	65
66	Balance on goods and services (lines 64 and 65)	3,508	2,254	−19,407	−78,381	−39,727	66
67	Balance on investment income (lines 11 and 25)	3,379	6,233	30,073	20,348	6,222	67
68	Balance on goods, services, and income (lines 1 and 15 or lines 64, 65, and 66)[13]	6,886	8,486	10,666	−58,034	−33,505	68
69	Unilateral transfers, net (line 29)	−4,062	−6,156	−8,349	−33,827	−32,895	69
70	Balance on current account (lines 1, 15, and 29 or lines 67 and 68)[13]	2,824	2,331	2,317	−91,861	−66,40070	70

FIGURE 2.1 (Continued)

value. For instance, suppose we record the sale of a machine from a U.S. manufacturer to a French importer and the manufacturer allows the buyer 90 days' credit to pay. The machinery export is recorded as a credit in the merchandise account, whereas the credit extended to the foreigner is a debit to short-term capital. The capital we speak of is financial capital. Thus credit extended belongs in the same broad account with stocks, bonds, and other financial instruments of a short-term nature. If, for any particular account, the value of the credit entries exceeds the debits, we say a *surplus* exists. On the other hand, where the debits exceed the credits, a *deficit* exists. Note that a surplus or deficit can apply only to a particular area of the balance of payments, since the sum of the credits and debits on all accounts will always be equal; in other words, the balance of payments always balances. This will become apparent in the following discussion.

Let us consider some of the popular summary measures of the balance of payments.

CURRENT ACCOUNT

The *current account* is defined as including the value of trade in merchandise, services, investment income, and unilateral transfers. Merchandise is the obvious trade in tangible commodities. *Services* refers to trade in the services of factors of production: land, labor, and capital. Included in this category are travel and tourism, royalties, transportation costs, and insurance premiums. The payment for the services of physical capital, or the return on investments, is recorded in the investment income account. Interest and dividends paid internationally are large and growing rapidly as the world financial markets become more integrated.

The final component of the balance of payments includes unilateral transfers like U.S. foreign aid, gifts, and retirement pensions. The United States always records a large deficit on these items, except for 1991 when several foreign countries transferred large sums of money to the United States to help pay for the expense of the war in the Mid-East.

Figure 2.2 illustrates how the various account balances have changed over time. The merchandise and current account deficits of the 1980s are unprecedented. In Figure 2.1, line 70 shows that

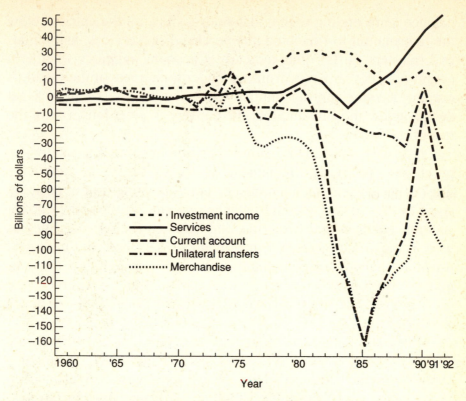

FIGURE 2.2 U.S. international transactions from 1960 to 1992.

there was a current account surplus of $2824 million in 1960 and a deficit of $66,400 million in 1992. The $66 billion current account deficit of 1992 is the sum of a $96 billion merchandise trade deficit, a $56 billion services surplus, a $6 billion investment income surplus, and a $33 billion transfers deficit. From 1955 to 1970, the United States ran a merchandise trade surplus. Following a $2 billion deficit in 1971, the merchandise account has been in deficit every year since, except 1973 and 1975. Even with this persistent merchandise trade deficit, U.S. earnings from foreign investments have had sizable surpluses so that the current account realized a surplus in the periods from 1973 to 1976 and from 1980 to 1981.

The balance of payments in Figure 2.1 actually ends at line 63. Lines 64 to 70 are summaries drawn from lines 1 to 63. We can draw a line in the balance of payments to sum the debit and credit items above that line. If we "draw the line" at the current account

balance items ending with unilateral transfers, all the entries below the line amount to financing the merchandise, services, and unilateral transfers (gifts); thus the current account indicates whether a country is a net borrower from, or lender to, the rest of the world. A current account surplus implies that a country is running a net deficit below the line and that the country is a net lender with the rest of the world.

The current account excludes capital account transactions—purchases and sales of financial assets. Since the items "below the line" of the current account must be equal in value (but opposite in sign) to the current account balance, we can see how the current account balance indicates financial activity (below the line) as well as the value of trade in merchandise, services, and unilateral transfers that are recorded above the line. In a period (year or quarter) during which a current account deficit is recorded, the country must borrow from abroad an amount sufficient to finance the deficit.

Since the balance of payments always balances, the massive current account deficits of recent years are matched by massive capital account surpluses. This means that foreign investment in U.S. securities has been at very high levels. Some analysts have expressed concern over the growing foreign indebtedness of the United States. The next section reviews the issue.

FINANCING THE CURRENT ACCOUNT

Large current account deficits imply large capital account surpluses. The capital account transactions are recorded below the current account items in the balance of payments. Referring back to Figure 2.1, lines 33 through 62 record capital account transactions. We see that capital account transactions include both official and private transactions. For ease of understanding, Table 2.1 provides a summary of U.S. capital account transactions since 1960. In this table, the debit and credit items are entered separately so that we can identify the sources of changes in net capital flows (capital inflows less capital outflows). For instance, in 1992 we see that U.S. security purchases abroad totaled $47,961 million. This is a capital account debit entry because it involves foreign exchange leaving

the United States. Security purchases in the United States by foreigners totaled $67,167 million in 1992. This is a credit item in the capital account since it brings foreign exchange to the United States. We can interpret the other capital account items in a similar manner.

Before interpreting the recent history of U.S. international capital flows, we should consider the definitions of the individual capital account items:

Direct investment: Private financial transactions that result in the ownership of 10 percent or more of a business firm.

Security purchases: Private sector net purchases of equity (stock) and debt securities.

Bank claims and liabilities: Claims include loans, collections outstanding, acceptances, deposits abroad, claims on affiliated foreign banks, foreign government obligations, and foreign commercial and finance paper; liabilities include deposits, certificates of deposit, liabilities to affiliated foreign banks, and other liabilities.

U.S. government assets abroad: Changes in U.S. official reserve assets (gold, SDRs, foreign currency holdings, and reserve position in the IMF).

Foreign official assets in the United States: Net purchases of U.S. government securities, obligations of U.S. government corporations and agencies, securities of U.S. state and local governments, and changes in liabilities to foreign official agencies reported by U.S. banks.

Some capital account transactions are a direct result of trade in merchandise and services. For instance, many goods are sold using trade credit. The exporter allows the importer a period of time—30, 60, or 90 days typically—before payment is due. This sort of financing will generally be reflected in bank claims and liabilities, because such transactions are handled by the exporter's bank. Other capital account items are a result of portfolio management by international investors. Security purchases would fall in this category. Official transactions involve governments and are motivated by a host of economic and political considerations.

In terms of financing current account deficits, Table 2.1 shows that, aside from the 1980s, only in the period from 1977 to 1978 were there sizable deficits to be financed. Table 2.1 shows that the

Table 2.1 U.S. CAPITAL ACCOUNT TRANSACTIONS
Capital Flows, in Millions of Dollars

Year	Direct investment abroad	Direct investment in U.S.	Security purchases abroad	Security purchases in U.S.	Bank claims on foreigners	Bank liabilities to foreigners	U.S. government assets abroad	Foreign official assets in U.S.
1961	2,653	311	762	475	1,261	928	303	765
1962	2,851	346	969	68	450	336	-450	1,270
1963	3,483	231	1,105	138	1,556	898	1,284	1,986
1964	3,760	322	677	-231	2,505	1,818	1,509	1,660
1965	5,011	415	759	-489	-93	503	380	134
1966	5,418	425	720	550	-233	2,882	973	-672
1967	4,805	698	1,308	881	495	1,765	2,370	3,451
1968	5,295	807	1,569	4,550	-233	3,871	3,144	-774
1969	5,690	1,263	1,459	3,062	570	8,886	3,379	-1,301
1970	7,590	1,464	1,076	2,270	967	-6,298	-892	6,908
1971	7,618	367	1,113	2,265	2,980	-6,911	-465	26,879
1972	7,747	949	618	4,468	3,506	4,754	1,572	10,475
1973	11,353	2,800	671	3,825	5,980	4,702	2,486	6,026
1974	9,052	4,760	1,854	1,075	19,516	16,017	1,101	10,546
1975	14,244	2,603	6,247	5,093	13,532	628	4,323	7,027
1976	11,949	4,347	8,885	4,067	21,368	10,990	6,772	17,693

Table 2.1 (continued)

1977	11,890	3,728	5,460	2,971	11,427	6,719	4,068	36,816
1978	16,056	7,897	3,626	4,432	33,667	16,141	3,928	33,678
1979	25,222	11,877	4,726	6,311	26,213	32,607	4,879	-13,665
1980	19,222	16,918	3,568	8,102	46,838	10,743	13,317	15,497
1981	9,624	25,195	5,699	9,832	84,175	42,128	10,272	4,960
1982	-991	12,464	7,983	13,112	111,070	65,633	11,096	3,593
1983	4,889	10,457	6,762	16,853	29,928	50,342	6,202	5,845
1984	10,948	24,748	4,756	35,569	11,127	33,849	8,620	3,140
1985	13,401	20,010	7,481	71,395	1,323	41,045	6,679	-1,119
1986	17,090	35,623	4,271	74,778	59,975	79,783	1,710	35,648
1987	27,181	58,219	5,251	34,477	42,119	89,026	-10,146	45,387
1988	15,448	57,278	7,846	46,592	53,927	70,235	943	39,758
1989	36,834	67,736	22,070	68,385	58,160	63,382	24,034	8,503
1990	27,109	48,014	28,765	-942	16,027	16,370	149	34,198
1991	29,113	23,975	44,740	53,970	3,278	-11,371	-8,668	17,564
1992	34,791	2,378	47,961	67,167	24,948	18,609	2,292	40,684

Source: International Economic Conditions, Federal Reserve Bank of St. Louis, June 1990, p. 4

deficits from 1977 to 1978 were financed in a manner different from the recent deficits. From 1977 to 1978, foreign official capital inflows largely financed the current account deficit. This was a period of large foreign exchange market intervention by foreign central banks aimed at supporting the dollar. U.S. government securities serve as an interest-bearing reserve asset for foreign governments accumulating dollar assets, so there were sizable official purchases during 1977 and 1978.

In the recent period, current account deficits were financed by private capital flows. As Table 2.1 shows, security purchases in the United States by foreigners increased dramatically through the 1980s. Moreover, U.S. bank claims on foreigners dramatically fell in the early 1980s. This result reflects an inward turn by U.S. banks. U.S. bank lending abroad fell as banks responded to the high returns and low risk available through domestic lending. Rapid economic growth in the United States coupled with large government borrowing requirements resulted in a rising demand for credit at home to which U.S. banks responded.

One implication of capital account transactions is the change in the net creditor or debtor status of a nation. A net debtor owes more to the rest of the world than it is owed, while a net creditor is owed more than it owes. The United States became a net international debtor in 1985 for the first time since World War I. The high current account deficits of the 1980s were matched by high capital account surpluses. This rapid buildup of foreign direct investment and purchases of U.S. securities led to a very rapid drop from being a net creditor of $147 billion in 1982 to net debtor status by 1985. Once again, we see that the current account is a useful measure because it summarizes the trend with regard to the net debtor position of a country. For this reason, international bankers focus on the current account trend as one of the crucial variables to consider when evaluating loans to foreign countries.

ADDITIONAL SUMMARY MEASURES

So far we have focused on the current account of the balance of payments. In terms of practical importance to economists, government policymakers, and business firms, this emphasis on the current account is warranted. However, there are other summary mea-

sures of balance-of-payments phenomena. Within the current account categories, the balance on merchandise trade is often cited in the popular press (because it is reported on a monthly basis by the United States). The *balance of trade* (line 2 plus line 16 in Figure 2.1) records a surplus when merchandise exports exceed imports. Domestic business firms and labor unions often use the balance of trade to justify a need to protect the domestic market from foreign competition. When a country is running a large balance-of-trade deficit, local industries that are being hurt by import competition will argue that the trade balance reflects the harm done to the economy. Because of the political sensitivity of the balance of trade, it is a popularly cited measure.

The *official settlements balance* (lines 34 plus 49 in Figure 2.1) measures short-term capital held by foreign monetary agencies and official reserve asset transactions. The official settlements balance serves as a measure of potential foreign exchange pressure on the dollar, in that official institutions may not hold increasing stocks of dollars but would rather sell them, thereby driving down the foreign exchange value of the dollar. Yet there may be a demand for the dollar so that official stocks of dollars build without any foreign exchange pressure. Furthermore, in the modern day it is not always clear whether official holdings are what they seem to be, since (as we will see in a later chapter) the Eurodollar market allows central banks to turn official claims against the United States into private claims.

Still, monetary economists have found the official settlement account to be useful, because changes in international reserves impinge on the money stock since reserves are one element on which the nation's money supply depends. (We will learn subsequently that "high-powered money" has a domestic credit component and an international reserves component.)

The foreign monetary agency holdings of the liabilities of most countries are trivial, so that the official settlements balance essentially measures international reserve changes. In the case of the United States, the official settlements balance primarily records changes in short-term U.S. liabilities held by foreign monetary agencies. This demand for dollar-denominated short-term debt by foreign central banks is what allows the United States to finance current account deficits largely with dollars. Other countries must finance deficits by selling foreign currency and, as a result, face a

greater constraint on their ability to run deficits as they eventually deplete their stocks of foreign currency.

TRANSACTIONS CLASSIFICATION

So far we have defined the important summary measures of the balance of payments and developed an understanding of the various categories included in a nation's international transactions. The actual classification of transactions is often confusing to those first considering such issues. To aid in understanding these classifying problems, we will analyze five transactions and their placement in a simplified balance of payments.

First, we must remember that the balance of payments is a balance sheet, so at the bottom line total credits equal total debits. This means that we use double-entry bookkeeping—every item involves two entries, a credit and a debit, to the balance sheet. The credits record items leading to inflows of payments. Such items are associated with a greater demand for domestic currency or supply of foreign currency to the foreign exchange market. The debits record items that lead to payments outflows. These are associated with a greater supply of domestic currency or demand for foreign currency in the foreign exchange market. Now consider the following five hypothetical transactions and their corresponding entries in Table 2.2:

Table 2.2 BALANCE OF PAYMENTS

	Credit (+)	Debit (−)	Net balance
Merchandise	$1,000,000 (2) 100,000 (5)		
Services	10,000 (3)	$10,000 (4)	
Unilateral transfers		100,000 (5)	
Current account			+ $1,000,000
Short-term capital	10,000 (4) 1,000,000 (1)	10,000 (3) 1,000,000 (2)	
Long-term capital		1,000,000 (1)	
Total	$2,120,000	$2,120,000	

Note: The numbers in parentheses refer to the five transactions we have analyzed.

1. *A 10-year loan of $1 million is made to Romania. The loan is funded by creating a $1 million deposit for Romania in a U.S. bank.* The loan represents a long-term capital outflow (long-term since it is over 1 year) and is recorded as a debit to long-term capital. The new deposit is recorded as a credit to short-term capital since an increase in foreign-owned bank deposits in U.S. banks is treated as a short-term capital inflow.

2. *A U.S. firm sells $1 million worth of wheat to Romania. The wheat is paid for with the bank account created in (1).* The wheat export represents a merchandise export of $1 million, and thus we credit merchandise $1 million. Payment using the deposit results in the decrease of foreign-owned deposits in U.S. banks; which is treated as a short-term capital outflow, leading to a $1 million debit to short-term capital.

3. *A U.S. resident receives $10,000 in interest from German bonds she owns. The $10,000 is deposited in a German bank.* Earnings on international investments represent a credit on the services account. The increase in U.S.-owned foreign bank deposits is considered a short-term capital outflow and is recorded by debiting short-term capital in the amount of $10,000.

4. *A U.S. tourist travels to Europe and spends the $10,000 German deposit.* Tourist spending is recorded in the services account. U.S. tourist spending abroad is recorded as a $10,000 debit to the services account. The decrease in U.S.-owned foreign deposits is considered a short-term capital inflow and is recorded by a $10,000 credit to short-term capital.

5. *The United States gives $100,000 worth of grain to Nicaragua.* The grain export is recorded as a $100,000 credit to the merchandise account. Since the grain was a gift, the balancing entry is unilateral transfers; in this case, there is a debit of $100,000 to unilateral transfers.

Note that the current account balance is the sum of the merchandise, services, and unilateral transfers accounts. Summing the credits and debits, we find that the credits sum to $1,110,000, whereas

the debits sum to $110,000, so that there is a positive or credit balance of $1 million.

The short-term capital entries are typically the most confusing, particularly those relating to changes in bank deposits. For instance, the third transaction we analyzed recorded the deposit of $10,000 in a German bank as a debit to the short-term capital account of the United States. The fourth transaction recorded the U.S. tourist spending the $10,000 German bank deposit as a credit to the short-term capital account of the United States. This may seem confusing because early in the chapter it was suggested that credit items are items that bring foreign exchange into a country while debit items involve foreign exchange leaving the country, yet neither of these transactions affected bank deposits in the United States, just foreign deposits. The key is to think of the deposit of $10,000 in a German bank as money that had come from a U.S. bank account. Increases in U.S.-owned deposits in foreign banks are debits whether the money was ever in the United States or not. What matters is not whether the money is physically ever in the United States, but the country of residence of the owner. Similarly, decreases in U.S.-owned foreign deposits are recorded as a credit to short-term capital, whether or not the money is actually brought from abroad to the United States.

The item called "Statistical discrepancy" (line 63) in Figure 2.1 is not the result of not knowing where to classify some transactions. The international transactions that are recorded are simply difficult to measure accurately. Taking the numbers from customs records and surveys of business firms will not capture all of the trade actually occurring. Some of this may be due to illegal or underground activity, but in the modern dynamic economy we would expect sizable measurement errors even with no illegal activity. It is simply impossible to observe every transaction, so we must rely on statistically valid sampling of international transactions.

BALANCE-OF-PAYMENTS EQUILIBRIUM AND ADJUSTMENT

So far we have focused on the accounting procedures and definitions that apply to the balance of payments. Now we want to consider the economic implications of the balance of payments. For instance, since merchandise exports earn foreign exchange while

imports involve outflows of foreign exchange, we often hear arguments for policy aimed at maximizing the trade or current account surplus. Is this in fact desirable? First, it must be realized that, because one country's export is another's import, it is impossible for everyone to have surpluses—on a worldwide basis the total value of exports equals the total value of imports, or there is globally balanced trade. Actually, the manner in which trade data are collected imparts a surplus bias to trade balances. Exports are recorded when goods are shipped, while imports are recorded upon receipt. Because there are always goods in transit from the exporter to the importer, if we sum the balance of trade for all nations we would expect a global trade surplus. However, the global current account balance has summed to a deficit in recent years. In 1992, the global current account deficit was $124 billion. The problem seems to involve accurate measurement of international financial transactions. Merchandise trade is measured fairly accurately, and the global sum of trade balances is roughly zero. But service transactions are more difficult to observe, and investment income flows, recorded in the services account, seem to be the major source of global current account discrepancies. Yet even with these bookkeeping problems facing government statisticians, the essential economic point is still true.

Since someone must always have a trade deficit when others have trade surpluses, is it necessarily true that surpluses are good and deficits bad so that one country benefits at another's expense? In one sense, it would seem that imports should be preferred to exports. In terms of current consumption, merchandise exports represent goods no longer available for domestic consumption that will be consumed by foreign importers. As we learn from studying international trade theory, the benefits of free international trade are more efficient production and increased consumption. If trade between nations is voluntary, then it is difficult to argue that deficit countries are harmed while surplus countries benefit by trade.

In general, it is not obvious whether a country is better or worse off to run payments surpluses rather than deficits. Consider the following simple example of a world with two countries, A and B. Country A is a wealthy creditor country that has extended loans to poor country B. In order for country B to repay these loans, B

must run trade surpluses with A to earn the foreign exchange required for repayment. Would you rather live in rich country A and experience trade deficits or in poor country B and experience trade surpluses? Although this is indeed a simplistic example, there are real-world analogues of rich creditor countries with trade deficits and poor debtor nations with trade surpluses. The point here is that you cannot analyze the balance of payments apart from other economic considerations. Deficits are not inherently bad, nor are surpluses necessarily good.

Balance-of-payments equilibrium is a condition in which exports equal imports or credits equal debits on some particular subaccount, like the current account or official settlements account. If we had a current account equilibrium, then the nation would find its net creditor or debtor position unchanging since there is no need for any net financing—the current account export items are just balanced by the current account import items. Equilibrium on the official settlements basis would mean no change in short-term capital held by foreign monetary agencies and reserve assets. For most countries, this would simply mean that their stocks of international reserves would be unchanging.

What happens if there is a disequilibrium in the balance of payments—say the official settlements basis? Now there will be reserve asset losses from deficit countries and reserve accumulation by surplus countries. International reserve assets comprise gold, IMF *special drawing rights* (a credit issued by the IMF and allocated to countries on the basis of their level of financial support for the IMF), and foreign exchange. To simplify matters (although this is essentially the case for most countries), let us consider foreign exchange alone. The concept of balance-of-payments equilibrium may be linked to a familiar diagram from principles of economics courses, the supply and demand diagram. Figure 2.3 depicts the hypothetical supply and demand diagram for the Japanese yen/U.S. dollar foreign exchange market. To further simplify matters, let's assume that Japan and the United States are the only two countries in the world.

Initially there is an official settlements balance-of-payments equilibrium and foreign exchange market equilibrium at point *A* in Figure 2.3. At this point the yen price of the dollar is 120 and quantity $\$_0$ (we don't care about a specific number here) is bought and sold. Notice that the demand is a familiar downward-sloping de-

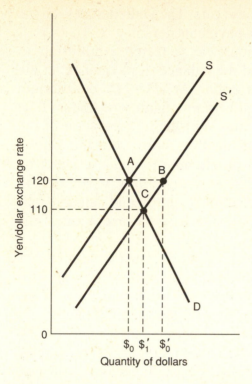

FIGURE 2.3 Balance-of-payments disequilibrium as reflected in the foreign exchange market.

mand curve. In this case, the demand for dollars comes from the Japanese demand for U.S. goods or financial assets. The higher the yen price of the dollar, the more expensive U.S. goods and the smaller the quantity of dollars demanded. The supply curve is the supply of dollars to this market from U.S. buyers of Japanese goods or financial assets. The upward-sloping supply curve reflects the fact that, as the dollar appreciates in value (so the exchange rate, ¥/$, rises), Japanese products are cheaper to U.S. buyers and more dollars will be supplied to this market.

Suppose the initial equilibrium at point *A* is disturbed by a change in market preferences for Japanese goods. For instance, suppose U.S. buyers now believe that Japanese automobiles are higher quality and now demand more auto imports from Japan. The supply of dollars to this market will shift to the right to *S'* so, at every level of the exchange rate, more dollars are offered for yen. In terms of the Japanese balance of trade, there is now a surplus resulting from

the higher U.S. demand for Japanese cars. The United States, on the other hand, now has a balance-of-payments deficit.

Figure 2.3 suggests an obvious way to restore equilibrium to the foreign exchange market and the balance of payments: let the dollar depreciate to 110 yen per dollar. At ¥/$=110, equilibrium is restored at point C. A new equilibrium quantity of dollars ($\$'_1$) is traded at the new exchange rate. With the appreciation of the yen, Japanese buyers are willing to buy more from the United States to balance the increased purchases of Japanese autos by U.S. buyers. In this case of *flexible exchange rates,* where the exchange rate is determined by free market supply and demand, balance-of-payments equilibrium is restored by the operation of the free market.

As we will learn in Chapter 3, exchange rates are not always free to adjust to changing market conditions. With *fixed exchange rates,* central banks set exchange rates at a particular level. If the exchange rate is fixed at 120, then after the shift in the supply curve the dollar will be overvalued, there will be an excess supply of dollars ($\$'_0 - \$_0$) on the foreign exchange market, and the United States will run a balance-of-trade deficit while Japan runs a surplus. The central banks must now finance the trade imbalance by international reserve flows. Specifically, the Federal Reserve (or the Bank of Japan) must sell yen for dollars to support the deficit. In this case, the U.S. deficit could continue only as long as the U.S. stock of yen lasts. Once the United States has depleted its stock of foreign exchange, the dollar would have to be devalued to 110 yen per dollar, at which time the trade imbalance would end and there would again be equilibrium in the foreign exchange market.

Besides these methods of adjusting to balance-of-payments disequilibrium, countries sometimes use direct controls on international trade to shift the supply and demand curves by government-mandated quotas or prices that induce balance-of-payments equilibrium. Such policies are particularly popular in developing countries where chronic shortages of international reserves will not permit financing the free-market-determined trade disequilibrium at the government-supported exchange rate.

The mechanism of adjustment to balance-of-payments disequilibrium is one of the most important practical problems in international economics. The discussion here is but an introduction; much of the analysis of Chapters 9 and 10 is related to this issue as well.

SUMMARY

1. If the value of the credit items on a particular balance-of-payments account exceeds (is less than) that of the debit items, a surplus (deficit) exists.
2. The current account is the sums of the merchandise, services, investment income, and unilateral transfers accounts.
3. Current account deficits are offset by capital account surpluses.
4. The United States became a net international debtor in 1985.
5. Merchandise exports minus imports equal the balance of trade.
6. The official settlements balance is equal to changes in short-term capital held by foreign monetary agencies and official reserve asset transactions.
7. Increases (decreases) in U.S.-owned deposits in foreign banks are debits (credits) to U.S. short-term capital. Increases (decreases) in foreign-owned deposits in U.S. banks are credits (debits) to short-term capital.
8. Deficits are not necessarily bad nor are surpluses necessarily good.
9. With floating exchange rates, balance-of-payments equilibrium is restored by exchange rate changes.
10. With fixed exchange rates, central banks must finance deficits, allow a devaluation, or else use trade restrictions to restore equilibrium.

EXERCISES

1. Under what circumstances could a country simultaneously have a balance-of-trade surplus and an official settlements balance-of-payments deficit?
2. Classify the following transactions in the German balance of payments:
    a. A U.S. tourist travels to Frankfurt and spends DM1000 on bratwurst and beer. He pays with a check drawn on a Tulsa, Oklahoma, bank.
    b. Mercedes-Benz sells DM400,000 of its cars to a U.S. distributor, allowing 90 days' trade credit until payment is due.
    c. Herr Schmidt in Bonn, Germany, sends his grandson in New York DM10 for a high school graduation present.
    d. A resident in Sun City, Arizona, receives a DM4000 dividend check from a German corporation and deposits it in a local bank.
3. What is the value of the current account in the preceding problem?
4. If a country has a current account deficit, is it a net lender or borrower to the rest of the world? Should a country necessarily be concerned if it experiences a current account deficit?
5. What is a balance-of-payments disequilibrium? Can a country run a balance-of-payments deficit indefinitely? Explain how balance-of-payments disequilibria are self-correcting.
6. Use the information in the table on Mexico's 1990 international transactions to answer the following questions (amounts are U.S. dollar values):

Merchandise imports	$29,799
Merchandise exports	$26,773
Services exports	$11,616
Services imports	$9,743

Investment income receipts	$3,201
Investment income payments	$10,776
Unilateral transfers	$3,473

a. What is the balance of trade?

b. What is the current account?

c. Did Mexico become a larger international net debtor during 1990?

REFERENCES

Glick, Reuven, "The Largest Debtor Nation," *Federal Reserve Bank of San Francisco Weekly Letter,* February 14, 1986.

Gonelli, Adam, *The Basics of Foreign Trade and Exchange,* Federal Reserve Bank of New York, 1993.

International Monetary Fund, *Report on the World Current Account Discrepancy,* September 1987.

Nawaz, Shuja, "Why the World Current Account Does Not Balance," *Finance and Development,* September 1987, 43–45.

Pigott, Charles, "Which Trade Balance?" *Federal Reserve Bank of San Francisco Weekly Letter,* April 20, 1984.

chapter 3

Past and Present International Monetary Arrangements

Like most areas of public policy, international monetary relations are subject to frequent proposals for change. Fixed exchange rates, floating exchange rates, and commodity-backed currency all have their advocates. Before considering the merits of alternative international monetary systems, we should understand the background of the international monetary system. Although an international monetary system has been in existence since monies have been traded, it is common for most modern discussions of international monetary history to start in the late nineteenth century. It was during this period that the gold standard began.

THE GOLD STANDARD: 1880 TO 1914

Although an exact date for the beginning of the gold standard cannot be pinpointed, we know that it started during the period from 1880 to 1890. Under a *gold standard,* currencies are valued in terms of a gold equivalent (an ounce of gold was worth $20.67 in terms of the U.S. dollar over the gold standard period). The gold standard is an important beginning for a discussion of international monetary systems because, when each currency is defined in terms of its gold value, all currencies are linked together in a system of fixed exchange rates. For instance, if currency A is worth 0.10

ounce of gold, whereas currency B is worth 0.20 ounce of gold, then 1 unit of currency B is worth twice as much as A, and thus the exchange rate of 1 currency $B = 2$ currency A is established.

Maintaining a gold standard requires a commitment from participating countries to be willing to buy and sell gold to anyone at the fixed price. To maintain a price of $20.67 per ounce, the United States had to buy and sell gold at that price.

Gold was used as the monetary standard because it is a homogeneous commodity (could you have a fish standard?) worldwide that is easily storable, portable, and divisible into standardized units like ounces. Since gold is costly to produce, it possesses another important attribute—governments cannot easily increase its supply. A gold standard is a *commodity money standard*. Money has a value that is fixed in terms of the commodity gold.

One aspect of a money standard based on a commodity with relatively fixed supply is long-run price stability. Since governments must maintain a fixed value of their money relative to gold, the supply of money is restricted by the supply of gold. Prices may still rise and fall with swings in gold output and economic growth, but the tendency is to return to a long-run stable level. Figure 3.1 illustrates graphically the relative stability of U.S. and U.K. prices over the gold standard period as compared to later years. Since currencies were convertible into gold, national money supplies were constrained by the growth of the stock of gold. As long as the gold stock grew at a steady rate, prices would also follow a steady path. New discoveries of gold would generate discontinuous jumps in the price level, but the period of the gold standard was marked by a fairly stable stock of gold.

People today often look back on the gold standard as a "golden era" of economic progress. It is common to hear arguments supporting a return to the gold standard. Such arguments usually cite the stable prices, economic growth, and development of world trade during this period as evidence of the benefits provided by such an orderly international monetary system. Others have suggested that the economic development and stability of the world economy in these years reflects not necessarily the existence of the gold standard but, instead, absence of any significant real shocks such as war. Although we may disagree on the merits of returning to a gold standard, it seems fair to say that the development of

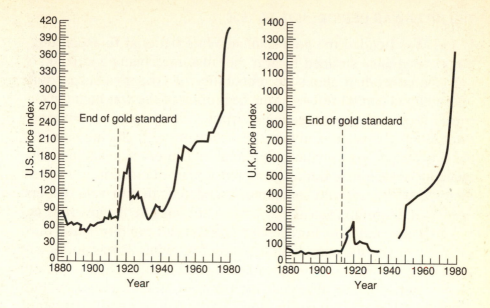

FIGURE 3.1 U.S and U.K. wholesale price indexes from 1880 to 1976. Data are missing for World War II years in the United Kingdom.
(*Source:* Roy W. Jastram, *The Golden Constant,* New York: Wiley, 1977.)

world trade was encouraged by the systematic linking of national currencies and the price stability of the system.

Since gold is like a world money during a gold standard, we can easily understand how a balance-of-payments disequilibrium may be remedied. A country running a balance-of-payments deficit would find itself with net outflows of gold, thus reducing its money supply and, in turn, its prices. A surplus country would find gold flowing in and expanding its money supply, so that prices rose. The fall in price in the deficit country would lead to greater net exports (exports minus imports), and the rise in price in the surplus country would reduce its net exports so that balance-of-payments equilibrium is restored.

In practice, actual flows of gold were not the only, or even necessarily the most important, means of settling international debts during this period. Since London was the financial center of the world, and England the world's leading trader and source of financial capital, the pound also served as a world money. International trade was commonly priced in pounds, and trade that never passed through England was often paid for with pounds.

THE INTERWAR PERIOD: 1918 TO 1939

World War I ended the gold standard. International financial relations are greatly strained by war, because merchants and bankers must be concerned about the probability of countries suspending international capital flows. At the beginning of the war both the patriotic response of each nation's citizens along with legal restrictions stopped private gold flows. Since wartime financing required the hostile nations to manage international reserves very carefully, private gold exports were considered unpatriotic. Central governments encouraged (and sometimes mandated) that private holders of gold and foreign exchange sell these holdings to the government.

Because much of Europe had experienced rapid inflation during the war and the period immediately following, it was not possible for a restoration of the gold standard at the old exchange values. However, the United States had experienced little inflation and thus returned to a gold standard by June 1919. The war ended Britain's financial preeminence, since the United States had risen to the status of the world's dominant banker country. In the immediate postwar years the pound fluctuated freely against the dollar in line with changes in the price level of each country.

In 1925, England returned to a gold standard at the old prewar pound per gold exchange rate even though prices had risen since the prewar period. As John Maynard Keynes had correctly warned, the overvalued pound hurt U.K. exports and led to a deflation of British wages and prices. By 1931, the pound was declared inconvertible because of a run on British gold reserves (a large demand to convert pounds into gold), and so ended the brief U.K. return to a gold standard. Once the pound was no longer convertible into gold, attention centered on the U.S. dollar. A run on U.S. gold at the end of 1931 led to a 15 percent drop in U.S. gold holdings. Although this did not lead to an immediate change in U.S. policy, by 1933 the United States abandoned the gold standard.

The Depression years were characterized by international monetary warfare. In trying to stimulate domestic economies by increasing exports, country after country devalued so that the early to mid-1930s may be characterized as a period of competitive devaluations. Governments also resorted to foreign exchange controls in an attempt to manipulate net exports in a manner that would increase GDP (gross domestic product). Of course, with the on-

slaught of World War II, the hostile countries utilized foreign exchange controls to aid the war-financing effort.

THE GOLD EXCHANGE STANDARD: 1944 TO 1970

Memories of the economic warfare of the interwar years led to an international conference at Bretton Woods, New Hampshire, in 1944. At the close of World War II there was a desire to reform the international monetary system to one based on mutual cooperation and freely convertible currencies. The Bretton Woods agreement required that each country fix the value of its currency in terms of gold (this established the "par" value of each currency and was to ensure parity across currencies). The U.S. dollar was the key currency in the system, and $1 was defined as being equal in value to $\frac{1}{35}$ ounce of gold. Since every currency had a defined gold value, all currencies were linked in a system of fixed exchange rates.

Nations were committed to maintaining the parity value of the currency within ± 1 percent of parity. The various central banks were to achieve this goal by buying and selling their currencies (usually against the dollar) on the foreign exchange market. When a country was experiencing difficulty maintaining its parity value because of balance-of-payments disequilibrium, it could turn to a new institution created at the Bretton Woods Conference: *the International Monetary Fund* (*IMF*). The IMF was created to monitor the operation of the system and provide short-term loans to countries experiencing temporary balance-of-payments difficulties. Such loans are subject to IMF conditions regarding changes in domestic economic policy aimed at restoring balance-of-payments equilibrium. In the case of a fundamental disequilibrium, when the balance-of-payments problems are not of a temporary nature, a country was allowed to devalue its currency, giving a permanent change in the parity rate of exchange. Table 3.1 summarizes the history of exchange rate adjustments over the Bretton Woods period for the major industrial countries.

We notice, then, that the Bretton Woods system, although essentially a fixed or pegged exchange rate system, allowed for changes in exchange rates when economic circumstances warranted such changes. In actuality, the system is best described as an *adjustable peg*. The system may also be described as a gold exchange

Table 3.1 EXCHANGE RATES OF THE MAJOR INDUSTRIAL COUNTRIES OVER THE PERIOD OF THE BRETTON WOODS AGREEMENT

Country	Exchange rates[a]
Canada	Floated until May 2, 1962, then pegged at Can$1.081 = $1. Floated again on June 1, 1970.
France	No official IMF parity value after 1948 (although the actual rate hovered around FF350 = $1) until December 29, 1958, when rate fixed at FF493.7 = $1 (old francs). One year later, rate was FF 4.937 = $1 when new franc (one new franc was equal to 100 old francs) was created. Devaluation to FF5.554 = $1 on August 10, 1969.
Germany	Revalued on March 6, 1961, from DM4.20 = $1 to DM4.0 = $1. Revalued to DM3.66 = $1 on October 26, 1969.
Italy	Pegged at Lit625 = $1 from March 30, 1960 until August 1971.
Japan	Pegged at ¥360 = $1 until 1971.
Netherlands	Pegged at F13.80 = $1 until March 7, 1961, when revalued at F13.62 = $1.
United Kingdom	Devalued from $2.80 = £1 to $2.40 = £1 on November 11, 1967.

[a]Relative to the U.S. dollar.

standard because the key currency, the dollar, was convertible into gold for official holders of dollars (such as central banks and treasuries).

The Bretton Woods system worked well through the 1950s and part of the 1960s. In 1960 there was a dollar crisis because the United States had run large balance-of-payments deficits in the late 1950s. Concern over large foreign holdings of dollars led to an increased demand for gold. Central bank cooperation in an international gold pool managed to stabilize gold prices at the official rate, but still the pressures mounted. Although the problem of chronic U.S. deficits and Japanese and European surpluses could have been remedied by revaluing the undervalued yen, mark, and franc, the surplus countries argued that it was the responsibility of the United States to restore balance-of-payments equilibrium.

The failure to realign currency values in the face of fundamental economic change spelled the beginning of the end for the gold exchange standard of the Bretton Woods agreement. By the late 1960s the foreign dollar liabilities of the United States were much larger than the U.S. gold stock. The pressures of this "dollar glut" finally culminated in August 1971, when President Nixon declared the dollar to be inconvertible and provided a close to the Bretton Woods era of fixed exchange rates and convertible currencies.

THE TRANSITION YEARS: 1971 TO 1973

In December 1971, an international monetary conference was held to realign the foreign exchange values of the major currencies. The Smithsonian agreement provided for a change in the dollar per gold exchange value from $35 to $38.02 per ounce of gold. At the same time that the dollar was being devalued by about 8 percent, the surplus countries saw their currencies revalued upward. After the change in official currency values the system was to operate with fixed exchange rates, under which the central banks would buy and sell their currencies to maintain the exchange rate within ±2.25 percent of the stated parity.

Although the realignment of currency values provided by the Smithsonian agreement allowed a temporary respite from foreign exchange crisis, the calm was short-lived. Speculative flows of capital began to put downward pressure on the pound and lira. In June 1972, the pound began to float according to supply and demand conditions. The countries experiencing large inflows of speculative capital, such as Germany and Switzerland, applied legal controls to slow further movements of money into their countries.

Although the gold value of the dollar had been officially changed, the dollar was still inconvertible into gold, and thus the major significance of the dollar devaluation was with respect to the foreign exchange value of the dollar, not to official gold movements. The speculative capital flows of 1972 and early 1973 led to a further devaluation of the dollar in February 1973, because the official price of an ounce of gold rose from $38 to $42.22. Still, the speculative capital flows persisted from the weak to the strong currencies. Finally, in March 1973, the major currencies began to float.

FLOATING EXCHANGE RATES: 1973 TO THE PRESENT

Although we refer to the exchange rate system in existence since 1973 as a floating rate system, exchange rates have not been determined solely by the free market forces of supply and demand. The system as operated is best described as a *managed float,* wherein central banks intervene at times to obtain a politically desirable exchange rate apart from that which would be determined by free market supply and demand. Such managed floating does not apply to all countries and currencies, as we observe several different exchange rate policies followed by countries today. Table 3.2 lists the exchange rate practices of the IMF member countries as of June 30, 1993. We observe some currencies, such as the U.S. dollar, to be freely floating, whereas others choose to maintain a fixed value (or peg) relative to a single currency such as the dollar or pound, and still others choose to peg to a composite or basket of currencies. There are several reasons for choosing a basket peg. If trade is not heavily concentrated with the United States but is instead diversified across several countries, then it may make more sense to alter the currency value relative to a weighted average of foreign currencies rather than any single currency. Note that some countries choose to peg to the SDR. *Special drawing rights,* or *SDR*s as they are commonly called, are special international reserve assets created by the IMF.

Note that the group of countries listed under "Cooperative arrangements" in Table 3.2 have combined to form the *European Monetary System* (*EMS*). Because these countries are very interdependent, they did not wish to float against one another. The EMS is a system in which the member countries maintain fixed exchange rates among themselves, yet float jointly against the rest of the world.

Finally, some countries have chosen an intermediate path between floating and pegging. A *crawling peg* is a system wherein the exchange rate is held fixed in the short run but is adjusted at regular intervals to reflect supply and demand pressures.

THE CHOICE OF AN EXCHANGE RATE SYSTEM

Perfectly fixed or pegged exchange rates would work much as a gold standard does. All currencies would fix their exchange rate in terms of another currency, say, the dollar, and thereby would fix

Table 3.2 EXCHANGE RATE PRACTICES OF IMF MEMBER COUNTRIES
(As of June 30, 1993)[1]

		Currency pegged to			
US dollar	French franc	Russian ruble	Other currency	SDR	Other composite[2]
Angola	Benin	Armenia	Bhutan	Libya	Algeria
Antigua &	Burkina Faso	Azerbaijan	(Indian	Myanmar	Austria
Barbuda	Cameroon	Belarus	Rupee)	Rwanda	Bangladesh
Argentina	C. African Rep.	Georgia	Estonia	Seychelles	Botswana
Bahamas, The	Chad	Kazakhstan	(deutsche		Burundi
Barbados			mark)		
	Comoros	Moldova	Kiribati		Cape Verde
Belize	Congo		(Australian		Cyprus
Djibouti	Côte d'Ivoire	Turkmenistan	dollar)		Fiji
Dominica	Equatorial		Lesotho		Hungary
Grenada	Guinea		(South		Iceland
Iraq	Gabon		African		
			Rand)		Jordan
Liberia	Mali		Namibia		Kenya
Marshall Islands	Niger		(South		Kuwait
Oman	Senegal		African		Malawi
Panama	Togo		Rand)		Malta
St. Kitts & Nevis					
			Swaziland		Mauritania
St Lucia			(South		Mauritius
St. Vincent and the			African		Morocco
Grenadines			Rand)		Nepal
Suriname					Papua New
Syrian Arab Rep.					Guinea
Yemen, Republic of					
					Solomon
					Islands
					Tanzania
					Thailand
					Tonga
					Vanuatu
					Western
					Samoa
					Zimbabwe

[1]For members with dual or multiple exchange markets, the arrangement shown is that in the major market.

[2]Comprises currencies which are pegged to various "baskets" of currencies of the members' own choice, as distinct from the SDR basket.

Table 3.2 (Continued)

Flexibility limited in terms of a single currency or group of currencies		More flexible		
Single currency[3]	Cooperative arrangements[4]	Adjusted according to a set of indicators[5]	Other managed floating	Independently floating
Bahrain	Belgium	Chile	Cambodia	Afghanistan
Qatar	Denmark	Colombia	China, P.R.	Islamic State
Saudi Arabia	France	Madagascar	Croatia	of
United Arab	Germany		Ecuador	Albania
Emirates	Ireland		Egypt	Australia
				Bolivia
	Luxembourg		Greece	Brazil
	Netherlands		Guinea	
	Portugal		Guinea-Bissau	Bulgaria
	Spain		Indonesia	Canada
			Israel	Costa Rica
				Dominican Rep.
			Korea	El Salvador
			Lao P.D. Rep	
			Malaysia	Ethiopia
			Maldives	Finland
			Mexico	Gambia, The
				Ghana
			Nicaragua	Guatemala
			Pakistan	
			Poland	Guyana
			Sao Tome &	Haiti
			Principe	Honduras
			Singapore	India
				Iran, I. R. of
			Slovenia	
			Somalia	Italy
			Sri Lanka	Jamaica
			Tunisia	Japan
			Turkey	Kyrgyz Rep.
				Latvia
			Uruguay	
			Venezuela	Lebanon
			Viet Nam	Lithuania
				Mongolia
				Mozambique
				New Zealand
				Nigeria
				Norway
				Paraguay
				Peru
				Philippines
				Romania
				Russia
				Sierra Leone
				South Africa
				Sudan
				Sweden
				Switzerland
				Trindad and
				Tobago
				Uganda
				Ukraine
				United Kingdom
				United States
				Zaïre
				Zambia

[3]Exchange rates of all currencies have shown limited flexibility in terms of the U.S dollar.

[4]Refers to the cooperative arrangement maintained under the European Monetary System.

[5]Includes exchange arrangements under which the exchange rate is adjusted at relatively frequent intervals, on the basis of indicators determined by the respective member countries.

Source: International Monetary Fund, *International Financial Statistics,* October 1993, p. 6.

their rate relative to every other currency. Under such an arrangement each country would have to follow the monetary policy of the key currency in order to experience the same inflation rate and keep the exchange rate fixed.

Flexible or floating exchange rates occur when the exchange rate is determined by the market forces of supply and demand. As the demand for a currency increases relative to supply, that currency will appreciate, whereas currencies in which the quantity supplied exceeds the quantity demanded will depreciate.

Economists do not all agree on the advantages and disadvantages of a floating as opposed to a pegged exchange rate system. For instance, some would argue that a major advantage of flexible rates is that each country can follow domestic macroeconomic policies independent of the policies of other countries. To maintain fixed exchange rates, countries have to share a common inflation experience, which was often a source of problems under the post–World War II system of fixed exchange rates. If the dollar, which was the key currency for the system, was inflating at a rate faster than, say, Germany desired, then the lower inflation rate followed by the Germans led to pressure for an appreciation of the mark relative to the dollar. Thus the existing pegged rate could not be maintained. Yet with flexible rates, each country can choose a desired rate of inflation and the exchange rate will adjust accordingly. Thus if the United States chooses 8 percent inflation and Germany chooses 3 percent, there will be a steady depreciation of the dollar relative to the mark (absent any relative price movements). Given the different political environment and cultural heritage existing in each country, it is reasonable to expect different countries to follow different monetary policies. Floating exchange rates allow for an orderly adjustment to these differing inflation rates.

Still there are those economists who argue that the ability of each country to choose an inflation rate is an undesirable aspect of floating exchange rates. These proponents of fixed rates indicate that fixed rates are useful in providing an international discipline on the inflationary policies of countries. Fixed rates provide an anchor for countries with inflationary tendencies. By maintaining a fixed rate of exchange to the dollar (or some other currency), each country's inflation rate is "anchored" to the dollar, and thus will follow the policy established for the dollar.

Critics of flexible exchange rates have also argued that flexible exchange rates would be subject to destabilizing speculation. By *destabilizing speculation* we mean that speculators in the foreign exchange market will cause exchange rate fluctuations to be wider than they would be in the absence of such speculation. Although it is doubtful that this is a serious criticism, the logic suggests that, if speculators expect a currency to depreciate, they will take positions in the foreign exchange market that will cause the depreciation as a sort of self-fulfilling prophecy. But speculators should lose money when they guess wrong, so that only successful speculators will remain in the market, and the successful players serve a useful role by "evening out" swings in the exchange rate. For instance, if we expect a currency to depreciate or decrease in value next month, we could sell the currency now, which would result in a current depreciation. This will lead to a smaller future depreciation than would occur otherwise. The speculator then spreads the exchange rate change more evenly through time and tends to even out big jumps in the exchange rate. If the speculator had bet on the future depreciation by selling the currency now and the currency appreciates instead of depreciates, then the speculator loses and will eventually be eliminated from the market if such mistakes are repeated.

Research has shown that there are systematic differences between countries choosing to peg their exchange rates and those choosing floating rates. One very important characteristic is country size in terms of economic activity or GDP. Large countries tend to be more independent and less willing to subjugate domestic policies with a view toward maintaining a fixed rate of exchange with foreign currencies. Since foreign trade tends to constitute a smaller fraction of GDP the larger the country is, it is perhaps understandable that larger countries are less attuned to foreign exchange rate concerns than are smaller countries.

The openness of the economy is another important factor. By openness, we mean the degree to which the country depends on international trade. The greater the fraction of tradable (i.e., internationally tradable) goods in GDP, the more open the economy will be. A country with little or no international trade is referred to as a *closed economy.* As previously mentioned, openness is related to size. The more open the economy, the greater the weight of tradable goods prices in the overall national price level, and therefore the greater the

impact of exchange rate changes on the national price level. To minimize such foreign-related shocks to the domestic price level, the more open economy tends to follow a pegged exchange rate.

Countries that choose higher rates of inflation than their trading partners will have difficulty maintaining an exchange rate peg. We find, in fact, those countries with inflation experiences different from the average following floating rates or a crawling-peg-type system in which the exchange rate is adjusted at short intervals to compensate for the inflation differentials.

Countries that trade largely with a single foreign country tend to peg their exchange rate to the foreign country's currency. For instance, since the United States accounts for the majority of Barbados trade, by pegging to the U.S. dollar, Barbados imparts to its exports and imports a degree of stability that would otherwise be missing. By maintaining a pegged rate between the Barbados dollar and the U.S. dollar, Barbados is not unlike another state of the United States as far as pricing goods and services in United States–Barbados trade. Countries with diversified trading patterns will not find exchange rate pegging so desirable.

The evidence from previous studies indicates quite convincingly the systematic differences between peggers and floaters, which is summarized in Table 3.3. But there are exceptions to these generalities because neither all peggers nor all floaters have the same characteristics. We can safely say that, in general, the larger the country is, the more likely it is to float its exchange rate; the more closed the economy is, the more likely the country will float; and so on. The point is that economic phenomena, and not just political maneuvering, ultimately influence foreign exchange rate practices.

Recently, researchers have focused on how the choice of an exchange rate system will affect the stability of the economy. If the

Table 3.3 CHARACTERISTICS ASSOCIATED WITH COUNTRIES CHOOSING TO PEG OR FLOAT

Peggers	Floaters
Small size	Large size
Open economy	Closed economy
Harmonious inflation rate	Divergent inflation rate
Concentrated trade	Diversified trade

domestic policy authorities seek to minimize unexpected fluctuations in the domestic price level, then they will choose an exchange rate system that best minimizes such fluctuations. For instance, the greater the foreign tradable goods price fluctuations are, the more likely there will be a float, since the floating exchange rate helps to insulate the domestic economy from foreign price disturbances. The greater the domestic money supply fluctuations are, the more likely there will be a peg, since international money flows serve as shock absorbers that reduce the domestic price impact of domestic money supply fluctuations. With a fixed exchange rate, an excess supply of domestic money will cause a capital outflow because some of this excess supply is eliminated via a balance-of-payments deficit. With floating rates, the excess supply of money is contained at home and reflected in a higher domestic price level and depreciating domestic currency. Once again, the empirical evidence supports the notion that real-world exchange rate practices are determined by such economic phenomena.

OPTIMUM CURRENCY AREAS AND THE EMS

The *optimum currency area* is the best area within which exchange rates are fixed and between which exchange rates are flexible. Looking at the real world, we might suggest that North America and Western Europe appear to be likely currency areas given the geographic proximity of Canada, Mexico, and the United States, as well as the geographic position of the Western European nations. Since exchange rates between U.S. and Canadian dollars and the Mexican peso seem closely linked (certainly the peso and the U.S. dollar had a long history of fixed exchange rates), we might expect these three countries to maintain pegged exchange rates with each other and to float versus the rest of the world. Western Europeans have, in fact, explicitly adopted such a regional optimum currency area arrangement. The European Monetary System (EMS) is characterized by relatively fixed rates within the system and floating rates between the EMS and the rest of the world.

One theory suggests that the optimum currency area is the region characterized by relatively costless mobility of the factors of production (labor and capital). As an illustration of this theory, suppose we have two countries, A and B, producing computers and cotton, respectively. Suddenly there is a change in tastes resulting

in a shift of demand from computers to cotton. Country A will tend to run a deficit balance of trade and have an excess supply of labor and capital since the demand for computers has fallen, whereas country B will run a surplus and have an excess demand for labor and capital because of the increase in demand for its cotton. What are the possibilities for international adjustment to these changes?

1. Factors of production could move from A to B and thereby establish new equilibrium wages and prices in each region.
2. Prices in A could fall relative to those in B, and the relative price change would eliminate the balance-of-trade disequilibrium if labor and capital cannot move between the countries. (We are ignoring the capital account now, in order to assume zero capital flows.)
3. The exchange rate could adjust and bring about the required change in relative prices if A and B have different currencies.

Now we can understand why the optimum currency area is characterized by mobile factors of production. If factors can freely and cheaply migrate from an area lacking jobs to an area where labor is in demand, then the factor mobility will restore equilibrium since the unemployment in one area is remedied by migration. Thus fixed exchange rates within the area will be appropriate because relative price movements are not the only means for restoring equilibrium.

When factors are immobile so that equilibrium is restored solely through relative price change, then there is an advantage to flexible exchange rates. If the monetary authorities in each country tend to resist any price changes, then the easiest way to adjust is with flexible exchange rates, because the adjustment can go largely through the exchange rate rather than through prices.

The optimum currency area literature suggests that in a regional setting like Western Europe a system of fixed exchange rates might be appropriate. In March 1979, the *European Monetary System* (*EMS*) was established. The EMS committed the member countries to maintaining small exchange rate fluctuations among themselves while allowing for large fluctuations against outside currencies. The EMS worked quite well through the 1980s and led to optimism that the member nations could eventually evolve into a

system with one European central bank and one money. It was in this spirit that the Maastricht Treaty was signed in December 1991 where the timetable for the evolution of the system was spelled out. The treaty called for:

- the immediate removal of restrictions on European flows of capital and greater coordination of monetary and fiscal policy.
- the establishment of a European Monetary Institute (EMI) in January 1994 to coordinate monetary policies of the individual central banks and make technical preparations for a single monetary policy.
- the irrevocable fixing of exchange rates among all member countries with the European Currency Unit (ECU) becoming a currency in its own right and the beginning of the European Central Bank in January 1997, at the earliest, and by January 1999, at the latest.

The achievement of monetary union under the EMS requires that all countries achieve a convergence of macroeconomic policies. They must have similar inflation rates, interest rates, and government budget deficits (as a fraction of GDP) in order to make a single currency possible. However, it was clear by the summer of 1993 that this convergence was not occurring. As a result the European Community (EC) officials modified the agreement to allow a greater fluctuation of exchange rates among member countries from 2.25 percent to 15 percent. This was presented as a temporary measure that would be eliminated as soon as economic conditions allowed. Critics of the move toward monetary union have argued that the recent difficulties point out the problems of having sovereign nations relinquish their discretionary policy powers and believe that the likelihood of ever having one European money is small. Supporters of one money for Europe see the recent setbacks as a mere bump in the road to ultimate monetary union.

INTERNATIONAL RESERVE CURRENCIES

International reserves are the means of settling international debts. Under the gold standard, gold was the major component of international reserves. Following World War II, we had a gold exchange standard in which international reserves included both gold and a

reserve currency, the U.S. dollar. The reserve currency country was to hold gold as backing for the outstanding balances of the currency held by foreigners. These foreign holders of the currency were then free to convert the currency into gold if they wished. However, as we observed with the dollar, once the convertibility of the currency becomes suspect, or once large amounts of the currency are presented for gold, the system tends to fall apart.

This appears to describe the dollar following World War II. At the end of the war, and throughout the 1950s, the world demanded dollars for use as an international reserve. During this time U.S. balance-of-payments deficits provided the world with a much-needed source of growth for international reserves. As the rest of the world developed and matured, over time U.S. liabilities to foreigners greatly exceeded the gold reserve backing these liabilities. Yet as long as the increase in demand for these dollar reserves equalled the supply, the lack of gold backing was irrelevant. Through the late 1960s, U.S. political and economic events began to cause problems for the dollar's international standing, and the continuing U.S. deficits were not matched by a growing demand, so that pressure to convert dollars into gold resulted in the dollar being declared officially no longer exchangeable for gold in August 1971.

Table 3.4 illustrates the diversification of the currency composition of foreign exchange reserves since the mid-1970s. There has been a trend of a falling share devoted to U.S. dollars along with a rising share devoted to the mark and yen.

At first glance it may appear very desirable to be the reserve currency and have other countries accept your balance-of-payments deficits as a necessary means of financing world trade. The difference between the cost to the reserve country of creating new balances and the real resources the reserve country is able to acquire with the new balances is called *seigniorage*. Seigniorage then is a financial reward accruing to the reserve currency as a result of the use of the currency as a world money.

The seigniorage return for being the dominant money must be quite low since the United States and the United Kingdom before it have not produced very high-quality reserve money. The seigniorage return to the United Kingdom was probably eroded by the dollar's growing dominance through the twentieth century, so that the United Kingdom did not have much to lose by following a domestic policy of high and variable inflation and thereby losing the in-

Table 3.4 SHARE OF NATIONAL CURRENCIES IN TOTAL IDENTIFIED OFFICIAL HOLDINGS OF FOREIGN EXCHANGE, END OF YEAR, 1977 TO 1992[a]

In Percentages

	1977	1979	1981	1983	1985	1987	1989	1992	Memorandum: ECUs treated separately[b] 1992
All countries									
U.S. dollar	80.3	75.2	73.1	72.2	65.1	67.2	60.2	64.4	55.3
Pound sterling	1.8	2.1	2.2	2.7	3.2	2.4	2.7	3.2	3.1
Deutsche mark	9.3	12.8	13.4	12.0	15.5	14.4	19.3	13.0	12.5
French franc	1.3	1.4	1.4	1.1	1.2	0.8	1.3	2.5	2.4
Swiss franc	2.3	2.6	2.8	2.4	2.4	2.0	1.7	1.3	1.3
Netherlands guilder	0.9	1.1	1.2	0.9	1.0	1.2	1.1	0.7	0.7
Japanese yen	2.5	3.7	4.3	5.0	7.6	7.5	7.9	8.1	7.8
Unspecified currencies[c]	1.6	1.2	1.4	3.5	3.9	4.4	5.7	6.8	16.9
Industrial countries									
U.S. dollar	89.4	83.4	78.7	76.0	63.2	70.3	59.4	64.9	49.9
Pound sterling	0.9	0.8	0.7	0.9	2.0	1.1	1.4	2.3	2.2
Deutsche mark	5.5	9.7	13.1	12.9	19.2	15.9	22.9	14.4	13.5
French franc	0.3	0.6	0.5	0.3	0.5	0.4	1.1	3.0	2.8
Swiss franc	0.8	1.5	1.8	1.5	1.8	1.6	1.5	0.6	0.5
Netherlands guilder	0.6	0.6	0.8	0.5	1.0	1.3	1.2	0.5	0.5
Japanese yen	1.8	2.6	3.7	5.1	8.5	7.1	8.2	7.4	7.0
Unspecified currencies[c]	0.7	0.7	0.7	2.9	3.9	2.3	4.4	6.9	23.5

Table 3.4 (continued)

Developing Countries[d]

U.S. dollar	70.9	66.3	67.1	68.0	67.5	60.4	62.1	63.6	64.6
Pound sterling	2.8	3.4	3.8	4.8	4.7	5.2	5.7	4.6	4.6
Deutsche mark	13.3	16.2	13.9	11.1	10.9	11.1	11.4	10.9	10.9
French franc	2.3	2.2	2.5	2.0	2.1	1.8	1.8	1.9	1.9
Swiss franc	3.9	3.8	3.9	3.6	3.1	2.7	2.4	2.5	2.5
Netherlands guilder	1.2	1.6	1.6	1.3	1.1	1.1	0.8	0.9	0.9
Japanese yen	3.2	4.8	5.0	4.9	6.5	8.6	7.1	9.0	9.0
Unspecified currencies[c]	2.5	1.7	2.2	4.2	4.0	9.0	8.7	6.7	6.7

[a]Starting with 1979, the SDR value of European currency units (ECUs) issued against U.S. dollars is added to the SDR value of U.S. dollars, but the SDR value of ECUs issued against gold is excluded from the total distributed here. Only selected countries that provide information about the currency composition of their official holdings of foreign exchange are included in this table.

[b]This column is for comparison and indicates the currency composition of reserves when holdings of ECUs are treated as a separate reserve asset, unlike the earlier columns starting with 1979 as is explained in the preceding footnote. The share of ECUs in total foreign exchange holdings was 9.4 percent for all countries and 17 percent for the industrial countries in 1992.

[c]This residual is equal to the difference between total identified reserves and the sum of the reserves held in the seven currencies listed in the table.

[d]The calculations here rely to a greater extent on Fund staff estimates than do those provided for the group of industrial countries.

Source: International Monetary Fund, *Annual Report*, 1993, p. 107.

ternational dominance of the pound. Likewise, the United States in the late 1960s and 1970s depreciated some of the dollar's international standing by a relatively high and variable U.S. inflation. Perhaps the growing use of external dollar markets (like the Eurodollar market) has reduced the seigniorage to the United States, so that the U.S. policy of depreciating the dollar's value was optimal. At any rate, the fact that we have not observed countries competing for reserve currency status indicates that the seigniorage return is likely to be quite small.

Although the dollar has lost some of its reserve currency market share since the 1970s, the dollar is still, by far, the dominant reserve currency. Since the U.S. international position has been somewhat eroded in the past few decades, the question arises, why have we not seen the German mark, Japanese yen, or Swiss franc emerge as the dominant reserve currency? Although the mark, yen, and Swiss franc have been popular currencies, the respective governments in each country have resisted a greater international role for their monies. Besides the apparent low seigniorage return to the dominant international money, there is another reason for these countries to resist. The dominant money producer (country) finds that international shifts in the demand for its money may have repercussions on domestic operations. For a country the size of the United States, domestic economic activity overwhelms international activity so that international capital flows of any given magnitude have a much smaller potential to disrupt U.S. markets than Japanese, German, or Swiss markets, where foreign operations are much more important. In this sense it is clear why these countries have withstood the movement of the yen, mark, and franc to reserve currency status.

In domestic monetary theory economists often identify three roles of money. Money is said to serve as (1) a unit of account, (2) a medium of exchange, and (3) a store of value. Likewise, in an international context we can explain the choice of a reserve currency according to criteria relevant for each role.

Table 3.5 summarizes the roles of a reserve currency. First, the role of the international unit of account results from information costs. We find that primary goods like coffee, tin, or rubber are quoted in terms of dollars worldwide. Since these goods are homogeneous, at least relative to manufactured goods, information regarding their value is conveyed more quickly when prices are quoted in terms of one currency worldwide. The private use as an

Table 3.5 ROLES OF A RESERVE CURRENCY

Function	Resulting from	Private role	Official role
1. International unit of account	Information costs	Invoicing currency	Pegging currency
2. International medium of exchange	Transaction costs	Vehicle currency	Intervention currency
3. International store of value	Stable value	Banking currency	Reserve currency

invoicing currency in international trade contracts arises from the reserve currency's informational advantage over other currencies. Besides being a unit of account for private contracts, the reserve currency also serves as a base currency to which other currencies peg exchange rates.

A currency's role as an international medium of exchange is the result of transaction costs. In the case of the U.S. dollar, the dollar is so widely traded that it is often cheaper to go from currency *A* to dollars to currency *B*, than directly from currency *A* to currency *B*. Thus it is efficient to use the dollar as an international medium of exchange, and the dollar serves as the "vehicle" for buying and selling nondollar currencies. The private (mainly interbank) role as a vehicle currency means that the dollar (or the dominant reserve currency) will also be used by central banks in foreign exchange market intervention aimed at achieving target levels for exchange rates.

Finally, a currency's role as an international store of value results from its stability of value. In other words, certainty of future value enhances a currency's role as a store of purchasing power. The U.S. dollar's role in this area has been diminished, and it seems likely that further instability in U.S. monetary policy would contribute to a further fall. The private market use of the dollar for denominating international loans and deposits indicates the role of the dominant reserve currency in banking. In addition, countries will choose to hold their official reserves largely in the dominant reserve currency.

As the preceding discussion indicates, market forces determine a currency's international role, and not a government's decree. It is important to realize, however, that just as the market chooses to elevate a currency like the U.S. dollar to reserve cur-

rency status, it can also take away some of that status, which happened to the U.K. pound earlier in this century and to the dollar to a lesser extent since the 1970s.

COMPOSITE RESERVE CURRENCIES

The previous section discussed the use of individual currencies as reserve currencies. However, sometimes it may be preferred to denominate bank accounts or trade contracts or peg to a combination or composite of currencies. With regard to exchange rate pegging practices, Table 3.2 indicated that 31 countries pegged to the SDR or some other composite of currencies.

There are many reasons why a country might choose to peg to an average of several currencies rather than a single currency. If a nation's trade is diversified across developed countries rather than concentrated with a single country, it may make sense to peg to an average of the trading partners' currencies rather than a single currency. In denominating bank deposits or bonds, there is a diversification gain to using a composite currency instead of a single currency. The value of the composite currency generally is more stable than that of a single currency.

Although one could construct a composite currency unit using any desired mix of currencies, two existing composites are frequently used: the SDR, issued by the IMF, and the European currency unit (ECU), created by the European Monetary System (EMS). The use of such existing composites that are maintained by official organizations lowers the costs of using composite currencies compared to a "basket of currencies" tailored for a specific transaction. Let's now consider the SDR and ECU in more detail.

Originally, SDRs were just traded between central banks, and when a country needed a particular currency, it could swap some of the SDRs allocated to it by the IMF for the desired currency. Recently, the private use of SDRs has expanded since private banks have issued SDR-denominated deposits and loans. Because the value of the SDR is a weighted average of the value of five major currencies (since January 1981 the currencies used are the U.S. dollar, German mark, French franc, Japanese yen, and U.K. pound), by denominating accounts in SDRs there is a diversification effect.

Prior to January 1981, the SDR was based on a weighted average of the currencies of the sixteen largest trading countries (those

whose share in world exports exceeded 1 percent of the total). In January 1981, the five-currency SDR was created. The move to a five-currency weighted average has made the SDR much more attractive as a unit of account in the private sector, because it is much easier to compute and comprehend expected changes in the value of five major world currencies than it is sixteen (which included some not so widely traded currencies). Table 3.6 shows how changes in the value of the dollar, mark, yen, franc, and pound will change the value of the SDR.

Column (2) of the table indicates the number of units of each currency that goes into the SDR. We see that one SDR is made up of 0.572 U.S. dollars, 0.453 German marks, 31.8 yen, and so on. As the value of each currency changes, the SDR's value will also change. Table 3.6 gives the computations determining the dollar value of the SDR on October 11, 1993. To determine the SDR's dollar value, we simply multiply column (2) by the dollar value of each currency as given in column (3), with the resulting product in column (4). Summing the dollar value of each component, we arrive at the dollar value of the SDR. On October 11, one SDR was equal to $1.4217.

Note that column (5) indicates how the various currencies are weighted in importance. These weights are found by dividing each single element of column (4) by the total of the column. We notice that on October 11, 1993 the dollar determined approximately 40 percent of the SDR's value, followed by the Japanese yen's 21.08 percent.

As stated earlier, the move to a five-currency SDR has encouraged private-sector use of SDR-denominated accounts. Although

Table 3.6 THE VALUATION OF SDRS ON OCTOBER 11, 1993

(1) Currency	(2) Units of currency	(3) Spot rate: $/domestic currency	(4) Dollar value of components	(5) Percentage value
U.S. dollar	0.572	1.0000	0.5720	40.23
German mark	0.453	0.6245	0.2829	19.90
Japanese yen	31.8	0.0094	0.2997	21.08
French franc	0.800	0.1780	0.1424	10.02
U.K. pound	0.0812	1.5367	0.1247	08.77
			1.4217	100.00

SDR1 = $1.4217

the SDR has grown in popularity, it must be made clear that the volume of business denominated in SDRs is dwarfed by the volume denominated in single currencies like the U.S. dollar. As for the official use of the SDR as a reserve currency, it is safe to say that countries prefer to receive reserve inflows in freely convertible currencies like the dollar or pound instead of SDRs.

The private use of SDRs is limited only by what market participants are willing to agree to. The first SDR-denominated bond was issued in June 1975. Between 1975 and 1981, there were 13 issues of SDR bonds for a total of SDR 563 million. Eleven of these issues were from official institutions and two were by private concerns. There were no SDR bonds issued between late 1981 and 1987. The first SDR-denominated bank deposit was issued by a London bank in June 1975. In March 1981, the Brussels branch of Morgan Guaranty Bank offered the first SDR-denominated demand deposits. By the end of 1981, 40 to 50 banks were offering SDR deposits with a volume that ranged from SDR5 to SDR7 billion. The volume of SDR deposits has declined since that time.

In June 1980, the London branch of Chemical Bank issued a certificate of deposit (CD) for SDR50 million. For a brief time through 1981, the issue of SDR CDs increased to around SDR700 million. Interest in SDR CDs has dwindled since the early 1980s and is now insignificant. In the early 1980s, some SDR-denominated syndicated bank loans were made. Since that time, no new loans have been made.

In general, private market use of the SDR seems to have peaked in the early 1980s. The little interest that has existed is in denominating financial contracts. Use of the SDR for pricing or invoicing goods has been very rare. One existing example is transit tolls for ships passing through the Suez Canal. Since 1975, such tolls have been denominated in SDRs.

Table 3.2 showed that several European countries follow a cooperative exchange rate agreement known as the European Monetary System (EMS). In March 1979, the EMS introduced a European composite currency unit, the *European currency unit* (*ECU*). The ultimate goal of the EMS is to have the ECU evolve as a monetary unit used in domestic economies to achieve a common European money. The ECU is the official unit of account for the European Communities (EC) and is used for EC budgets and trans-

actions. It also serves as the reserve asset of the EMS. In this role it is analogous to the SDR in that there is no physical ECU currency. ECUs are simply accounting entries whose ownership is transferred by credits and debits to the financial statements of the concerned parties.

Unlike the SDR, the private market use of the ECU has grown over time. And as a composite currency unit, we should expect the ECU to gain a more stable value than any other single currency because of the diversification effect it enjoys.

The first ECU-denominated bank deposit was opened by the European Commission in March 1976, and the ECU deposit market has grown to include a broad range of deposits, ranging from savings and demand deposits at the retail level to 5-year deposits in the interbank market. By mid-1985, ECU-denominated deposits exceeded ECU45 billion and by late 1991 they were approximately $193 billion. The first ECU-denominated syndicated bank loan was made in June 1980. Through 1985, more than 91 syndicated loans had been made in excess of ECU6.4 billion. The first ECU-denominated bond issue occurred in April 1981. In the 5 years following, over 260 bond issues worth almost ECU16 billion occurred. The ECU is now the fifth-most important unit of account for new bond issues (behind the U.S. dollar, Swiss franc, yen, and mark). In addition, there is a thriving spot and forward exchange market in ECUs; there are ECU-denominated travelers checks in Europe, ECU-denominated life insurance issued in Italy, and ECU options and futures contracts offered on several exchanges.

Why has the ECU won private market acceptance where the SDR failed? The ECU is considered to be a more effective hedge against the dollar than the SDR, since the ECU valuation excludes the dollar completely while the dollar is the most important currency in determining the value of the SDR. Furthermore, the EMS commitment to stabilizing European exchange rates has made the ECU quite stable relative to national currencies.

MULTIPLE EXCHANGE RATES

Most countries conduct all foreign exchange transactions at a single exchange rate. But some countries (25 as of June 30, 1992) maintain multiple exchange rates. A typical arrangement is a dual exchange

rate system with a free-market-determined floating exchange rate for capital account transactions and a fixed exchange rate, overvaluing the domestic currency, for current account transactions. Some countries have much more complex arrangements involving three or more exchange rates applied to various transactions.

The IMF has generally sought to unify exchange rates in those countries where multiple rates exist. The argument is that multiple exchange rates harm both the countries that impose them as well as other countries. With different exchange rates for different types of transactions, domestic relative prices of internationally traded goods tend to differ from international relative prices. This results in distorted decision making in consumption, production, and investment as domestic residents respond to artificial relative prices rather than the true prices set on world markets. Multiple exchange rates are also costly in that people devote resources to finding ways to profit from the tiered exchange rates (like having transactions classified to the most favorable exchange rate category). Finally, the maintenance of a multiple exchange rate system requires a costly administrative structure.

Research has generally found that multiple exchange rates are a form of protectionism, originally introduced to improve a country's balance of payments. The elimination of a multiple exchange rate system could simply involve allowing all transactions to occur at the market-determined rate. If a unified fixed exchange rate is desired, the floating rate will suggest an appropriate level for the new fixed rate. Of course, after the fixed rate is established, monetary and fiscal policy must be consistent with the maintenance of the new exchange rate.

SUMMARY

1. Under a gold standard, currencies are convertible into gold at fixed exchange rates.
2. The IMF and a system of fixed exchange rates were created at the Bretton Woods Conference in 1944.
3. In March 1973, the major developed countries began floating exchange rates.
4. Countries with floating exchange rates tend to have large, closed economies, with inflation rates that differ from those of their trading partners and trade diversified across many countries.
5. The optimum currency area is characterized by mobile factors of production.

6. Reserve currencies serve as an international unit of account, a medium of exchange, and a store of value.
7. Composite currency units have more stable values than individual currencies.
8. Multiple exchange rates are used to encourage exports and discourage imports.

EXERCISES

1. What is seigniorage? Does the United States possess an unfair advantage in world commerce due to seigniorage?
2. With a gold standard, is it feasible for a country to continuously change the value of its currency in terms of gold to achieve faster and faster money supply growth?
3. How does a gold standard eliminate the possibility of continuous balance-of-payments disequilibria?
4. What are the fundamental differences between the ECU and the SDR? Why has the ECU become the more popular unit of account of the two?
5. Discuss the common economic arguments germane to whether, in general, exchange rates should float or be fixed.
6. How did the Bretton Woods international monetary system differ from the gold standard? What was the primary purpose of the IMF under Bretton Woods? Why did the Bretton Woods agreement finally break down?

REFERENCES

Bordo, Michael David, "The Classical Gold Standard: Lessons from the Past," in Michael B. Connolly, ed., *The International Monetary System: Choices for the Future.* New York: Praeger, 1982.

deVries, Margaret, "The IMF: 40 Years of Challenge and Change," *Finance and Development,* September 1985.

Edison, Hali J., and Michael Melvin, "The Determinants and Implications of the Choice of an Exchange Rate System," in William S. Haraf and Thomas D. Willett, eds., *Monetary Policy for a Volatile Global Economy.* Washington, D.C.: The AEI Press, 1990.

Flood, Robert P., "Exchange Rate Expectations in Dual Exchange Markets," *Journal of International Economics,* February 1978.

Glick, Reuven, "ECU, Who?" *Federal Reserve Bank of San Francisco Weekly Letter,* January 9, 1987.

Magee, Stephen P., and Ramesh K. S. Rao, "Vehicle and Nonvehicle Currencies in International Trade," *American Economic Review,* May 1980.

McKinnon, Ronald I., *An International Standard for Monetary Stabilization.* Washington, D.C.: Institute for International Economics, March 1984.

Mundell, Robert A., "A Theory of Optimum Currency Areas," *American Economic Review,* September 1961.

The Role of the SDR in the International Monetary System. Washington, D.C.: International Monetary Fund, March 1987.

chapter 4

Forward-Looking Market Instruments

In Chapter 1, we considered the problem of a U.S. importer buying French wine. Since the importer requires payment in French francs, the transaction requires an exchange of U.S. dollars for francs. The discussion in Chapter 1 was related to the *spot market*—exchanging dollars for francs today at the current spot exchange rate.

Suppose we now return to the example of the U.S. wine importer. Earlier, the importer purchased francs in the spot market to settle a contract payable now. Yet much of international trade is contracted in advance of delivery and payment. It would not be unusual for the importer to place an order for French wine for delivery at a future date. For instance, suppose the order calls for delivery of the goods and payment of the invoice in 3 months. Specifically, let's say that the order is for FF100,000.

What options does the importer have with respect to payment? One option is to wait 3 months and then buy the francs. A disadvantage of this strategy is that the exchange rate could change over the next 3 months in a way that makes the deal unprofitable. Looking at Figure 4.1, the foreign exchange quotes that appeared earlier as Figure 1.1, we see that the current spot rate (on September 23) is $0.17487 = FF1. At the current spot rate, FF100,000 = $17,487. Yet there is no guarantee that this exchange rate (and consequent dollar value of the contract) will prevail in the

EXCHANGE RATES
Thursday, September 23, 1993
The New York foreign exchange selling rates below apply to trading among banks in amounts of $1 million and more, as quoted at 3 p.m. Eastern time by Bankers Trust Co., Telerate and other sources. Retail transactions provide fewer units of foreign currency per dollar.

Country	U.S. $ equiv.		Currency per U.S. $	
	Thurs.	Wed.	Thurs.	Wed.
Argentina (Peso)	1.01	1.01	.99	.99
Australia (Dollar)	.6543	.6555	1.5284	1.5256
Austria (Schilling)	.08648	.08727	11.56	11.46
Bahrain (Dinar)	2.6536	2.6536	.3769	.3769
Belgium (Franc)	.02855	.02871	35.03	34.83
Brazil (Cruzeiro real)	.0088067	.0089334	113.55	111.94
Britain (Pound)	1.5060	1.5178	.6640	.6588
30-Day Forward	1.5025	1.5142	.6656	.6604
90-Day Forward	1.4956	1.5074	.6686	.6634
180-Day Forward	1.4878	1.4995	.6721	.6669
Canada (Dollar)	.7561	.7580	1.3226	1.3193
30-Day Forward	.7552	.7571	1.3242	1.3209
90-Day Forward	.7530	.7550	1.3280	1.3245
180-Day Forward	.7498	.7517	1.3337	1.3303
Czech. Rep. (Koruna)				
Commercial rate	.0353257	.0356888	28.3000	28.0200
Chile (Peso)	.002516	.002523	397.49	396.42
China (Renminbi)	.174856	.174856	5.7190	5.7190
Colombia (Peso)	.001453	.001451	688.79	689.25
Denmark (Krone)	.1508	.1509	6.6315	6.6264
Ecuador (Sucre)				
Floating rate	.000525	.000525	1904.00	1904.00
Finland (Markka)	.17159	.17095	5.8279	5.8496
France (Franc)	.17487	.17632	5.7185	5.6715
30-Day Forward	.17425	.17568	5.7389	5.6921
90-Day Forward	.17309	.17449	5.7774	5.7310
180-Day Forward	.17184	.17330	5.8195	5.7705
Germany (Mark)	.6085	.6141	1.6435	1.6285
30-Day Forward	.6065	.6121	1.6487	1.6338
90-Day Forward	.6031	.6086	1.6580	1.6432
180-Day Forward	.5993	.6049	1.6685	1.6533
Greece (Drachma)	.004233	.004281	236.25	233.60
Hong Kong (Dollar)	.12921	.12925	7.7395	7.7370
Hungary (Forint)	.0109075	.0109678	91.6800	91.0100
India (Rupee)	.03212	.03212	31.13	31.13
Indonesia (Rupiah)	.0004757	.0004757	2102.21	2102.21
Ireland (Punt)	1.4217	1.4341	.7034	.6973
Israel (Shekel)	.3591	.3598	2.7846	2.7797
Italy (Lira)	.0006291	.0006344	1589.50	1576.32
Japan (Yen)	.009438	.009416	105.95	106.20
30-Day Forward	.009442	.009420	105.91	106.15
90-Day Forward	.009453	.009431	105.79	106.03
180-Day Forward	.009477	.009455	105.52	105.76
Jordan (Dinar)	1.4810	1.4810	.6752	.6752
Kuwait (Dinar)	3.3400	3.3400	.2994	.2994
Lebanon (Pound)	.000580	.000580	1724.50	1724.50
Malaysia (Ringgit)	.3917	.3922	2.5530	2.5496
Malta (Lira)	2.6560	2.6560	.3765	.3765
Mexico (Peso)				
Floating rate	.3219575	.3219575	3.1060	3.1060
Netherland (Guilder)	.5419	.5468	1.8453	1.8289
New Zealand (Dollar)	.5540	.5548	1.8051	1.8025
Norway (Krone)	.1396	.1408	7.1632	7.1035
Pakistan (Rupee)	.0336	.0336	29.78	29.78
Peru (New Sol)	.4919	.4955	2.03	2.02
Philippines (Peso)	.03593	.03593	27.83	27.83
Poland (Zloty)	.00005297	.00005304	18879.00	18854.00
Portugal (Escudo)	.005950	.006001	168.08	166.63
Saudi Arabia (Riyal)	.26665	.26665	3.7503	3.7503
Singapore (Dollar)	.6275	.6276	1.5935	1.5934
Slovak Rep. (Koruna)	.0310945	.0312891	32.1600	31.9600
South Africa (Rand)				
Commercial rate	.2917	.2919	3.4285	3.4253
Financial rate	.2191	.2155	4.5650	4.6400
South Korea (Won)	.0012362	.0012350	808.90	809.70
Spain (Peseta)	.007612	.007685	131.36	130.12
Sweden (Krona)	.1240	.1231	8.0614	8.1221
Switzerland (Franc)	.6979	.7036	1.4328	1.4213
30-Day Forward	.6970	.7026	1.4348	1.4233
90-Day Forward	.6954	.7009	1.4381	1.4267
180-Day Forward	.6938	.6994	1.4413	1.4298
Taiwan (Dollar)	.037538	.037594	26.64	26.60
Thailand (Baht)	.03975	.03975	25.16	25.16
Turkey (Lira)	.0000839	.0000841	11918.00	11891.00
United Arab (Dirham)	.2723	.2723	3.6725	3.6725
Uruguay (New Peso)				
Financial	.233863	.233863	4.28	4.28
Venezuela (Bolivar)				
Floating rate	.01046	.01047	95.64	95.54
SDR	1.41366	1.41204	.70738	.70820
ECU	1.16050	1.16920	....	....

Special Drawing Rights (SDR) are based on exchange rates for the U.S., German, British, French and Japanese currencies. Source: International Monetary Fund.
European Currency Unit (ECU) is based on a basket of community currencies.

FIGURE 4.1 Foreign exchange rate quotations for September 23, 1993. (*Source: The Wall Street Journal,* September 24, p C13. Reprinted by permission of *The Wall Street Journal,* © 1993, Dow Jones and Company, Inc. All rights reserved worldwide.)

future. If the dollar should *depreciate* against the franc, then it would take more dollars to buy any given quantity of francs. For instance, suppose the future spot rate (which is currently unknown) is $0.20 = FF1. Then it would take $20,000 to purchase FF100,000, and the wine purchase would not be as profitable for the importer. Of course, if the dollar should *appreciate* against the franc, then the profits would be larger. As a result of this uncertainty regarding the

dollar/franc exchange rate in the future, the importer may not want to choose the strategy of waiting 3 months to buy francs.

Another alternative is to buy the francs now and hold or invest them for 3 months. This alternative has the advantage that the importer knows exactly how many dollars are needed to buy FF100,000. But the importer is faced with a new problem of coming up with cash now and investing the francs for 3 months. Another alternative that ensures a certain dollar price of francs is using the *forward exchange market.* As will be shown in Chapter 5, there is a close relationship between the forward market and the former alternative of buying francs now and investing them for 3 months. For now, we will focus on the operation of the forward market.

FORWARD RATES

The forward exchange market refers to buying and selling currencies to be delivered at a future date. Figure 4.1 includes forward exchange rates for the major traded currencies, including the French franc. Note that the 90-day forward rate on the franc is $0.17309 = FF1. To buy francs for delivery in 90 days would cost $0.17309 per franc. Note that a 30-day and 180-day forward rate is also quoted.

The advantage of the forward market is that we have established a set exchange rate between the dollar and the franc and do not have to buy the francs until they are needed in 90 days. This may be preferred to buying francs now and investing them for 3 months, because it is neither necessary to part with any funds now nor to have knowledge of investment opportunities in francs. (However, the selling bank may require that the importer hold "compensating balances" until the 90-day period is up—that is, leave funds in an account at the bank, allowing the bank to use the money until the forward date.) With a forward rate of $0.17309 = FF1, FF100,000 will sell for $17,309. The importer now knows with certainty how many dollars the wine will cost in 90 days.

If the forward exchange price of a currency exceeds the current spot price, that currency is said to be selling at a *forward premium.* A currency is selling at a *forward discount* when the forward rate is less than the current spot rate. The forward rates in Figure 4.1 indicate that the French franc, British pound, and

Canadian dollar are selling at a discount against the dollar, but the Japanese yen is selling at a premium. The implications of a currency selling at a discount or premium will be explored in coming chapters. In the event that the spot and forward rates are equal, the currency is said to be *flat*.

SWAPS

Commercial banks rarely use forward exchange contracts for interbank trading; instead, swap agreements are arranged. A *currency swap* is a trade involving two currencies. For example, suppose Citibank wants pounds now. They could borrow the pounds, arranging to repay in 3 months. Then they could buy pounds in the forward market to ensure a certain price to be paid when the pounds are needed in 3 months. Alternatively, Citibank could enter into a swap agreement wherein they trade dollars for pounds now and pounds for dollars in 3 months. The terms of the arrangement are obviously closely related to conditions in the forward market, since the swap rates will be determined by the discounts or premiums in the forward exchange market.

Suppose Citibank wants pounds for 3 months and works a swap with Lloyds. Citibank will trade dollars to Lloyds and in return will receive pounds. In 3 months the trade is reversed. Citibank will pay out pounds to Lloyds and receive dollars (of course, there is nothing special about the 3-month period used here—swaps could be for any period). Suppose the spot rate is $/£ = \$2.00$ and the 3-month forward rate is $/£ = \$2.10$, so that there is a \$0.10 premium on the pound. These premiums or discounts are actually quoted in basis points when serving as swap rates (a *basis point* is $\frac{1}{100}$ percent, or 0.0001). Thus the \$0.10 premium converts into a swap rate of 1000 points, which is all the swap participants are interested in; they do not care about the actual spot or forward rate since only the difference between them matters for a swap.

Swap rates are usefully converted into percent per annum terms to make them comparable to other borrowing and lending rates (remember a swap is the same as borrowing one currency while lending another currency for the duration of the swap period). The swap rate of 1000 points or 0.1000 was for a 3-month period. To convert this into annual terms, we find the percentage

return for the swap period and then multiply this by the reciprocal of the fraction of the year for which the swap exists. The percentage return for the swap period is equal to the

Premium (discount) ÷ spot rate = 0.10/$2.00 = 0.05

The fraction of a year for which the swap exists is

3 months/12 months = ¼

And the reciprocal of the fraction is

1/(¼) = 4

Thus the percent per annum premium (discount) or swap rate = 0.05 × 4 = 0.20. This swap then yields a return of 20 percent per annum, which can be compared to the other opportunities open to the bank.

Swaps allow firms to obtain long-term foreign currency financing at lower costs than they can obtain from direct borrowing. Suppose a Canadian firm wants to receive German marks today with repayment in 5 years. If the Canadian firm is not well known to German banks, the firm will pay a higher interest rate than firms that actively participate in German financial markets. The Canadian firm may approach a bank to arrange a currency swap that will reduce its borrowing costs. The bank will find a German firm desiring Canadian dollars. The Canadian firm is able to borrow Canadian dollars more cheaply than the German firm, and German firm is able to borrow marks more cheaply than the Canadian firm. The intermediary bank will arrange for each firm to borrow its domestic currency and then swap the domestic currency for the desired foreign currency. The interest rates paid on the two currencies will reflect the forward premium in existence at the time the swap is executed. When the swap agreement matures, the original principal amounts are traded back to the source firms. Both firms benefit by having access to foreign funds at a lower cost than they could directly obtain.

Swaps are an efficient way to meet the firm's need for foreign currencies because they combine two separate transactions into one. We will learn later that the firm avoids any foreign exchange risk by matching the liability created by borrowing foreign currencies with the asset created by lending domestic currency, both to be repaid at the known future exchange rate. This is known as *hedging* the foreign exchange risk.

Table 4.1 presents data on the volume of activity in the foreign exchange market. Over half of the transactions reported by the banks surveyed were spot transactions. Swaps constitute almost 40 percent of the business, with forward purchases or sales of a single currency constituting around 7 percent of total transactions and options accounting for around 5 percent. We can see that foreign exchange activity is dominated by the spot market.

In foreign exchange dealing, banks do not always trade directly with one another, but often use someone in the middle—a *broker.* If a bank wants to buy a particular currency, several other banks could be called for quotes, or the bank representative could call a broker who is in contact with many banks and able to reveal the best price at the current time among those banks with whom he or she conducts business. If a bank contacts the broker with an offer to buy a currency and the broker has no offers to sell, then the broker will call around and try to find an interested seller. The broker's role, obviously, is to reduce the information costs to the banks. While trading in the broker's market is in progress, the names of the banks making bids and offers are not known until a deal is reached. This anonymity may be very important to the trading banks, because it allows banks of different sizes and market positions to trade on an equal footing. The broker's reward, the commission, is split by the buyer and seller and is usually less than 0.01 percent of the selling price.

Table 4.1 FOREIGN EXCHANGE MARKET TURNOVER IN BILLIONS OF U.S. DOLLARS

Type of transaction	Average daily turnover
Spot	394
Swaps	324
Forwards	59
Options	38
Futures	9
Other*	8
	832

*Some countries do not provide a breakdown of data between swaps and forwards, so this amount includes both swap and forward activity.

Source: Bank for International Settlements, *Central Bank Survey of Foreign Exchange Market Activity,* Basle, March 1993.

A 1992 survey by the Bank for International Settlements found that in the major countries, brokers handled about one–third of the value of foreign exchange trades. In addition to brokers, some trades are facilitated by automated dealing systems that electronically link traders. Rather than talking directly over the telephone dealer–to–dealer, computer networks allow for trades to be executed electronically. The use of electronic dealing systems varies greatly across countries. The 1992 survey found that 32 percent of trading in the United States went through such networks, compared to 24 percent in the United Kingdom and 42 percent in Japan.

FUTURES

The foreign exchange market we have discussed (spot, forward, and swap transactions) is a global market. Commercial banks, business firms, and governments in various locations buy and sell using telephone and telegraph with no geographical market location. However, there exist additional institutions that have not yet been covered, one of which is the foreign exchange futures market. The *futures market* is a market where foreign currencies may be bought and sold for delivery at a future date. The futures market differs from the forward market in that only a few currencies are traded; moreover, trading occurs in standardized contracts and in a specific geographic location, such as the International Monetary Market (IMM) of the Chicago Mercantile Exchange, which is the largest currency futures market.

IMM futures are traded on the British pound, Canadian dollar, Japanese yen, Swiss franc, Australian dollar, and German mark. The contracts involve a specific amount of currency to be delivered at specific maturity dates. Figure 4.2 displays the foreign exchange futures quotes for September 23, 1993. In this market, contracts mature on the third Wednesday of March, June, September, and December. In the forward market, contracts are typically 30, 90, or 180 days long and are maturing every day of the year. Forward market contracts are written for any amount agreed upon by the parties involved. In the futures market the contracts are written for fixed amounts as indicated in Figure 4.2: £62,500, Can $100,000, ¥12,500,000, SF125,000, and DM125,000.

The first column of Figure 4.2 gives the maturity month of the contract; the remaining columns yield the following information:

CURRENCY

	Open	High	Low	Settle	Change	Lifetime High	Lifetime Low	Open Interest
JAPAN YEN (CME) — 12.5 million yen; $ per yen (.00)								
Dec	.9420	.9477	.9400	.9448	+ .0014	.9950	.7970	63,404
Mr94	.9450	.9492	.9430	.9471	+ .0014	.9930	.8700	2,194
Est vol 26,428; vol Wed 31,176; open int 65,640, +6,349.								
DEUTSCHEMARK (CME) — 125,000 marks; $ per mark								
Dec	.6088	.6103	.6020	.6041	− .0050	.6650	.5657	79,592
Mr94	.6049	.6053	.5988	.6000	− .0050	.6200	.5646	1,205
June	....	....	....	.5969	− .0051	.6160	.5607	115
Est vol 58,128; vol Wed 54,052; open int 80,912, +625.								
CANADIAN DOLLAR (CME) — 100,000 dirs.; $ per Can $								
Dec	.7544	.7545	.7520	.7534	− .0018	.8310	.7470	32,550
Mr94	.7508	.7508	.7495	.7500	− .0018	.7860	.7450	1,022
June	.7460	.7467	.7457	.7464	− .0018	.7805	.7425	784
Sept	.7425	.7435	.7424	.7428	− .0018	.7740	.7395	205
Est vol 4,688; vol Wed 1,990; open int 34,581, −192.								
BRITISH POUND (CME) — 62,500 pds.; $ per pound								
Dec	1.5112	1.5112	1.4928	1.4972	− .0104	1.5670	1.3930	25,780
Mr94	1.4900	1.4900	1.4850	1.4890	− .0105	1.5550	1.3950	194
Est vol 11,642; vol Wed 10,816; open int 25,988, −980.								
SWISS FRANC (CME) — 125,000 francs; $ per franc								
Dec	.7015	.7015	.6930	.6960	− .0056	.7212	.6400	53,128
Mr94	.6970	.6970	.6920	.6944	− .0056	.7195	.6470	391
Est vol 23,895; vol Wed 20,138; open int 53,541, −554.								
AUSTRALIAN DOLLAR (CME) — 100,000 dirs.; $ per A.$								
Dec	.6515	.6545	.6488	.6531	+ .0001	.7117	.6408	5,912
Est vol 380; vol Wed 1,126; open int 5,926, −247.								

FIGURE 4.2 Foreign currency futures prices for September 23, 1993. (*Source: The Wall Street Journal,* September 24, 1993, p. C13. Reprinted by permission of *The Wall Street Journal,* © 1993, Dow Jones and Company, Inc. All rights reserved worldwide.)

Open: Price of contract at beginning of business that day.

High: High price of contract on that trading day.

Low: Low price of contract on that trading day.

Settle: Price at which contracts are settled at the close of trading that day.

Change: Change in the settlement price from the previous day.

Lifetime high: Highest price at which this contract has ever traded.

Lifetime low: Lowest price at which this contract has ever traded.

Open interest: Number of outstanding contracts on the previous trading day.

To review each of these values specifically, consider the December pound contract. On September 23, the contract began trading at $1.5112 per pound (so for £62,500, the contract value was $94,450). Over the course of the day, the price rose to a high of $1.5112, sank to a low of $1.4928, and settled at $1.4972. The settlement price was down $0.0104 from the previous day. Over the life of trading in this contract, the highest price ever was $1.5670. The lowest price ever was $1.3930. On the previous day there were 25,780 outstanding contracts.

The daily settlement is an interesting feature of futures markets. Traders are required to realize any losses in cash on the day they occur. In order to trade in the futures market, a trader must deposit money with a broker. The amount required varies with the broker and the contract, and is called the *margin requirement*. Suppose the December pound contract requires an initial margin of $5000. If the price fell $0.0175 on one day, then the fall in the settlement price of $0.0175 represents a loss of $1093.75 on the £62,500 contract ($0.0175 \times 62,500 = 1093.75$). The daily settlement involves deducting this daily loss from the margin deposited with the broker. If the value of the margin account falls below a certain level (typically 75 percent of the initial margin), the trader must deposit sufficient funds to raise the margin to its initial level. With a $5000 margin, the loss of $1093.75 in a single day reduces the margin account to $3906.25—a value that would be close to the level warranting a call for additional funds.

The last line for each currency in Figure 4.2 provides information regarding the estimated volume of trading on the current day, the actual volume on the previous day, the current number of contracts (open interest) across all maturity dates for this currency, and the change in the number of contracts since the previous day.

Futures markets provide a hedging facility for firms involved in international trade as well as a speculative opportunity. Speculators will profit when they accurately forecast a future price for a currency that differs significantly (by more than the transaction cost) from the current contract price. For instance, if we believe that, in December, the pound will sell for $1.40, and the December futures contract is currently priced at $1.4972, we would sell a December contract. Then, at maturity, we will receive $1.4972 per pound, or $93,575. If the actual price of the pound falls below $1.4972, we will realize a profit (less transaction costs).

Suppose the actual price in December is $1.40. We could then buy 62,500 pounds for $87,500 (1.40 × 62,500). The difference of $93,575 − $87,500 = $6,075, less transactions costs, will be our profit.

Since futures contracts involve daily cash flow settlements while forward contracts do not, prices in the two markets will differ slightly even for the same contract maturity date. Futures contracts are for smaller amounts of currency than are forward contracts and therefore serve as a useful hedging vehicle for relatively small firms. Forward contracts are within the realm of wholesale banking activity and are typically used only by large financial institutions and other large business firms that deal in very large amounts of foreign exchange.

OPTIONS

Besides forward and future contracts, there is an additional market where future foreign currency assets and liabilities may be hedged; it is called the *options market.* A foreign currency option is a contract that provides the right to buy or sell a given amount of currency at a fixed exchange rate on or before the maturity date (these are known as "American" options; "European" options may be exercised only at maturity). A *call option* gives the right to buy currency and a *put option* gives the right to sell. The prices at which currency can be bought or sold is the *striking price* or *exercise price.*

The use of options for hedging purposes is straightforward. Suppose a U.S. importer is buying equipment from a German manufacturer with DM1 million payment due in December. The importer can hedge against a mark appreciation by buying a call option that confers the right to purchase marks over the next 3 months until December maturity at a specified price. Specifically, assume that the current spot exchange rate is $0.60 per mark. At this exchange rate, DM1 million would cost $600,000. If the mark appreciated to $0.65 over the next 3 months, then using the spot market in 3 months would change the value of the imports to $650,000 (0.65 × DM1,000,000), an increase in the price of the imports of $50,000. The call option will provide insurance against such change. To add realism to our example, refer to the options quotes displayed in Figure 4.3.

OPTIONS
PHILADELPHIA EXCHANGE

		Calls Vol.	Calls Last	Puts Vol.	Puts Last
FFranc					**174.81**
250,000 French Franc EOM-European style.					
17	Oct	...	...	3647	1.26
18	Oct	3647	0.94	...	...
DMark					**60.86**
62,500 German Mark EOM-European style.					
61	Sep	10	0.26	...	...
62,500 German Marks EOM-European style.					
56½	Oct	...	...	50	0.04
66½	Oct	50	0.04	...	...
Australian Dollar					**65.51**
50,000 Australian Dollars-cents per unit.					
64	Oct	...	...	100	0.33
British Pound					**150.56**
31,250 British Pound EOM-cents per unit.					
147½	Sep	...	...	20	0.05
150	Sep	28	0.75	60	0.62
31,250 British Pounds-European Style.					
152½	Oct	5	1.20	...	...
152½	Nov	5	2.01	...	...
155	Oct	...	...	1	4.20
31,250 British Pounds-cents per unit.					
130	Dec	...	...	43	0.04
145	Nov	...	...	10	1.20
147½	Nov	...	...	4	1.82
150	Oct	2	2.10	4	1.84
150	Dec	...	...	1	3.70
152½	Oct	115	1.04	...	...
155	Dec	13	1.90	...	...
170	Dec	30	0.14	...	...
British Pound-GMark					**247.67**
31,250 British Pound-German Mark cross.					
244	Dec	...	...	16	2.20
248	Dec	16	3.70	...	...
250	Oct	64	1.10	...	...
250	Dec	28	2.60	...	...
256	Dec	16	1.00	...	...
31,250 British Pound-German mark EOM.					
246	Sep	...	...	130	0.16
248	Sep	160	0.20	...	...
252	Oct	10	0.84	...	...
Canadian Dollar					**75.62**
50,000 Canadian Dollars EOM-cents per unit.					
75½	Sep	50	0.19	...	...
50,000 Canadian Dollars-cents per unit.					
75	Oct	...	...	25	0.30
76	Nov	...	...	200	1.18
77	Dec	...	...	1	2.09
ECU					**116.64**
62,500 European Currency Units-cents per unit.					
114	Oct	...	...	16	0.82
French Franc					**174.81**
250,000 French Francs-10ths of a cent per unit.					
16½	Oct	...	...	63	0.20
17	Oct	...	...	63	0.74
17½	Oct	...	...	126	2.64
17¾	Oct	63	1.14	...	...
18	Oct	63	0.60	...	...
250,000 French Francs-European Style.					
		Calls Vol.	**Calls Last**	**Puts Vol.**	**Puts Last**
16¼	Dec	3200	11.40	...	...
17	Dec	...	...	3647	2.68
19	Dec	3647	0.40	...	...
GMark-JYen					**64.58**
62,500 German Mark-Japanese Yen cross.					
63½	Oct	...	...	16	0.35
64	Oct	...	...	30	0.52
German Mark					**60.86**
62,500 German Marks EOM-cents per unit.					
60	Sep	...	...	200	0.07
60½	Sep	50	0.46	290	0.19
61	Sep	320	0.22	700	0.40
61	Oct	...	...	380	1.00
61½	Sep	195	0.08	75	0.81
61½	Oct	380	0.72	130	1.47
62	Sep	200	0.03	...	...
62½	Sep	...	...	250	1.20
62,500 German Marks-European Style.					
57½	Oct	...	...	100	0.04
59	Oct	10	2.16	...	...
60½	Oct	20	1.07	...	...
60½	Nov	...	...	10	0.97
61	Oct	...	...	15	0.89
61	Dec	...	...	272	1.66
61½	Oct	20	0.56	...	...
61½	Nov	...	...	10	1.47
62	Nov	...	...	25	1.76
62½	Nov	...	...	3	2.11
62,500 German Marks-cents per unit.					
56½	Dec	...	...	10	0.27
57	Oct	...	...	128	0.05
57	Dec	...	...	3	0.35
58	Oct	...	...	7	0.10
58	Dec	...	...	141	0.60
58½	Oct	...	...	250	0.16
58½	Nov	...	...	10	0.30
59	Nov	...	...	52	0.59
59	Dec	66	2.78	35	0.86
59½	Nov	...	...	45	0.75
60	Oct	7	1.31	456	0.51
60	Nov	...	...	100	0.94
60	Dec	21	1.66	78	1.27
60½	Oct	1005	0.88	...	...
60½	Nov	...	...	67	1.15
60½	Dec	...	...	9	1.50
61	Oct	1251	0.69	1026	0.99
61	Nov	17	0.98	8	1.45
61	Dec	9	1.14	7	1.83
61½	Oct	80	0.47	20	1.29
61½	Nov	23	0.79	77	1.80
61½	Dec	...	...	8	2.07
62	Oct	62	0.35	100	1.45
62	Nov	10	0.83	...	...
62	Dec	16	0.85	58	2.18
62½	Oct	1625	0.23	309	2.00
62½	Nov	135	0.49	...	...
62½	Dec	210	0.68	...	...
		Calls Vol.	**Calls Last**	**Puts Vol.**	**Puts Last**
63	Oct	13	0.16	100	2.46
63	Nov	10	0.46	...	...
63	Dec	751	0.64	...	...
64	Dec	2026	0.34	3	3.94
Japanese Yen					**94.27**
6,250,000 Japanese Yen EOM-100ths of a cent per unit.					
93	Sep	...	...	50	0.05
95	Sep	500	0.10	...	...
6,250,000 Japanese Yen EOM.					
93½	Sep	...	...	50	0.13
95½	Sep	10	0.07	...	...
6,250,000 Japanese Yen-100ths of a cent per unit.					
90	Nov	...	...	90	0.44
90	Dec	...	...	11	0.80
91	Nov	...	...	5	0.74
91	Dec	...	...	15	0.97
92	Oct	...	...	320	0.44
92	Nov	...	...	59	0.99
92	Dec	...	...	2	1.20
93	Oct	...	...	40	0.76
93½	Oct	...	...	5	1.06
94	Oct	...	...	300	1.08
94	Dec	...	...	1	2.25
94½	Dec	...	...	1	2.51
95	Oct	...	...	50	1.66
98	Nov	10	0.68	...	...
99	Nov	20	0.48	...	...
100	Oct	10	0.10	...	...
100	Dec	10	0.54	...	...
101	Oct	10	0.07	...	...
Swiss Franc					**69.82**
62,500 Swiss Franc EOM-cents per unit.					
68	Oct	...	...	50	0.60
70	Sep	7	0.19	...	...
72	Oct	50	0.40	...	...
62,500 Swiss Francs EOM.					
70½	Sep	10	0.27	...	...
71½	Sep	...	...	22	1.74
62,500 Swiss Francs-European Style.					
65	Dec	...	...	25	0.33
68	Oct	...	...	35	0.34
70	Oct	...	...	10	1.15
71½	Oct	40	0.32	...	...
72	Oct	35	0.22	...	...
74	Oct	40	0.06	...	...
62,500 Swiss Francs-cents per unit.					
69	Nov	...	...	3	1.16
69	Dec	...	...	2	1.47
69½	Oct	12	0.97	10	0.85
70	Nov	1	1.29	...	...
70	Dec	2	1.56	136	2.05
70½	Oct	20	0.62	12	1.09
71½	Oct	1	0.46	...	...
71½	Nov	30	0.47	...	...
72	Oct	4	0.33	10	2.62
73	Nov	1	0.37	...	...
74	Dec	43	0.51	...	...
78	Dec	15	0.12	...	...
Call Vol 60,696			**Open Int ... 558,337**		
Put Vol 56,121			**Open Int ... 546,156**		

FIGURE 4.3 Foreign currency options for September 23, 1993.
(*Source: The Wall Street Journal,* September 24, 1993, p. C13. Reprinted by permission of the *The Wall Street Journal,* © 1993, Dow Jones and Company, Inc. All Rights Reserved Worldwide.)

Figure 4.3 reports options prices for the largest exchange in the United States where such trading occurs. Foreign currency options have been traded only since December 1982, when the Philadelphia Stock Exchange offered a market. While the Philadelphia market is the largest, options are also traded on the Chicago Board Options Exchange. The Philadelphia exchange offers contracts for A$50,000, £31,250, Can$50,000, DM62,500, FF250,000, ¥6,250,000, and SF62,500. The first row of the options quotations for each currency gives the currency being traded and its current spot exchange rate. The first column lists alternative strik-

ing prices available for different months. The next two columns list the call option volume and prices or premiums existing at the close of business for different maturity months. The final two columns list the put option volume and prices or premiums for different maturity months. Note that the prices are "cents per unit" of currency so a price of .85 is .85 cents or $.0085.

An option is said to be "in the money" if the striking price is less than the current spot rate for a call or greater than the current spot rate for a put. Note that the prices of options in Figure 4.3 rise for those that are in the money.

Returning to our example of the U.S. importer buying DM1 million of equipment to be paid for in December, the current spot rate is $0.6086 per mark. At this rate DM1 million is equal to $608,600. To hedge against unexpected exchange rate change, the importer could buy a December option. Suppose he wants a striking price of $0.62, so that the upper bound on the value of the imports is $620,000. In figure 4.3, a December option with a striking price of 62 sells for $0.0085 per mark, so one contract for DM62,500 costs $531.25. To cover DM1 million, the importer must buy 16 contracts ($16 \times 62,500 = 1,000,000$) at a cost of $8,500. If the mark appreciates above $0.62, the option will be exercised. For instance, if the December spot price is $0.65, then using the spot market would mean a cost of $650,000 for the imports. Exercising the option contracts ensures a price of $620,000, so that the firm saves $30,000 less the $8,500 premium compared to an unhedged position. If the mark does not appreciate to the level of the striking price, then the option is allowed to expire. For instance, if the December spot price is $0.61, then using the spot market would mean a cost of $610,000 for the imports. This is $10,000 less than the cost using the option contracts. In this case the firm is out the $8,500 it paid for the options.

Aside from trading options on organized exchanges, like the Philadelphia Exchange, large multinational firms often buy options directly from banks. Such custom options may be for any size or date agreed to and therefore provide greater flexibility than is possible on organized exchanges.

If we knew with certainty what the future exchange rate would be, there would be no market for options, futures, or forward contracts. In an uncertain world, risk-averse traders willingly pay to avoid the potential loss associated with adverse movements in ex-

change rates. An advantage of options over futures or forwards is greater flexibility. A futures or forward contract is an obligation to buy or sell at a set exchange rate. An option offers the right to buy or sell if desired in the future and is not an obligation.

RECENT PRACTICES

The growth of options contracts since the early 1980s has stimulated the development of new products and techniques for managing foreign exchange assets and liabilities. One recent development combines the features of a forward contract and option contract. Terms such as "break forward," "participating forward," or "FOX" (forward with option exit) refer to forward contracts with an option to break out of the contract at a future date. In this case, the forward exchange rate price includes an option premium for the right to break the forward contract. The incentive for such a contract comes from the desire of customers to have the insurance provided by a forward contract when the exchange rate moves against them and yet not lose the potential for profit available with favorable exchange rate movements.

One might first wonder whether a break-forward hedge could not be achieved more simply by using a straight option contract. There are several attractive features of the break-forward contract that do not exist with an option. For one thing, an option requires an up-front premium payment. The corporate treasurer may not have a budget for option premiums or may not have management approval for using options. The break forward hides the option premium in the forward rate. Since the price at which the forward contract is broken is fixed in advance, the break forward may be treated as a simple forward contract for tax and accounting purposes, whether the contract is broken or not.

One of the more difficult problems in hedging foreign exchange risk arises in bidding on contracts. The bidder submits a proposal to perform some task to a firm or government agency seeking to award a contract to the successful bidder. Since there may be many other bidders, the bidding firms face the foreign exchange risk associated with the contract only if they, in fact, are awarded the contract. Suppose a particular bidder assesses only a 20 percent chance of winning the contract. Should they buy a forward contract or option today to hedge the foreign exchange risk

they face in the event they are the successful bidder? If substantial foreign exchange risk is involved for the successful bidder, then both the bidders and the contract awarder face a dilemma. The bids will not be as competitive with the outstanding foreign exchange risk as they would be if the exchange rate uncertainty were hedged.

One approach to this problem is the "Scout" contract. Midland Bank developed the Scout (share currency option under tender) as an option that is sold to the contract awarder, who then sells it to the successful bidder. The awarding agency now receives more competitive and, perhaps, a greater number of bids since the bidders now know that the foreign exchange hedge is arranged.

Over time, we should expect a proliferation of new financial market products aimed at dealing with future transactions involving foreign exchange. If there is a corporate interest in customizing an option or forward arrangement to a specific type of transaction, an innovative bank will step in and offer a product. The small sample of new products discussed in this section is intended to suggest the practical use of these financial innovations.

SUMMARY

1. The forward exchange market is formed by commercial banks buying and selling foreign currency for delivery at a future date.
2. If the forward price of a currency is greater than (less than) the spot price, the currency is said to sell at a forward premium (discount).
3. Swap contracts allow participants to borrow the currency of a market where they receive favorable credit terms and then trade for another currency required for financing activities.
4. Foreign currency futures are standardized contracts traded on established exchanges for delivery of currencies at a specified future date.
5. Foreign currency options are contracts for the right to buy or sell currencies on or before a certain date.
6. Futures and options are traded on exchanges and are also available on a customized basis from commercial banks.

EXERCISES

1. Use Figure 4.1 to determine whether each of the currencies listed here is selling at a forward premium or discount against the dollar:
   a. Pound
   b. German mark

    c. Yen

    d. Canadian dollar

    e. French franc

2. Calculate the per annum premium (discount) of a 1-month forward contract on German marks based on information in Table 4.1.

3. List at least three ways in which a futures contract differs from a forward contract.

4. A straddle is a combination of put and call options in the same contract in which the strike price and maturity are identical for both options. Under what circumstances would a straddle be profitable to the investor?

5. Assume U.S. corporation XYZ needs to arrange to have £10,000 in 90 days. Discuss the alternatives available to the corporation in meeting this obligation. What factors are important in determining which strategy is best?

REFERENCES

Andersen, Torben Juul, *Currency and Interest Rate Hedging.* New York: New York Institute of Finance, 1987.

Bank for International Settlements, *Central Bank Survey of Foreign Exchange Market Activity in April 1992,* Basle, March 1993.

Chang, Jack S. K., and Latha Shanker, "Hedging Effectiveness of Currency Options and Currency Futures," *The Journal of Futures Markets,* 2, 1986, 289–305.

Smith, Clifford W., Jr., Charles W. Smithson, and Lee M. Wakeman, "The Evolving Market for Swaps," *Midland Corporate Finance Journal,* Winter 1986, pp. 20–32.

"Supplement on Foreign Exchange," *Euromoney,* May 1993, p. 71–76.

Warren, Geoffrey, "Quick Brown Fox Breaks Forward over Lazy Scout," *Euromoney,* May 1987, 245–263.

chapter 5

Exchange Rates, Interest Rates, and Interest Parity

International trade occurs in both goods and financial assets. Exchange rates change in a manner to accommodate this trade. In this chapter, we study the relationship between interest rates and exchange rates, and consider how exchange rates adjust to achieve equilibrium in financial markets.

INTEREST PARITY

The interest parity relationship results from profit-seeking arbitrage activity, specifically *covered interest arbitrage*. Let us go through an example of how covered interest arbitrage works. For expositional purposes

$$i_\$ = \text{interest rate in the United States}$$

$$i_\pounds = \text{interest rate in the United Kingdom}$$

$$F = \text{forward exchange rate (dollars per pound)}$$

$$E = \text{spot exchange rate (dollars per pound)}$$

Where the interest rates and the forward rate are the same term to maturity (e.g., 3 months or 1 year). The investor in the United States can earn $(1 + i_\$)$ at home by investing \$1 for 1 period (for instance, 1 year). Alternatively, the U.S. investor can invest in the United Kingdom by converting dollars to pounds and then investing the pounds. \$1 is equal to $1/E$ pounds. Thus, by investing in the United Kingdom, the U.S. resident can earn $(1 + i_£)/E$. This is the quantity of pounds resulting from the \$1 invested. Remember, \$1 buys $1/E$ pounds, and £1 will return $1 + i_£$ after 1 period. Thus, $1/E$ pounds will return $(1 + i_£)/E$ after 1 period.

Since the investor is a resident of the United States, the investment return will ultimately be converted into dollars. But since future spot exchange rates are not known with certainty, the investor can eliminate the uncertainty regarding the future dollar value of $(1 + i_£)/E$ by *covering* the £ currency investment with a forward contract. By selling $(1 + i_£)/E$ pounds to be received in a future period in the forward market today, the investor has guaranteed a certain dollar value of the pound investment opportunity. The *covered return* is equal to $(1 + i_£)F/E$ dollars. The U.S. investor can earn either $1 + i_\$$ dollars by investing \$1 at home or $(1 + i_£)F/E$ dollars by investing the dollar in the United Kingdom. Arbitrage between the two investment opportunities results in

$$1 + i_\$ = (1 + i_£)\frac{F}{E}$$

which may be rewritten as

$$\frac{1 + i_\$}{1 + i_£} = \frac{F}{E} \tag{5.1}$$

Equation (5.1) can be put in a more useful form by subtracting 1 from both sides, giving us the *interest rate parity* equation:

$$\frac{i_\$ - i_£}{1 + i_£} = \frac{F - E}{E} \tag{5.2}$$

which is sometimes approximated as

$$i_\$ - i_£ = \frac{F - E}{E} \tag{5.3}$$

The smaller $i_£$, the better the approximation of Equation (5.3) to (5.2). Equation (5.3) indicates that the interest differential be-

tween a comparable U.S. and U.K. investment is equal to the forward premium or discount on the pound. (We must remember that since interest rates are quoted at annual rates or percent per annum, the forward premiums or discounts must also be quoted at annual rates.)

Now let's consider an example. Ignoring bid-ask spreads, we observe the following interest rates:

$$\text{Euro \$: 15\%}$$

$$\text{Euro £: 10\%}$$

The exchange rate is quoted as the dollar price of pounds and is currently $E = 2.00$. Given the previous information, what do you expect the 12-month forward rate to be?

Using Equation (5.3), we can plug in the known values for the interest rates and spot exchange rate and then solve for the forward rate:

$$0.15 - 0.10 = \frac{F - 2.00}{2.00} \rightarrow$$

$$0.05 = \frac{F - 2.00}{2.00} \rightarrow$$

$$0.10 = F - 2.00 \rightarrow F = 2.10$$

Thus we would expect a 12-month forward rate of $2.10 to give a 12-month forward premium equal to the 0.05 interest differential.

Suppose the actual 12-month forward rate is not $2.10, but instead $2.15. What would profit-seeking arbitragers do? They could buy pounds at the spot rate, then invest and sell the pounds forward for dollars, because the future price of pounds is higher than that implied by the interest parity relation. These actions would tend to increase the spot rate and lower the forward rate, thereby bringing the forward premium back in line with the interest differential. The interest rates could also move, because the movement of funds into pound investments would tend to depress the pound interest rate, whereas the shift out of dollar investments would tend to raise the dollar rate.

The interest parity relationship can also be used to illustrate the concept of the *effective return* on a foreign investment. Equation (5.3) can be rewritten so that the dollar interest rate is equal to the pound rate plus the forward premium. Thus

$$i_\$ = i_\pounds + \frac{F - E}{E} \qquad (5.4)$$

Interest parity ensures that Equation (5.4) will hold. But suppose we do not use the forward market, yet we are U.S. residents who buy U.K. bonds. The interest rate on the bond $i_\pounds$ is not the relevant return measure, since this is the return in terms of a U.K. investment. The effective return on the bond is given by the interest rate plus the expected change in the exchange rate. In other words, the return on a U.K. investment plus the expected change in the value of U.K. currency is our expected return on a pound investment. If the forward exchange rate is equal to the expected future spot rate, then the forward premium is also the expected change in the exchange rate. (The next chapter introduces a reason this might not hold—foreign exchange risk.)

Even though foreign exchange traders quote forward rates based on interest differentials and current spot rates so that the forward rate will yield a forward premium equal to the interest differential, we may ask: How well does interest rate parity hold in the real world? Since deviations from interest rate parity would seem to present profitable arbitrage opportunities, we would expect profit-seeking arbitragers to eliminate any deviations. Still, careful studies of the data indicate that small deviations from interest rate parity do occur. Do these deviations indicate unexploited profit opportunities for the astute investor? It appears the answer is no. There are several reasons why interest rate parity may not hold exactly, and yet we can earn no arbitrage profits from the situation. The most obvious reason is the cost of transacting in the markets. Because buying and selling foreign exchange and international securities involves a cost for each transaction, there may exist deviations from interest rate parity that are equal to, or smaller than, these transaction costs. In this case, speculators cannot profit from these deviations, since the price of buying and selling in the market would wipe out any apparent gain. Studies indicate that, for comparable financial assets that differ only in terms of currency of denomination (like dollar- and pound-denominated deposits in a

London bank), 100 percent of the deviations from interest rate parity can be accounted for by transaction costs.

Besides transaction costs, there are other reasons interest rate parity may not hold perfectly. These include differential taxation, government controls, political risk, and time lags between observing a profit opportunity and actually trading to realize the profit. If taxes differ according to the investor's residence, which they surely do, then the same investment opportunity will yield a different return to residents of different countries. Thus it will be misleading to simply consider pretax effective returns to decide if profitable arbitrage is possible.

If government controls on financial capital flows exist, then an effective barrier between national markets is in place. If an individual cannot freely buy or sell the currency or securities of a country, then the free market forces that work in response to effective return differentials will not function. Indeed, even the serious threat of controls, or more generally any national emergency impinging on international trade in financial assets could make the political risk of investing in a country prohibitive. Political risk is often mentioned as a reason why interest rate parity does not hold. We should note, however, that the external or Eurocurrency market often serves as a means of avoiding political risk, since an individual can borrow and lend foreign currencies outside the home country of each currency. For instance, the Eurodollar market provides a market for U.S. dollar loans and deposits in major financial centers outside the United States. We will investigate in detail the Eurocurrency markets in Chapter 13.

INTEREST RATES AND INFLATION

To better understand the relationship between interest rates and exchange rates, we now consider how inflation can be related to both. To link exchange rates, interest rates, and inflation, we must first understand the role of inflation in interest rate determination. Economists distinguish between real and nominal rates of interest. The *nominal interest rate* is the rate actually observed in the market. The *real rate* is a concept that measures the return after adjusting for inflation. If you loan someone money and charge that person 5 percent interest on the loan, the real return on your loan is negative if the inflation rate exceeds 5 percent. For instance, if the rate of inflation is 10 percent, then the debtor is repaying the loan

with dollars that are worth less, so much less that the loan is going to wind up providing you, the creditor, with less purchasing power after you are repaid the principal and interest than you had when you initially made the loan.

This all means that the nominal rate of interest will tend to incorporate inflation expectations in order to provide lenders with a real return for the use of their money. The expected effect of inflation on the nominal interest rate is often called the *Fisher effect* (after Irving Fisher, an early pioneer of the determinants of interest rates), and the relationship between inflation and interest rates is given by the *Fisher equation:*

$$i = r + \pi \tag{5.5}$$

where i is the nominal interest rate, r the real rate, and π the expected rate of inflation. Thus an increase in π will tend to increase i. The fact that interest rates in the 1970s and 1980s were much higher than in the 1950s and 1960s is the result of higher inflation rates in recent years. Across countries, at a specific time, we should expect interest rates to vary with inflation. Table 5.1 shows that nominal interest rates tend to be higher in countries with higher rates of inflation.

EXCHANGE RATES, INTEREST RATES, AND INFLATION

If we combine the Fisher equation (5.5) and the interest parity equation (5.3) we can determine how interest rates, inflation, and

Table 5.1   INTEREST RATES AND INFLATION RATES FOR SELECTED COUNTRIES, 1992

Country	Inflation rate	Interest rate
Japan	1.7%	2.71%
United States	3.0	3.68
United Kingdom	3.7	7.30
Germany	4.8	8.01
Greece	15.9	19.92

Note: The inflation rate is equal to the annual rate of change in the consumer price index. Interest rate is equal to the annual average of bank deposit rates.
Source: International Monetary Fund, *International Financial Statistics.*

exchange rates are all linked. First, consider the Fisher equation for the United States and the United Kingdom:

$$i_\$ = r_\$ + \pi_\$ \qquad\qquad i_£ = r_£ + \pi_£$$

If the real rate of interest is the same internationally, then $r_\$ = r_£$. In this case, the nominal interest rates, $i_\$$ and $i_£$, differ solely by expected inflation, so we can write

$$i_\$ - i_£ = \pi_\$ - \pi_£ \qquad\qquad (5.6)$$

The interest parity condition of Equation (5.3) indicates that the interest differential is also equal to the forward premium, or

$$i_\$ - i_£ = \pi_\$ - \pi_£ = \frac{F - E}{E} \qquad\qquad (5.7)$$

Equation (5.7) summarizes the link among interest, inflation, and exchange rates.

In the real world the interrelationships summarized by Equation (5.7) are determined simultaneously, because interest rates, inflation expectations, and exchange rates are jointly affected by new events and information. For instance, suppose we begin from a situation of equilibrium where interest parity holds. Suddenly, there is a change in U.S. policy that leads to expectations of a higher U.S. inflation rate. The increase in expected inflation will cause dollar interest rates to rise. At the same time exchange rates will adjust to maintain interest parity. If the expected future spot rate is changed, we would expect F to carry much of the adjustment burden. If the expected future spot rate is unchanged, the current spot rate would tend to carry the bulk of the adjustment burden. Finally, if central bank intervention is "pegging" exchange rates at fixed levels by buying and selling to maintain the fixed rate, the domestic and foreign currency interest rates will have to adjust to parity levels. The fundamental point is that the initial U.S. policy change led to changes in inflationary expectations, interest rates, and exchange rates simultaneously, since they all adjust to new equilibrium levels.

EXPECTED EXCHANGE RATES AND THE TERM STRUCTURE OF INTEREST RATES

There is no such thing as *the* interest rate for a country. Interest rates within a country vary for different investment opportunities

and for different maturity dates on similar investment opportunities. The structure of interest rates existing on investment opportunities over time is known as the *term structure of interest rates.* For instance, in the bond market we observe 3-month, 6-month, 1-year, 3-year, and even longer-term bonds. If the interest rates rise with the term to maturity, then we observe a rising term structure. If the interest rates were the same regardless of term, then the term structure would be flat. We describe the term structure interest rates by describing the slope of a line connecting the various points in time at which we observe interest rates.

There are several competing theories that explain the term structure of interest rates; we will discuss three:

1. *Expectations:* This theory suggests that the long-term interest rate tends to equal an average of short-term rates expected over the long-term holding period. In other words, an investor could buy a long-term bond or a series of short-term bonds, so that the expected return from the long-term bond will tend to be equal to the return generated from holding the series of short-term bonds.

2. *Liquidity premium:* Underlying this theory is the idea that long term bonds incorporate a risk premium since risk-averse investors would prefer to lend short-term. The premium on long-term bonds would tend to result in interest rates rising with the holding period of the bond.

3. *Preferred habitat:* This approach contends that the bond markets are segmented by maturities. In other words, there is a separate market for short- and long-term bonds, and the interest rates are determined by supply and demand in each market.

Although we could use these theories to explain the term structure for interest rates in any one currency, in international finance we use the term structures on different currencies to infer expected exchange rate changes. For instance, if we compared Eurodollar and Euromark deposit rates for different maturities like 1-month and 3-month deposits, the difference between the two term structures should reflect expected exchange rate changes. Of course, if there are capital controls, then the various national mar-

kets become isolated and there would not be any particular relationship between international interest rates.

Figure 5.1 plots the Eurocurrency deposit rates at a particular time for 1- to 12-month terms. We know from our previous discussion that when one country has higher interest rates than another, the high-interest-rate currency is expected to depreciate relative to the low-interest-rate currency. Since effective returns will tend to be equal everywhere, the only way an interest rate can be above another one is if the high-interest-rate currency is expected to depreciate; thus the effective rate, $i + (F - E)/E$ [as shown in Equation (5.4), with the forward rate used as a predictor of the future spot rate], is lower than the observed rate, i, because of the expected depreciation of the currency ($F < E$).

If the distance between two of the term structure lines is the same at each point, then the expected change in the exchange rate

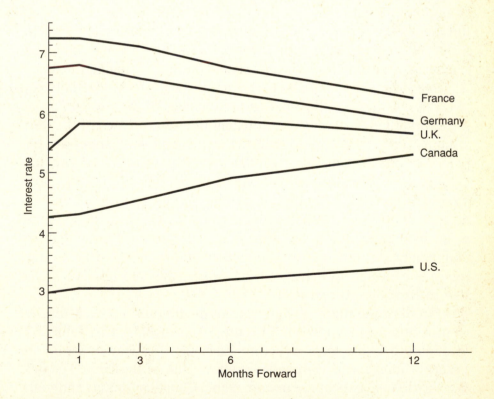

FIGURE 5.1 Eurocurrency interest rates for September 23, 1993. (*Source: Financial Times,* September 24, 1993.)

is constant. To see this more clearly, let us once again consider the interest parity relation given by Equation (5.3):

$$i_\$ - i_\pounds = \frac{F - E}{E}$$

This expression indicates that the difference between the interest rate in two countries will be equal to the forward premium or discount when the interest rates and the forward rate have the same term to maturity. If the forward rate is considered a market forecast of the future spot rate, which it often is, then we can say that the interest differential is also approximately equal to the expected change in the spot rate. This means that at each point in the term structure, the difference between the national interest rates should reflect the expected change in the exchange rate for the two currencies being compared. By examining the different points in the term structure, we can determine how the exchange rate expectations are changing through time. One implication of this is that, even if we did not have a forward exchange market in a currency, the interest differential between the interest rate on that currency and other currencies would allow us to infer expected future exchange rates.

Now we can understand why a constant differential between two interest rates implies that future changes in the exchange rate are expected to occur at some constant rate. Thus if two of the term structure lines are parallel, then the exchange rate changes are expected to be constant (the currencies will appreciate or depreciate against each other at a constant rate). On the other hand, if two term structure lines are diverging, or moving farther apart from one another, then the high-interest-rate currency is expected to depreciate at an increasing rate over time. For term structure lines that are converging, or moving closer together, the high-interest-rate currency is expected to depreciate at a declining rate relative to the low-interest-rate currency.

To illustrate the exchange rate-term structure relationship, let us look at the data underlying Figure 5.1 as displayed in Table 5.2. In Figure 5.1, the term structure lines for the United Kingdom, France, Canada, and Germany lie above that of the United States. We should then expect the pound, franc, Canadian dollar, and mark to depreciate against the U.S. dollar. Table 5.2 indicates that the negative interest differentials between Eurodollars and these other

**Table 5.2   INTEREST DIFFERENTIAL AND FORWARD PREMIUM OR
DISCOUNT VERSUS U.S. DOLLAR**

Term	U.K. pound	Canadian dollar	German mark	French franc
1 month	−.0271	−.0127	−.0372	−.0421
	(−.0275)	(−.0125)	(−.0375)	(−.0419)
3 month	−.0278	−.0162	−.0342	−.0402
	(−.0275)	(−.0150)	(−.0350)	(−.040)

Note: Figures in parentheses are interest differentials.
Source: The exchange rate data and the interest rates are from *Financial Times,*
September 24, 1993.

currencies are reflected in forward discounts. With regard to the
shapes of the curves, the term structure line for the United States is
basically flat, while the Canadian term structure is rising. The convergence of the Canadian dollar line toward the French, German,
and U.K. lines suggests that the Canadian dollar is expected to appreciate against the other currencies at a slower rate over time. The
fact that the term structure line for Canada is closest to the U.S.,
and then the U.K., Germany, and France lie farther away from the
U.S. curve, indicates that the Canadian dollar should have the
smallest expected depreciation against the U.S. dollar, followed by
the pound, mark, and franc. Table 5.2 indicates that the forward
discount on the Canadian dollar is the smallest and we see that the
term structure of interest rates roughly reflects expected exchange
rate changes as the forward discounts are larger on the pound,
mark, and franc.

SUMMARY

1. The interest parity relation indicates that the interest differential between investments in two currencies will equal the forward premium or discount between the currencies.
2. Covered interest arbitrage ensures interest parity.
3. Deviations from interest rate parity could be the result of transaction costs, differential taxation, government controls, or political risk.
4. The real interest rate is equal to the nominal interest rate minus expected inflation.
5. If real interest rates are equal in two countries, then the interest differential on
   their currencies will equal the inflation differential, which will equal the forward premium or discount.

6. Differences between the term structure of interest rates in two countries will reflect expected exchange rate changes.

EXERCISES

1. Suppose you want to infer expected future exchange rates in a less developed country that has free-market-determined interest rates, but the country does not have a forward exchange market. Is there any other way of inferring expected future exchange rates? Under what assumptions?

2. a. Show that there is a direct relationship between the forward premium and the "real" interest rate differential between two currencies.

   b. Under what conditions will the forward premium equal the expected "inflation" differential between two currencies?

3. Give four reasons why, when interest parity does not hold exactly, we are unable to take advantage of arbitrage to earn profits.

4. Suppose the 1-year interest rate on British pounds is 11 percent, the dollar interest rate is 6 percent, and the current $/£ spot rate is $1.80.

   a. What do you expect the spot rate to be in 1 year?

   b. Why can we not observe the expected future spot rate?

   c. Suppose both the United States and United Kingdom implement new policies that lead to an expected future spot rate of $1.75. What would you expect the pound interest rate to be now if the dollar interest rate increases to 7 percent?

5. Expected inflation differentials cause interest rate changes, which in turn bring about exchange rate changes. Is this statement true? Explain very carefully.

6. The British pound is selling in the spot market for $1.76, while in the 180-day forward market it sells for $1.74.

   a. Is the dollar selling at a premium or discount?

   b. What is the forward premium (discount) on the pound at an annual rate?

REFERENCES

McKinnon, Ronald I., *Money in International Exchange,* New York: Oxford, 1979.
Solnik, Bruno, "International Parity Conditions and Exchange Risk," *Journal of Banking and Finance,* 2, 1978, 281–293.

APPENDIX: WHAT ARE LOGARITHMS, AND WHY ARE THEY USED IN FINANCIAL RESEARCH?

Although this is not a course in mathematics, there are certain techniques that are so prevalent in modern financial research that not to use them would be a disservice to the student. Logarithms are a prime example. One major reason financial researchers use logarithms is to make calculations easier.

WHAT ARE LOGARITHMS?

Logarithms are a means to transform numbers to simplify mathematical analysis of a problem. One way of viewing a logarithm is as the *power* to which some *base* must be raised to give a certain number. For example, we all know that the square of 10 is 100, or $10^2 = 100$. Therefore, if 10 is our base, we know that 10 must be raised to the second power to equal 100. We could then say that the logarithm of 100 to the base 10 is 2. This is written as

$$\log_{10} 100 = 2$$

What then is the $\log_{10}$ of 1000? Of course, $\log_{10} 1000 = 3$, because $10 \times 10 \times 10 = 10^3 = 1000$.

In general, any number greater than 1 could serve as the base by which we could write all positive numbers. So picking any arbitrary number designated as a, where a is greater than 1, we could write any positive number b as

$$\log_a b = c$$

where c is the power to which a must be raised to equal b.

Rather than pick any arbitrary number for our base a, there is a particular number that arises naturally in economic phenomenon. This number is approximately 2.71828, and it is called e. The value of e arises in the continuous compounding of interest. Specifically, $e = \lim_{n \to \infty} (1 + 1/n)^n$, where n is the number of times interest is compounded per year. The value of some principal amount P in 1 year, compounded continuously at r percent interest, is $V = Pe^r$. If $r = 100$ percent, then the amount of principal and interest after 1 year is $V = Pe$. Since e comes *naturally* out of continuous compounding, we refer to e as the base of the *natural logarithms*.

Financial researchers utilize logarithms to the base e. Rather than write the log of some number b as $\log_e b = c$, it is common to express $\log_e$ as ln, so that we write

$$\ln b = c$$

In all uses of logarithms in this text, we assume log b is actually ln b or the natural logarithm; it is for convenience that we drop the e subscript and simply write log b rather than $\log_e b$.

WHY USE LOGARITHMS IN FINANCIAL RESEARCH?

If the lesson so far has seemed rather esoteric and unrelated to your interests, here is the payoff. There are three extremely helpful properties of logarithms that are used frequently in international finance:

1. The log of a product of two numbers is equal to the sum of the logs of the individual numbers:

$$\log (MN) = \log M + \log N$$

2. The log of a quotient is equal to the difference of the logs of the individual numbers:

$$\log (M/N) = \log M - \log N$$

3. The log of some number M raised to the N power is equal to N times the log of M:

$$\log (M^N) = N \log M$$

Since many relationships in financial research are products or ratios, by taking the logs of these relationships, we are able to analyze simple linear, additive relationships rather than more complex phenomena involving products and quotients.

Another useful feature of logarithms is that the change in the logarithm of some variable is commonly used to measure the percentage change in the variable (the measure is precise for compound changes and approximate for simple rates of change). If we want to calculate the percentage change in the $/£ exchange rate ($E$) between today (period t) and yesterday (period $t - 1$), we could

calculate $(E_t - E_{t-1})/E_{t-1}$. Alternatively, we could calculate $\log E_t - \log E_{t-1}$. This is a very convenient feature of logarithms that will appear in later chapters.

This appendix serves as a brief introduction or review of logarithms. Rather than provide more illustrations of the specific use of logarithms in international finance, at this point it is preferable to study the examples that arise in the context of the problems, as analyzed in subsequent chapters. More general examples of the use of logarithms may be found in the text listed in the references.

REFERENCES

Chiang, Alpha C., *Fundamental Methods of Mathematical Economics*. New York: McGraw-Hill, 1984.

chapter 6

Foreign Exchange Risk and Forecasting

International business involves foreign exchange risk since the value of transactions in different currencies will be sensitive to exchange rate changes. Although it is possible to manage a firm's foreign-currency-denominated assets and liabilities to avoid exposure to exchange rate changes, the benefit involved is not always worth the effort.

The appropriate strategy for the corporate treasurer and the individual speculator will be at least partly determined by expectations of the future path of the exchange rate. As a result, exchange rate forecasts are an important part of the decision-making process of international investors.

In this chapter, we first consider the issue of foreign exchange risk, which is the presence of risk that arises from uncertainty regarding the future exchange rate; this uncertainty makes forecasting necessary. If future exchange rates were known with certainty, there would be no foreign exchange risk.

TYPES OF FOREIGN EXCHANGE RISK

One problem we encounter when trying to evaluate the effect of exchange rate changes on a business firm arises in determining the appropriate concept of exposure to foreign exchange risk.

We can identify three popular concepts of *exchange risk exposure:*

1. *Translation exposure:* This is also known as accounting exposure and is the difference between foreign-currency-denominated assets and foreign-currency-denominated liabilities.
2. *Transaction exposure:* This is exposure resulting from the uncertain domestic currency value of a foreign-currency-denominated transaction to be completed at some future date.
3. *Economic exposure:* This is exposure of the firm's value to changes in exchange rates. If the value of the firm is measured as the present value of future after-tax cash flows, then economic exposure is concerned with the sensitivity of the real domestic currency value of long-term cash flows to exchange rate changes.

Economic exposure is the most important to the firm. Rather than worry about how accountants will report the value of our international operations (translation exposure), it is far more important to the firm (and to rational investors) to focus on the purchasing power of long-run cash flows insofar as these determine the real value of the firm.

Let us consider an example of a hypothetical firm's situation to illustrate the differences among the alternative exposure concepts. Suppose we have the balance sheet of XYZ-France, a foreign subsidiary of the parent U.S. firm XYZ, Inc. The balance sheet in Table 6.1 initially shows the position of XYZ-France in terms of French francs. A balance sheet is simply a recording of the firm's assets (listed on the left side) and liabilities (listed on the right side). A balance sheet must balance. In other words, the value of assets must equal the value of liabilities so that the sums of the two columns are equal. Equity is the owner's claim on the firm and is a sort of residual in that the value of equity will change to keep liabilities equal to assets.

Although the balance sheet at the top of Table 6.1 is stated in terms of francs, the parent company, XYZ, Inc., consolidates the financial statements of all foreign subsidiaries into its own statements. Thus the franc-denominated balance sheet items must be

Table 6.1 BALANCE SHEET OF XYZ-FRANCE, MAY 31

Cash	FF 1,000,000	Debt	FF 5,000,000
Accounts receivable	3,000,000	Equity	6,000,000
Plant & equipment	5,000,000		
Inventory	2,000,000		
	FF 11,000,000		FF11,000,000

Dollar translation on May 31		FF4 = $1	
Cash	$ 250,000	Debt	$1,250,000
Accounts receivable	750,000	Equity	1,500,000
Plant & equipment	1,250,000		
Inventory	500,000		
	$2,750,000		$2,750,000

Dollar translation on June 1		FF5 = $1	
Cash	$200,000	Debt	$1,000,000
Accounts receivable	600,000	Equity	1,200,000
Plant & equipment	1,000,000		
Inventory	400,000		
	$2,200,000		$2,200,000

translated into dollars to be included in the parent company's balance sheet. *Translation* is the process of expressing financial statements measured in one unit of currency in terms of another unit of currency.

Assume that initially the exchange rate equals FF4 = $1. The balance sheet in the middle of Table 6.1 uses this exchange rate to translate the balance sheet items into dollars. We might mention here that under the old accounting standards used in the United States, only monetary assets and liabilities (cash, accounts receivable, and debt) were translated at current exchange rates, whereas other items were translated at historic rates existing at the time of their acquisition. The current standards, introduced in 1981, require all foreign-denominated assets and liabilities to be translated at current exchange rates.

In the United States, accounting standards are set by the Financial Accounting Standards Board (FASB). On December 7, 1981, the FASB issued Financial Accounting Standard No. 52, commonly referred to as FAS 52. FAS 52 essentially requires that balance sheet accounts be translated at the exchange rate prevailing

at the date of the balance sheet. The issue in translation exposure is the sensitivity of the equity account of the balance sheet to exchange rate changes. The equity account equals assets minus liabilities and measures the accounting or book value of the firm. As the domestic currency value of the foreign-currency-denominated assets and liabilities of the foreign subsidiary changes, the domestic currency book value of the subsidiary will also change.

The top two balance sheets in Table 6.1 give us the French franc and dollar position of the firm on May 31. However, suppose there is a devaluation of the franc on June 1 from FF4 = $1 to FF5 = $1. The balance sheet in terms of dollars will change as illustrated by the new translation at the bottom of the table. Now the owner's claim on the firm in terms of dollars or the book value measured by equity has fallen from $1.5 million to $1.2 million. Given the current method of translating exchange rate changes, when the currency used to denominate the foreign subsidiaries' statements is depreciating relative to the dollar, then the owner's equity will fall. We must realize that this drop in equity does not necessarily represent any real loss to the firm or real drop in the value of the firm. The franc position of the firm is unchanged; only the dollar value to the U.S. parent is altered by the exchange rate change.

Since the balance sheet translation of foreign assets and liabilities does not by itself indicate anything about the real economic exposure of the firm, we must look beyond the balance sheet and the translation exposure. Transaction exposure can be viewed as a kind of economic exposure, since the profitability of future transactions is susceptible to exchange rate change, and these changes can have a big effect on future cash flows—as well as on the value of the firm. Suppose XYZ-France has contracted to deliver goods to an Italian firm and allows 30 days' credit before payment is received. Furthermore, suppose at the time the contract was made the exchange rate was 120 Italian lire (the plural of *lira* is *lire*) per French franc (Lit120 = FF1). Suppose also that the contract called for payment in lire of exactly Lit120,000 in 30 days. At the current exchange rate the value of Lit120,000 is FF1000. But if the exchange rate changes in the next 30 days, the value of Lit120,000 would also change. Should the lira depreciate unexpectedly, then in 30 days XYZ-France will receive Lit120,000; however, this will be worth

less than FF1000, so that the transaction is not as profitable as originally planned. This is transaction exposure. XYZ has committed itself to this future transaction, thereby exposing it to exchange risk. Had the contract been written to specify payment in francs, then the transaction exposure to XYZ-France would have been eliminated; the Italian importer would now have the transaction exposure. Firms can, of course, hedge against future exchange rate uncertainty in the forward-looking markets discussed in Chapter 4. The Italian firm could buy francs in the forward market to be delivered in 30 days and thus eliminate the transaction exposure.

The example of transaction exposure just analyzed illustrates how exchange rate uncertainty can affect the future profitability of the firm. The possibility that exchange rate changes can affect future profitability, and therefore the current value of the firm, is indicative of economic exposure. Managing foreign exchange risks involves the sorts of operations considered in Chapter 4. There we covered the use of forward markets, swaps, options, futures, and borrowing and lending in international currencies and so will not review that information here. Note, however, that firms should manage cash flows carefully, with an eye toward expected exchange rate changes, and should not always try to avoid all risks since risk taking can be profitable. Firms practice risk minimization subject to cost constraints and eliminate foreign exchange risk only when the expected benefits from it exceed the costs.

Although forward exchange contracts may be an important part of any corporate hedging strategy, there exist other alternatives that are frequently used. For example, suppose a firm has both assets and liabilities denominated in weak currency X, which is expected to depreciate, and strong currency Y, which is expected to appreciate. The firm's treasurer would try to minimize the value of accounts receivable denominated in X, which could mean tougher credit terms for customers paying in currency X. The firm may also delay the payment of any accounts payable denominated in X, because it expects to be able to buy X for repayment at a cheaper rate in the future. Insofar as is possible, the firm will try to reinforce these practices on payables and receivables by invoicing its sales in currency Y and its purchases in X. Although institutional constraints may exist on the ability of the firm to specify the invoicing currency, it would certainly be desirable to implement such policies.

We see, then, that corporate hedging strategies involve more than simply minimizing holdings of currency X and currency-X-denominated bank deposits. Managing cash flows, receivables, and payables will be the daily activity of the financial officers of a multinational firm. In instances when it is not possible for the firm successfully to hedge a foreign currency position internally, there is always the forward or futures market. If the firm has a currency-Y-denominated debt and it wishes to avoid the foreign exchange risk associated with the debt, it can always buy Y currency in the forward market and thereby eliminate the risk.

In summary, foreign exchange risk may be hedged or eliminated by the following strategies:

1. Trading in forward, futures, or options markets
2. Invoicing in the domestic currency
3. Speeding (slowing) payments of currencies expected to appreciate (depreciate)
4. Speeding (slowing) collection of currencies expected to depreciate (appreciate)

FOREIGN EXCHANGE RISK PREMIUM

Let us now consider the effects of foreign exchange risk on the determination of forward exchange rates. As mentioned previously, the forward exchange rate may serve as a predictor of future spot exchange rates. We may question whether the forward rate should be equal to the expected future spot rate, or whether there is a *risk premium* incorporated in the forward rate that serves as an insurance premium inducing others to take the risk, in which case the forward rate would differ from the expected future spot rate by this premium. The empirical work in this area has dealt with the issue of whether the forward rate is an unbiased predictor of future spot rates. An *unbiased* predictor is one that is correct on average, so that over the long run the forward rate is just as likely to overpredict the future spot rate as it is to underpredict. The property of unbiasedness does not imply that the forward rate is a good predictor. For example, there is the story of an old lawyer who says, "When I was a young man I lost many cases that I should have won; when I

was older I won many that I should have lost. Therefore, on average, justice was done." Is it comforting to know that on average the correct verdict is reached when we are concerned with the verdict in a particular case? Likewise, the forward rate could be unbiased and "on average" correctly predict the spot rate without ever actually predicting the future realized spot rate. All we need for unbiasedness is that the forward rate is just as likely to guess too high as it is to guess too low.

The effective return differential between two countries' assets should be dependent on the perceived risk of each asset and the risk aversion of the investors. Now let us clarify what we mean by *risk* and *risk aversion.* The risk associated with an asset is the contribution of that asset to the overall portfolio risk of the investor. Modern financial theory has commonly associated the riskiness of a portfolio with the variability of the returns from that portfolio. This is reasonable in that investors are concerned with the future value of any investment, and the more variable the return from an investment is, the less certain we can be about its value at any particular future date. Thus we are concerned with the variability of any individual asset insofar as it contributes to the variability of our portfolio return (our portfolio return is simply the total return from all our investments).

Risk aversion is the real-world phenomenon of preferring less risk to more risk. In terms of investments, two individuals may agree on the degree of risk associated with two assets, but the more risk-averse individual would require a higher interest rate on the more risky asset to induce him or her to hold it than would the less risk-averse individual. Risk aversion implies that people must be paid to take risk—individuals and corporations with bad credit must pay a higher interest rate than those with good credit. The interest differential is required to induce creditors to make loans to the bad credit risks.

It was already stated that the effective return differential between assets of two countries is a function of risk and risk aversion. The effective return differential between a U.S. security and a security in the United Kingdom is

$$i_{US} - \frac{E_{t+1}^* - E_t}{E_t} - i_{UK} = f(\text{risk aversion, risk}) \qquad (6.1)$$

The left-hand side of the equation is the effective return differential measured as the difference between the domestic U.S. return, i_{US}, and the foreign asset return, $(E_{t+1}^* - E_t) / E_t + i_{UK}$. We must remember that the effective return on the foreign asset is equal to the interest rate in terms of foreign currency plus the expected change in the exchange rate, where E_{t+1}^* is the expected dollar currency price of pounds next period. The right-hand side of Equation (6.1) indicates that the return differential is a function of risk aversion and risk. In this case, to say that the return differential is a function of risk and risk aversion means that changes in risk and risk aversion will cause changes in the return differential.

We can view the effective return differential shown in Equation (6.1) as a risk premium. Let us begin with the approximate interest parity relation

$$i_{US} - i_{UK} = \frac{F - E_t}{E_t} \tag{6.2}$$

To convert the left-hand side to an effective return differential, we must subtract the expected change in the exchange rate (but since this is an equation, whatever is done to the left-hand side must also be done to the right-hand side):

$$i_{US} - \frac{E_{t+1}^* - E_t}{E_t} - i_{UK} = \frac{F - E_t}{E_t} - \left(\frac{E_{t+1}^* - E_t}{E_t} \right) \tag{6.3}$$

or

$$i_{US} - \frac{E_{t+1}^* - E_t}{E_t} - i_{UK} = \frac{F - E_{t+1}^*}{E_t}$$

Thus we find that the effective return differential is equal to the percentage difference between the forward and expected future spot exchange rate. The right-hand side of Equation (6.3) may be considered a measure of the risk premium in the forward exchange market. Therefore, if the effective return differential is zero, then there would appear to be no risk premium. If the effective return differential is positive, then there is a positive risk premium on the domestic currency, since the expected future spot price of pounds is less than the prevailing forward rate. In other words, traders offering to sell pounds for dollars in the future will receive a premium, in that pounds are expected to depreciate (relative to dollars) by an amount greater than the current forward rate. Conversely, traders

wishing to buy pounds for delivery next period will pay a premium to the future sellers to ensure a set future price.

For example, suppose $E_t = \$2.10$, $E^*_{t+1} = \$2.00$, and $F = \$2.05$. The foreign exchange risk premium is

$$\frac{F - E^*_{t+1}}{E_t} = \frac{\$2.05 - \$2.00}{\$2.10} = 0.024$$

The expected change in the exchange rate is equal to

$$\frac{E^*_{t+1} - E_t}{E_t} = \frac{\$2.00 - \$2.10}{\$2.10} = -0.048$$

The forward discount on the pound is

$$\frac{F - E_t}{E_t} = \frac{\$2.05 - \$2.10}{\$2.10} = -0.024$$

Thus, the dollar is expected to appreciate against the pound by approximately 4.8 percent, but the forward premium indicates an appreciation of only 2.4 percent if we use the forward rate as a predictor of the future spot rate. The discrepancy results from the presence of a risk premium that makes the forward rate a biased predictor of the future spot rate. Specifically, the forward rate over-predicts the future dollar price of pounds in order to allow the risk premium.

Given the positive risk premium on the dollar, the expected effective return from holding a U.K. bond will be less than the domestic return to U.S. residents holding U.S. bonds. This nonzero effective return differential can be an equilibrium result consistent with rational investor behavior.

To continue the previous example, let us suppose that the U.K. interest rate is 0.124, whereas the U.S. rate is 0.100. Then the interest differential is

$$i_{US} - i_{UK} = -0.024$$

The expected return from holding a U.K. bond is

$$i_{UK} + \frac{E^*_{t+1} - E_t}{E_t} = 0.124 - 0.048 = 0.076$$

The return from the U.S. bond is 0.10, which exceeds the expected effective return on the foreign bond; yet this can be an equilibrium solution given the risk premium. Investors are willing to hold U.K.

investments yielding a lower expected return than comparable U.S. investments because there is a positive risk premium on the dollar. Thus, the higher dollar return is necessary to induce investors to hold the riskier dollar-denominated investments.

MARKET EFFICIENCY

A market is said to be *efficient* if prices reflect all available information. In the foreign exchange market this means that spot and forward exchange rates will quickly adjust to any new information. For instance, an unexpected change in U.S. economic policy that informed observers feel will be inflationary (like an unexpected increase in money supply growth) will lead to an immediate depreciation of the dollar. If markets were inefficient, then prices would not adjust quickly to the new information, and it would be possible for a well-informed investor to make profits consistently from foreign exchange trading that would be excessive relative to the risk undertaken.

With efficient markets, the forward rate would differ from the expected future spot rate by only a risk premium. If this were not the case and the forward rate exceeded the expected future spot rate plus a risk premium, an investor could realize certain profits by selling forward currency now, being able to buy the currency in the future at a lower price than the forward rate at which the currency will be sold. Although profits are most certainly earned from foreign exchange speculation in the real world, it is also true that there are no sure profits. The real world is characterized by uncertainty regarding the future spot rate, since the future cannot be foreseen. Yet forward exchange rates adjust to the changing economic picture according to revisions of what the future spot rate is likely to be (as well as changes in the risk attached to the currencies involved). It is this ongoing process of price adjustments in response to new information in the efficient market that rules out any certain profits from speculation. Of course, the fact that the future will bring unexpected events ensures that profits and losses will result from foreign exchange speculation. If an astute investor possessed an ability to forecast exchange rates better than the rest of the market, the profits resulting would be enormous. Foreign exchange forecasting will be discussed in the next section.

Many studies have tested the efficiency of the foreign exchange market. The fact that they have often reached different con-

clusions regarding the efficiency of the market emphasizes the difficulty involved in using statistics in the social sciences. Such studies have usually investigated whether the forward rate contains all the relevant information regarding the expected future spot rate. They test whether the forward rate alone predicts the future spot rate well or whether additional data will aid in the prediction. If further information adds nothing beyond that already embodied in the forward rate, the market is said to be efficient. On the other hand, if some data are found that would permit a speculator consistently to predict the future spot rate better than the forward rate allows (including a risk premium), then this speculator would earn a consistent profit from foreign exchange speculation, and one could conclude that the market is not efficient.

It must be recognized that such tests have their weaknesses. Although a statistical analysis must make use of past data, speculators must actually predict the future. The fact that a researcher could find a forecasting rule that would beat the forward rate in predicting past spot rates is not particularly useful for current speculation and does not rule out market efficiency. The key point is that such a rule was not known during the time the data were actually being generated. So if a researcher in 1995 claims to have found a way to predict the spot rates observed in 1990 better than the 1990 forward rates, this does not mean that the foreign exchange market in 1990 was necessarily inefficient. Speculators in 1990 did not have this forecasting rule developed in 1995, and thus could not have used such information to outguess the 1990 forward rates consistently.

FOREIGN EXCHANGE FORECASTING

Since future exchange rates are uncertain, participants in international financial markets can never know for sure what the spot rate will be one month or one year ahead. As a result, forecasts must be made. If we could forecast more accurately than the rest of the market, the potential profits would be enormous. An immediate question is: What makes a good forecast? In other words, how should we judge a forecast of the future spot rate.

We can certainly raise objections to rating forecasts on the basis of simple forecast errors. Even though we should prefer a smaller forecast error to a larger one, other things equal, in practice other things are not equal. To be successful, a forecast should be on

the correct side of the forward rate. For instance, consider the following example:

Current spot rate: ¥120 = $1

Current 12-month forward rate: ¥115 = $1

Mr. A forecasts: ¥106 = $1

Ms. B forecasts: ¥116 = $1

Future spot rate realized in 12 months: ¥113 = $1

A Japanese firm has a $1 million payment due in 12 months and uses the forecasts to help decide whether to cover the dollar payable with a forward contract or wait and sell the dollars in the spot market in 12 months. In terms of forecast errors, Mr. A's prediction of ¥106 = $1 yields an error of 6.2 percent with a realized future spot rate of ¥113. Ms. B's prediction of ¥116 = $1 is much closer to the realized spot rate with a error of only 2.6 percent. While Ms. B's forecast was closer to the rate eventually realized, this is not the important feature of a good forecast. Ms. B forecasts a future spot rate in excess of the forward rate, so following her prediction the Japanese firm would wait and sell the dollars in the spot market in 12 months. (or would take a *long position* in dollars). Unfortunately, since the future spot rate ¥113 = $1 is less than the forward rate at which the dollars could be sold (¥115 = $1) the firm receives ¥113 million rather than ¥115 million for the $1 million.

Following Mr. A's forecast of a future spot rate below the forward rate, the Japanese firm would sell dollars in the forward market (or take a *short position* in dollars). The firm would then sell dollars at the forward rate of ¥115 per dollar rather than wait and only receive ¥113 per dollar in the spot market. The forward contract yields ¥2 million more than the uncovered position. The important lesson is that a forecast should be on the correct side of the forward rate; otherwise a small forecasting error is not useful. Corporate treasurers or individual speculators want a forecast that will give them the direction the future spot rate will take relative to the forward rate.

If the foreign exchange market is efficient so that prices reflect all available information, then we may wonder why anyone would pay for forecasts. There is some evidence that advisory services

have been able to "beat the forward rate" at certain times. If such services could consistently offer forecasts that are better than the forward rate, what can we conclude about market efficiency? Evidence that some advisory services can consistently beat the forward rate is not necessarily evidence of a lack of market efficiency. If the difference between the forward rate and the forecast represents transaction costs, then there is no abnormal return from using the forecast. Moreover, if the difference is the result of a risk premium, then any returns earned from the forecasts would be a normal compensation for risk bearing. Finally, we must realize that the services are rarely free. Although the economics departments of larger banks sometimes provide free forecasts to corporate customers, professional advisory services charge anywhere from several hundred to many thousands of dollars per year for advice. If the potential profits from speculation are reflected in the price of the service, then once again we cannot earn abnormal profits from the forecasts.

Although the returns to a superior forecaster would be considerable, there is no evidence to suggest that abnormally large profits have been produced by following the advice of professional advisory services. But then if you ever developed a method that consistently outperformed other speculators, would you tell anyone else?

SUMMARY

1. Foreign exchange risk may be analyzed as translation exposure, transaction exposure, or economic exposure to exchange rate change.
2. Exchange risk hedges are accomplished by using the forward, futures, or options market; invoicing in domestic currency; speeding (slowing) payments of currencies expected to appreciate (depreciate); and speeding (slowing) collection of currencies expected to depreciate (appreciate).
3. The foreign exchange risk premium is equal to the difference between the forward rate and the expected future spot rate.
4. In an efficient market, the prices reflect all available information.
5. A good spot rate forecast should be on the correct side of the forward rate.

EXERCISES

1. Distinguish among translation exposure, transaction exposure, and economic exposure. Define each concept and then indicate how they may be interrelated.
2. The 6-month interest rate in the United States is 10 percent; in France it is 12 percent. The current spot rate (dollars per franc) is $0.40.

  a. What do you expect the 6-month forward rate to be?

  b. Is the franc selling at a premium or discount?

  c. If the expected spot rate in 6 months is $0.38, what is the risk premium?

3. We discussed risk aversion as being descriptive of investor behavior. Can you think of any real-world behavior that you might consider evidence of the existence of risk preferrers?

4. Does an efficient market rule out all opportunities for speculative profits? If so, why? If not, why not?

5. You are the treasurer of a U.S. firm that has a DM1 million commitment due to a German firm in 90 days. The current spot rate is $0.35 per mark. Ali forecasts that the spot rate in 90 days will be $0.40. Jahangir forecasts that the spot rate will be $0.44 in 90 days. The 90-day forward rate is $0.43 and the actual spot rate in 90 days turns out to be $0.42. Who had the best forecast and why?

REFERENCES

Bekaert, Geert, and Robert J. Hodrick, "On Biases in the Measurement of Foreign Exchange Risk Premiums," *Journal of International Money and Finance,* April 1993.

Boothe, Paul, and David Longworth, "Foreign Exchange Market Efficiency Tests: Implications of Recent Empirical Findings," *Journal of International Money and Finance,* June 1986.

Kenyon, Alfred, *Currency Risk Management.* New York: Wiley, 1981.

Levich, Richard M., "Empirical Studies of Exchange Rates: Price Behavior, Rate Determination, and Market Efficiency," in R. Jones and P. Kenen, eds., *Handbook of International Economics.* Amsterdam: North-Holland, 1984.

"Managing Corporate Risk," *Euromoney,* May 1990. pp. 138–141.

chapter 7

International Investment and Capital Flows

In the early 1960s international investment was thought to be motivated by interest differentials among countries. If the interest rate in one country exceeded that of another, then financial capital was expected to flow between the countries until the rates were equal. Modern capital market theory provided a new basis for analysis. There were obvious problems with the old theory, since interest differentials can explain one-way flows of capital, from the low- to the high-interest-rate country; yet, realistically, capital flows both ways between most pairs of countries.

In this chapter we apply some basic ideas of modern finance to understand and analyze the incentives for international investment.

PORTFOLIO DIVERSIFICATION

No doubt, the differences in the returns on various countries' assets provide an incentive for capital flows. However, we would not expect interest rates to be equalized throughout the world, since risk differs from one asset to another. Furthermore, we would anticipate a certain random component in international capital flows because money flows to new investment opportunities as they open up in various countries. Given the short time needed to shift funds

around the world, the expected profit (adjusted for risk differences) from investing in different assets should be equal. If this were not the case, then money would flow internationally until it was true.

Yet even with constant interest rates internationally, there would still be an incentive for international capital flows. This additional incentive is provided by the desire to hold diversified portfolios. It is this diversification motive that leads to the two-way flows of capital between countries. Besides the return on an investment, investors are also concerned with the risk attached to the investment. It is very unlikely that an individual who has $100,000 to invest will invest the entire amount in one asset. By choosing several investment alternatives and holding a *diversified portfolio,* the investor can reduce the risk associated with his or her investments. The modern finance literature has emphasized the concept of variability of return as a measure of risk. This is reasonable in that investors are interested in the future value of their portfolio, and the more variable the value of the portfolio, the less certain they can be of the future value.

By diversifying and selecting different assets (including assets of different countries) for a portfolio, we can reduce the variability of the portfolio. To see the effects of diversification, let us consider a simple example of an investor facing a world with two investment opportunities: asset A and asset B. The investor will hold a portfolio of A and B, with the share of the portfolio devoted to A denoted by a and the share devoted to B denoted by b. Thus, if the investor holds only A, then $a = 1$ and $b = 0$. If only B is held, then $a = 0$ and $b = 1$. Most likely the investor will choose some amount of diversification by holding both A and B.

The return on the portfolio (R_p) can be written as a weighted average of the returns on the individual assets $(R_A$ and $R_B)$:

$$R_p = aR_A + bR_B \qquad (7.1)$$

The expected future return on the portfolio will then be determined by the expected future return on the individual assets:

$$R_p^* = aR_A^* + bR_B^* \qquad (7.2)$$

where R_p^*, R_A^*, and R_B^* are the expected values of the portfolio and individual asset returns, respectively. We said earlier that the idea of portfolio risk was associated with the variability of the return on the portfolio. The measure of the degree to which a variable varies

about its mean or average value is known as the *variance*. The variance of the portfolio will depend on the portfolio share taken by the assets and the variance of the individual assets, as well as their covariance. Specifically,

$$\text{var}(R_p) = a^2 \, \text{var}(R_A) + b^2 \, \text{var}(R_B) + 2ab \, \text{cov}(R_A, R_B) \quad (7.3)$$

where *var* stands for variance and *cov* stands for covariance. The *covariance* is a measure of the degree to which the two assets move together. If when one return is higher than average the return on the other asset is lower than average, the covariance is negative. Looking at Equation (7.3), we see that a negative covariance could contribute greatly to reducing the overall portfolio variance and, therefore, risk.

To see the effects of diversification more clearly, let us use a simple example:

Probability	R_A (%)	R_B (%)
.25	−2	16
.25	9	9
.25	19	−4
.25	14	11

Note: $R_A{}^* = 10\%$; $R_B{}^* = 8\%$; $\text{var}(R_A) = 0.00605$; $\text{var}(R_B) = 0.00545$; $\text{cov}(R_A, R_B) = -0.004825$.

This table is a hypothetical assessment of the investment opportunity that is available. If we only hold asset A, our expected return is 10 percent with a variance of 0.00605. If we only hold asset B, our expected return is 8 percent with a variance of 0.00545. By holding 50 percent of our portfolio in A and 50 percent in B, our expected return is $R_p = 0.5(10 \text{ percent}) + 0.5(8 \text{ percent}) = 9$ percent with a variance of [using Equation (7.3)]

$$\text{var}(R_p) = .25(0.00605) + .25(0.00545)$$
$$+ 2(.25)(-0.004825) = 0.0004625$$

We need not be concerned with the statistical theory underlying the example. The important result for our use is the large reduction in variability of return achieved by diversification. By invest-

ing half of our wealth in A and half in B, we expect to receive a return on our portfolio that is halfway between what we would expect
from just holding A or B alone. However, the variance of our return
is much less than half the variance of either R_A or R_B. The substan-
tially lower risk achieved by diversification will lead investors to
hold many different assets, including assets from different countries.

As the size of the investor's portfolio grows, the investor will
want to buy more assets in the proportions that are already held in
order to maintain the desired degree of diversification. This means
that, as wealth increases, we could anticipate international capital
flows between countries as investors maintain these optimal portfolios. Thus, even with constant international interest rates, we
should expect to observe two-way flows of capital as international
wealth increases.

We should recognize that diversification will not eliminate all
risk to the investor, since there will still exist *systematic risk*—the
risk present in all investment opportunities. For instance, in the domestic context we know that different industries have different time
patterns of performance. While one industry is enjoying increasing
sales and profits, another industry might be languishing in the dol-
drums. Then, at some later period, the reverse might be true, and
the once-thriving industry is now the stagnant one. This is similar
to the example of opportunities A and B previously presented. The
negative covariance between them indicates that, when one is enjoying better-than-average times, the other is suffering, and vice
versa. Yet there is still a positive portfolio variance even when we
diversify and hold both assets. The variance that can be eliminated
through diversification is called the *nonsystematic risk;* this is the
risk that is unique to a particular firm or industry. The systematic
risk is common to all firms and remains even in diversified portfolios. Systematic risk results from events that are experienced jointly
by all firms, like the overall business cycle of recurrent periods of
prosperity and recession that occur at the national level.

By extending our investment alternatives internationally, we
can gain by international diversification. There appears to be nonsystematic risk at the national level that can be reduced with international portfolio diversification. Business cycles do not happen
uniformly across countries, so when one country is experiencing

rapid growth, another may be in a recession. By investing across countries, we eliminate part of the cyclical fluctuation in our portfolio that would arise from the domestic business cycle. Therefore, some of what would be considered systematic risk, in terms of strictly domestic investment opportunities, becomes nonsystematic risk when we broaden our opportunities to include foreign as well as domestic investment. Thus we can say that not only will investors tend to diversify their portfolio holdings across industries, but they can also realize additional gains by diversifying across countries.

In an interesting application of the kinds of ideas presented here, Bertrand Jacquillat and Bruno Solnik investigated whether the gains from international diversification could be realized by investing in domestic multinational firms. If we consider a multinational firm—a firm doing business in many countries—to be affected significantly by foreign factors, then we may view multinational stock as similar to an international portfolio. Since multinational firms have operations in many countries, we may hypothesize that multinational stock prices behave more like an internationally diversified portfolio than like just another domestic stock.

To examine this hypothesis, they compared the variability of returns on three types of portfolios:

1. Those invested in U.S. firms with little foreign activity.
2. Those invested in U.S. multinationals.
3. Those invested in major national stock markets.

Jacquillat and Solnik discovered that the variability of returns from a portfolio of U.S. multinational stock is 90 percent of the variability of a portfolio of purely domestically oriented stocks. However, a portfolio invested equally among different national stock markets reduced the portfolio return variance by 30 to 50 percent relative to the purely domestic portfolio.

Although the investor risk considered so far has focused on the variability of portfolio return, it should be realized that in international investment there is always the potential for political risk, which may involve the confiscation of foreigners' assets. Chapter 13 explicitly considers the analysis of such risk and includes a recent

ranking of countries in terms of the perceived political risk attached to investments made in that country.

INTERNATIONAL INVESTMENT OPPORTUNITIES

As with domestic markets, there are international investment opportunities in stocks, bonds, and mutual funds. The United States is the largest market, with financial investment opportunities well in excess of the next-largest market, Japan. The different size of the various national markets can (and does at times) prove problematic for investors seeking to trade quickly in the smaller markets.

A good example of the problems that can arise in turbulent times is provided by the stock market collapse of October 1987. In mid-October, prices collapsed dramatically in all stock markets around the world. The price fall brought huge orders to sell stocks as investors liquidated their positions and mutual funds raised cash to pay off customers' redemption requests. Stock exchanges in the United States are relatively *deep*—meaning that there are enough potential buyers and sellers and a large number of securities traded so that the market permits trading at all times. Other markets are relatively *thin*—with a much smaller number of potential buyers and sellers and a smaller volume of securities traded.

During the stock market collapse in 1987, the New York Stock Exchange was able to trade 600 million shares, while markets in Hong Kong, Singapore, Italy, Spain, France, and Germany weren't nearly as liquid. In fact, at the peak of the trading frenzy, the Hong Kong market closed for a week. Can you imagine the frustration of a U.S. portfolio manager wanting to sell shares in Hong Kong while trading has stopped?

It is not always necessary to transfer funds abroad to buy foreign securities. Many foreign stocks are traded in the United States in the form of *American depositary receipts,* or *ADRs,* as they are called. ADRs are negotiable instruments certifying that 1 to 10 shares of a foreign stock are being held by a foreign custodian. There are 56 foreign stocks listed on the New York Stock Exchange, 49 on the American Stock Exchange, and 260 more stocks traded in the "over-the-counter" market. Even though these stocks are bought and sold on the U.S. market, they are still subject

to foreign exchange risk because the dollar price of the ADR shares reflects the dollar value of the foreign currency price of the stock in the foreign country of origin. Furthermore, foreign government policy will have an impact on the value of ADRs. In April 1987, the British government imposed a 5 percent tax on conversion of British stocks into ADRs. Trading in these ADRs dropped dramatically until the British government reduced the tax.

DIRECT FOREIGN INVESTMENT

So far we have considered international investment in the form of portfolio investment, like the purchase of a stock or bond issued in a foreign currency. There is, however, another type of international investment activity called direct foreign investment. *Direct foreign investment* is the money spent by a domestic firm in establishing foreign operating units. In the U.S. balance of payments, direct investment is distinguished from portfolio investment solely on the basis of fraction of ownership. Capital flows are designated as direct investment when a foreign entity owns 10 percent or more of a firm regardless of whether the capital flows are used to purchase new plant and equipment or to buy an ownership position in an existing firm. The growth of direct investment spending corresponds to the growth of the multinational firm. Although direct investment is properly emphasized in international trade discussions of the international movement of factors of production, students should be able to distinguish portfolio investment from direct investment.

The motives for portfolio investment are easily seen in terms of the risk and return concepts already examined. In a general sense, the concern with a firm's return, subject to risk considerations, may be thought of as motivating all firm decisions, including those of direct investment. However, a literature has developed to offer more specific motives for desiring domestic ownership of foreign production facilities. Theories of direct foreign investment typically explain the incentive for such investment in terms of some imperfection in free market conditions. If markets were perfectly competitive, rather than actually establishing a foreign operating unit, the domestic firm would just as well buy foreign securities to transfer capital abroad. One line of theorizing on direct

investment is that individual firms may not maximize profits, which would be in the interest of such a firm's stockholders; instead, they would maximize growth in terms of firm size. This is a concept that relies on an oligopolistic nature of industry that would allow a firm to survive without maximizing profits. In this case direct investment is preferred since domestic firms cannot depend on foreign-managed firms to operate in their best interests.

Other theories of direct foreign investment are based on the domestic firm possessing superior skills, knowledge, or information as compared to foreign firms. Such advantages would allow the foreign subsidiary of the domestic firm to earn a higher return than is possible by a foreign-managed firm.

Direct investment may become an increasingly important source of finance for developing countries. Prior to the rapid growth of bank lending following the oil price shocks of 1973 and 1974, direct investment exceeded bank lending as a source of funds in developing countries. Through the late 1970s, bank lending grew in size and came to dominate direct investment by the early 1980s. In more recent years that trend has been reversed. Table 7.1 illustrates how sources of funds to developing countries changed over time. In 1970, direct investment in developing countries accounted for 19 percent of money inflows. By 1980 this figure fell to 12 percent. More recently direct investment has risen in importance again.

The growth of bank lending in the early 1980s was a result of the growth of the Eurodollar market associated with the "recycling" of dollars earned by oil exporters through international banks, which in turn lent to developing countries. Bank lending was preferred by developing countries because it allowed great flexibility in the use of funds in the borrowing country. Direct investment was often politically unpopular in developing countries

Table 7.1 NET SOURCES OF FUNDS TO DEVELOPING COUNTRIES

	1970	1980	1992
Direct investment	19%	12%	18%
Official Development Aid	43	28	40
Nonconcessional loans and credits	38	60	42

Source: The World Bank, *World Development Report,* various issues.

because it is associated with an element of foreign control over domestic resources. Nationalist sentiment combined with a fear of exploitation often resulted in laws restricting direct investment. In such a setting, it is understandable that countries readily embraced the low-cost availability of bank loans in the 1970s. In contrast to direct investment decisions that are made by foreign firms, funds loaned by banks could be used by the nation to follow whatever economic or political strategy existed.

In the mid-1980s, bank lending to large-debtor developing countries was sharply curtailed because of problems of nonrepayment. As a result, direct investment has become an important source of funds in developing countries. It may be that direct investment contributes more to economic development than bank loans, since more of the funds go to actual investment in productive resources. Bank loans to sovereign governments were (and are) often used for consumption spending rather than investment. In addition, direct investment may involve new technologies and productive expertise not available in the domestic economy. If foreign firms make a bad decision regarding a direct investment expenditure, the loss is sustained by the foreign firm. If the domestic government uses bank loans inefficiently, the country still faces a repayment obligation to the banks.

CAPITAL FLIGHT

In the discussion of portfolio investment, we emphasized expected risk and return as determinants of foreign investment. When the risk of doing business in a country rises sharply or the expected return falls, we sometimes observe large outflows of investment funds so that the country experiences massive capital account deficits. Such outflows of funds are often descriptively referred to as *capital flight*. The change in the risk-return relationship that gives rise to capital flight may be the result of political or financial crisis, tightening capital controls, tax increases, or fear of a domestic currency devaluation.

Table 7.2 provides estimates of the magnitude of capital flight from 1977 to 1987 for selected countries. The third column, "Gross external debt (1984)," is provided to indicate the size of the capital

**Table 7.2 ESTIMATED CAPITAL FLIGHT,
1977 TO 1987**
Billions of U.S. Dollars

(1) Country	(2) Capital flight	(3) Gross external debt (1984)
Argentina	$20 billion	$ 46 billion
Brazil	20	104
Mexico	45	97
Venezuela	28	34
Nigeria	9	20
Phillipines	8	24

Source: Morgan Guaranty Trust Company and World Bank.

flows relative to the debt incurred. One of the issues arising from the developing-country debt crisis of the 1980s was an assertion by bankers that some of the borrowed money was not put to use in the debtor nations but, instead, was misappropriated by individuals and deposited back in the developed countries. In addition to alleged misappropriated funds, wealthy individuals and business firms often shipped capital out of the debtor nations at the same time that these nations were pleading for additional funds from developed-country banks.

Table 7.2 suggests that over the period from 1977 to 1987, $20 billion of flight capital left Argentina. This $20 billion is almost half of the debt incurred through 1984 that totaled $46 billion. Since some of the debt was accumulated prior to 1977, the data suggest a crude interpretation that, for every $1 borrowed by Argentina, about 50 cents came out of the country as flight capital. Similar statements might be made for the other countries in the table. An important aspect of the capital outflows is that less resources are available at home to service the debt, and more borrowing is required. In addition, capital flight may be associated with a loss of international reserves and greater pressure for devaluation of the domestic currency.

The discussion of capital flight serves to highlight the importance of economic and political stability for encouraging domestic investment. Business firms and individuals respond to lower risk and higher return. The stable and growing developing country faces

little, if any, capital flight and attracts foreign capital to aid in expanding the productive capacity of the economy. Several of the countries in Table 7.2 have seen a repatriation of flight capital as their economies stabilized in the late 1980s and early 1990s.

SUMMARY

1. Even with constant interest rates, portfolio diversification provides an incentive for international capital flows.
2. The less variable the return on a portfolio, the more certain the return.
3. Portfolio diversification eliminates the nonsystematic risk that is unique to an individual asset. The systematic risk, common to all assets, will remain.
4. American depositary receipts (ADRs) are negotiable instruments sold in the United States that represent ownership of shares in a foreign firm.
5. Direct foreign investment is spending to establish foreign operating units.
6. Capital flight arises from the increased risk of doing business in a country.

EXERCISES

1. How can investment flows be motivated by interest differentials and yet two-way capital flows be observed between countries?
2. How does diversification reduce risk? Give an example.
3. Why might we expect the stock of a domestic multinational firm to have different risk characteristics than the stock of a firm with purely domestic operations? If the difference does not exist, why might that be?
4. Why might U.S. investors prefer to invest in U.S. assets rather than foreign assets?
5. What is the difference between direct foreign investment and financial portfolio investment? In what ways are the motives for direct investment similar to the motives for portfolio investment? In what ways are they different?
6. What policy would you recommend to a country facing substantial capital flight? In other words, knowing nothing about the details of the country, what do you suppose is the most important policy change it should make?

REFERENCES

Black, Fischer, "The Ins and Outs of Foreign Investment," *Financial Analysts Journal,* 34, May–June 1978.

Grauer, Robert R., and Nils H. Hakkansson, "Gains from International Diversification: 1968–85 Returns on Portfolios of Stocks and Bonds," *Journal of Finance,* July 1987.

Khan, Mohsin S., and Nadeem Ul Haque, "Capital Flight from Developing Countries," *Finance and Development,* March 1987.

Mann, Catherine L., "Determinants of Japanese Direct Investment in U.S. Manufacturing Industries," International Finance Discussion Paper No. 362, Federal Reserve Board, 1989.

Solnik, Bruno, *International Investments,* 2nd ed., Reading, Mass.: Addison-Wesley, 1991.

Walter, Ingo, *Secret Money.* London: Allen and Unwin, 1985.

chapter 8

Prices and Exchange Rates: Purchasing Power Parity

Chapter 1 discussed the role of foreign exchange market arbitrage in keeping foreign exchange rates the same in different locations. If the dollar price of a yen is higher at Bank of America in San Francisco than at Morgan Guaranty Bank in New York, we would expect traders to buy yen from Morgan Guaranty and simultaneously sell yen to Bank of America. This activity would raise the dollar/yen exchange rate quoted by Morgan Guaranty and lower the rate at Bank of America until the exchange rate quotations are transaction costs close. Such arbitrage activity is not limited to the foreign exchange market. We would expect arbitrage to be present in any market where similar goods are traded in different locations. For instance, the price of gold is roughly the same worldwide at any point in time. If gold sold at a higher price in one location than in another, arbitragers would buy gold where it is cheap and sell where it is high until the prices are equal (allowing for transaction costs). Similarly, we would expect the price of tractors or automobiles or sheet steel to be related across geographically disparate markets. However, there are good economic reasons why some goods prices are more similar across countries than others.

This tendency for similar goods to sell for similar prices globally provides a link between prices and exchange rates. If we wanted to know why exchange rates change over time, one obvious

answer is that, as prices change internationally, exchange rates must also change to keep the prices measured in a common currency equal across countries. In other words, exchange rates should adjust to offset differing inflation rates between countries. This relationship between the prices of goods and services and exchange rates is known as *purchasing power parity*. Although we are hesitant to refer to purchasing power parity as a theory of the exchange rate, for reasons that will be made apparent shortly, it is important to study the relationship between price levels and exchange rates in order to understand the role of goods markets (as separate from financial asset markets) in international finance.

ABSOLUTE PURCHASING POWER PARITY

Our first view of purchasing power parity (PPP) is absolute purchasing power parity. Here we consider the exchange rate to be given by the ratio of price levels between countries. If E is the spot exchange rate (domestic currency units per foreign unit), P the domestic price index, and P^F the foreign price index, the absolute PPP relation is written as

$$P/P^F = E \tag{8.1}$$

For those readers who are not familiar with price indexes, P and P^F may be thought of as consumer price indexes, or producer price indexes, or price indexes used to convert the gross domestic product (GDP) from nominal to real magnitudes—known as GDP deflators. A price index is supposed to measure average prices in an economy and therefore is subject to the criticism that in fact it measures the actual prices faced by no one. To construct such an index, we must first determine which prices to include—that is, which goods and services are to be monitored. Then these various items need to be assigned weights reflecting their importance in total spending. Thus, the consumer price index would weight housing prices very heavily, but bread prices would have only a very small weight. The final index is a weighted average of the prices of the goods and services surveyed.

Phrased in terms of price indexes, absolute PPP, as given in Equation (8.1), indicates that the exchange rate between any two currencies is equal to the ratio of their price indexes. Therefore, the exchange rate is a *nominal* magnitude, dependent on prices. We

should be careful when using real-world price index data that the various national price indexes are comparable in terms of goods and services covered as well as base year (the reference year used for comparisons over time). If changes in the world were only nominal, the results of price level change, then we would expect PPP to hold if we had true price indexes. The significance of this last sentence will be illustrated soon.

Equation (8.1) can be rewritten as

$$P = EP^F \tag{8.2}$$

so that the domestic price level is equal to the product of the domestic currency price of foreign currency and the foreign price level. Equation (8.2) is called the *law of one price* and indicates that goods sell for the same price worldwide. For instance, we might observe a shirt selling for $10 in the United States and £4 in the United Kingdom. If the $/£ exchange rate is $2.50 per pound, then $P = EP^F = (2.50)(4) = 10$. Thus, the price of the shirt in the United Kingdom is the same as the U.S. price once we convert the pound price into dollars using the exchange rate and compare prices in a common currency.

Unfortunately for this analysis, the world is more complex than the simple shirt example. The real world is characterized by differentiated products, costly information, and all sorts of impediments to the equalization of goods prices worldwide. Certainly, the more homogeneous goods are, the more we expect the law of one price to hold. Some commodities, which retain essentially the same form worldwide, provide the best examples of the law of one price. Gold, for instance, is quoted in dollar prices internationally, and so we would be correct in stating that the law of one price holds quite closely for gold. However, shirts come in different styles, brand names, and prices, and we do not expect the law of one price to hold domestically for shirts, let alone internationally.

Figure 8.1 illustrates some international price differences of comparable goods and services across countries. We might be able to quarrel with the international comparability of the goods and services chosen, but any international traveler is aware that wide discrepancies exist between prices of similar products and services across countries.

One might wonder why we would ever expect PPP to hold since we know international trade involves freight charges and tar-

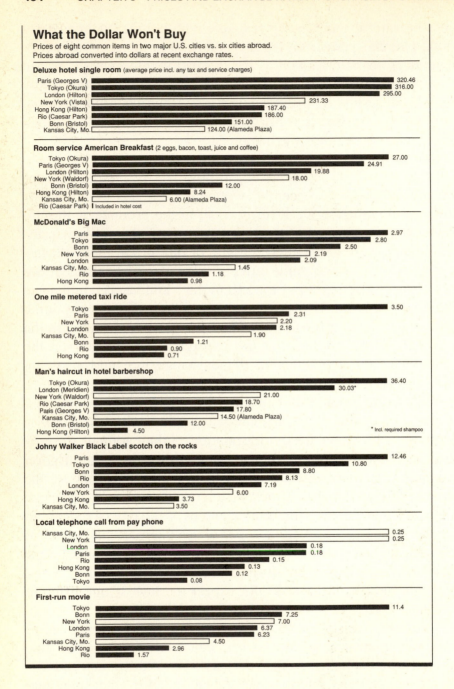

FIGURE 8.1
International price comparisons (all foreign prices converted to U.S. dollar equivalents); prices and exchange rates as of December 1987.
(*Source: The Wall Street Journal,* December 4, 1987, p. 37. Reprinted by permission of the *The Wall Street Journal,* © 1987, Dow Jones and Company, Inc. All rights reserved worldwide.)

iffs. Given these costs associated with shipping goods, we would not expect PPP to hold for any particular good—so why would we anticipate the relationship phrased in terms of price indexes to hold as in Equation (8.1)? Furthermore, not all goods are traded internationally, yet the prices of these goods are captured in the national price indexes. As the prices of nontraded goods change, the price indexes change. But the exchange rates may not vary, since the changing price of nontraded goods would not give rise to international trade flows, and so no change in the supply and demand for currencies need result. Recently, economists have added many refinements to the analysis of PPP that we need not consider here. The important lesson to be learned is the potential problem associated with using price indexes to explain exchange rate changes.

So far we have emphasized variations in the exchange rate brought about by changing price indexes or nominal changes. However, it is reasonable to assume that much of the week-to-week change in exchange rates is the result of real rather than nominal events. Besides variations in the price level due to general inflation, we can also identify *relative price changes*. Inflation results in an increase in all prices, but *relative* price changes indicate that not all prices move together. Some prices increase faster than others, and some rise while others fall. An old analogy that students often find useful is to think of inflation as an elevator carrying a load of tennis balls, representing the prices of individual goods. As the inflation continues, the balls are carried higher by the elevator, which means that all prices are rising. But as the inflation continues and the elevator rises, the balls, or individual prices, are bouncing up and down. So while the elevator raises all the balls inside, the balls do not bounce up and down together. The balls bouncing up have their prices rising relative to the balls going down.

If we think of different elevators as representing different countries, then if the balls were still and the elevators rose at the same rate, the exchange rate would be constant as suggested by purchasing power parity. Moreover, if we looked for sufficiently long intervals, we could ignore the bouncing balls, since the large movements of the elevators would dominate the exchange rate movements. If, however, we observed very short intervals during which the elevators move only slightly, we would find that the bouncing balls, or relative price changes of individual goods, would largely determine the exchange rate.

Arbitrage in goods markets makes it easy to understand why price level changes affect exchange rates, but the effect of relative price changes is more subtle. The following example will illustrate how exchange rates can change because of relative price change even though there is no change in the overall price level (no inflation). Table 8.1 summarizes the argument. Let us suppose there are two countries, France and Japan, and each consumes wine and sake. Initially, in period 0, wine and sake each sell for 1 franc in France and 1 yen in Japan. In a simple world of no transport costs or other barriers to the law of one price, the exchange rate, $E = FF/¥$, must equal 1. Note initially the relative price of one bottle of wine is equal to one bottle of sake (since sake and wine sell for the same price in each country). To determine the inflation rate in each country, we must calculate price indexes that indicate the value of the items consumed in each country for each period. Suppose that initially France consumes 9 units of wine and 1 unit of sake, whereas Japan consumes 1 wine and 9 sake. At the domestic prices of 1 unit of domestic currency per unit of wine or sake, we can see that the total value of the basket of goods consumed in France is 10 francs, whereas the total value of the goods consumed in Japan is 10 yen.

Now let us suppose that there is a bad grape harvest, so that in the next period wine is more expensive. In terms of relative prices, we know that the bad harvest will make wine rise in price relative to sake. Suppose now that, instead of the original relative price of 1 sake = 1 wine, we now have 1.5 sake = 1 wine. Consumers will recognize this change in relative prices and tend to decrease their consumption of wine and increase consumption of sake. Suppose in period 1 the French consume 8 wine and 1.5 sake, whereas the Japanese consume 0.333 wine and 9.5 sake. Let us further assume that the central banks of Japan and France follow a policy of zero inflation, where inflation is measured by the change in the cost of current consumption. With no inflation, the value of the consumption basket will be unchanged from period 0 and will equal 10 in each country. Thus, although average prices have not changed, we know that individual prices must change because of the rising price of wine relative to sake.

The determination of the individual prices is a simple exercise in algebra but is not needed to understand the central message of the example; therefore, students could skip this paragraph and still

Table 8.1 THE EFFECT OF A RELATIVE PRICE CHANGE ON THE EXCHANGE RATE

	France				Japan			
	Period 0		Period 1		Period 0		Period 1	
	Price in francs	Quantity consumed	Price in francs	Quantity consumed	Price in yen	Quantity consumed	Price in yen	Quantity consumed
Wine	1	9	1.111	8	1	1	1.5	0.333
Sake	1	1	0.741	1.5	1	9	1	9.5
Value of consumption	10		10		10		10	

Note: Exchange rate, FF/¥, in period 0 = 1; exchange rate, FF/¥, in period 1 = 0.741.
Source: Bruno Solnik, "International Parity Conditions and Exchange Risk," *Journal of Banking and Finance,* 2, October 1978, p. 289.

retain the benefit of the lesson. Since we know that France consumes 8 wine and 1.5 sake with a total value of 10 francs and that the relative price is 1.5 sake = 1 wine, we can solve for the individual prices by letting $1.5P_s = P_w$, and we can then substitute this into our total spending equation ($8P_w + 1.5P_s = 10$) to determine the prices. In other words, we have a system with two equations and two unknowns that is solvable:

$$8P_w + 1.5P_s = 10 \qquad (8.3)$$

$$1.5P_s = P_w \qquad (8.4)$$

Substituting Equation (8.4) into the previous equation, we obtain

$$8P_w + 1P_w = 10 \rightarrow P_w = {}^{10}\!/_9 = 1.111 \qquad (8.5)$$

Since $P_w = 1.111$, we can use this to determine P_s:

$$1.5P_s = 1.111 \rightarrow P_s = {}^{1.1111}\!/_{1.5} = 0.741 \qquad (8.6)$$

Thus we have our prices in France in period 1. For Japan it is even easier:

$$\tfrac{1}{3}P_w + 9.5P_s = 10 \qquad (8.7)$$

$$1.5P_s = P_w \qquad (8.8)$$

Substituting Equation (8.8) into the preceding equation, we obtain

$$\tfrac{1}{3}P_w + 6\,\tfrac{1}{3}P_w = 10 \rightarrow P_w = 1.5 \qquad (8.9)$$

Thus

$$1.5P_s = 1.5 \rightarrow P_s = 1 \qquad (8.10)$$

Given the new prices in period 1, we can now determine the exchange rate implied by the law of one price. Since sake sells for 0.741 franc in France and 1 yen in Japan, the franc price of yen must be FF/¥ = 0.741.

In summary, this example has shown how exchange rates can change because of real economic events, even with average price levels constant. Since PPP is usually discussed in terms of price indexes, we find that real events, such as the relative price changes brought about by a poor harvest, will cause deviations from absolute PPP as the exchange rate changes, even though the price indexes are constant. Note also that the relative price effect leads to an appreciation of the currency where consumption of the good in-

creasing in price is heaviest. In our example the franc appreciates as a result of the increased relative price of wine.

The previous discussion has illustrated why absolute PPP probably fails to hold at most points in time. Stating that the level of the exchange rate is equal to the ratio of price indexes is quite a strong statement to make. In the next section, a less restrictive relationship between prices and exchange rates is discussed.

RELATIVE PURCHASING POWER PARITY

There is an alternative view of PPP besides the absolute PPP just discussed. Relative PPP is said to hold when

$$\hat{E} = \hat{P} - \hat{P}^F \tag{8.11}$$

where a hat ($\wedge$) over a variable denotes percentage change. So Equation (8.11) says that the percentage change in the exchange rate ($\hat{E}$) is equal to the percentage change in the domestic price level ($\hat{P}$) minus the percentage change in the foreign price level ($\hat{P}^F$). Therefore, although absolute PPP states that the exchange rate is equal to the ratio of the price indexes, relative PPP deals with percentage changes in these variables.

We usually refer to the percentage change in the price level as the rate of inflation. So another way of stating the relative PPP relationship is by saying that the percentage change in the exchange rate is equal to the inflation differential between the domestic and foreign country. If we say that the percentage change in the exchange rate is equal to the inflation differential, then we can ignore the actual level of E, P, and P^F and consider the changes, which is not so strong an assumption as absolute PPP. It should be noted that, if absolute PPP holds, then relative PPP will also hold. But if absolute PPP does not hold, relative PPP still may. This is because the level of E may not equal P/P^F, but the change in E could still equal the inflation differential.

Having observed in the last section how relative prices can determine exchange rates, we can, with reason, believe that these relative price changes will, over time, decrease in importance as compared to inflation rates, so that in the long run inflation differentials will dominate exchange rate movements. The idea is that real events causing relative price movements are often random and short run in nature. By *random,* we mean they are unexpected and

equally likely to raise or lower the exchange rate. Given this characterization, it follows that these random relative price movements will tend to cancel out over time (otherwise, we would not consider them equally likely to raise or lower E).

TIME, INFLATION, AND PPP

Several researchers have found that PPP holds better for high-inflation countries. When we say "holds better," we mean that the equalities stated in Equations (8.1) and (8.11) are more closely met by actual exchange rate and price level data observed over time in high-inflation countries compared to low-inflation countries. In high-inflation countries changes in exchange rates are highly correlated with inflation differentials because the sheer magnitude of inflation overwhelms the relative price effects, whereas in low- or moderate-inflation countries the relative price effects dominate exchange rate movements and lead to discrepancies from PPP. In terms of our earlier example, when the elevator is moving faster (high inflation), the movement of the balls inside (relative prices) is less important; however, when the elevator is moving slowly (low inflation), the bouncing balls will be quite important.

Besides the rate of inflation, the period of time analyzed will also have an effect on how well PPP holds. We expect PPP to hold better for annual data than for monthly data, since the longer time frame will allow for more inflation. Thus, the random relative price effects are relatively unimportant, and we find exchange rate changes closely related to inflation differentials. Using the elevator analogy, the longer the time frame analyzed, the farther the elevator will move, and the more the elevator moves, the less important will be the balls inside. This suggests that studies of PPP covering many years will be more likely to yield evidence of PPP than studies based on a few years' data.

The literature on PPP is voluminous and tends to confirm the conclusions we have made. Researchers have presented evidence that real relative price shifts can have an important role in the short run, but over time the random nature of the relative price changes minimizes the importance of these unrelated events. Investigations

over long periods of time (100 years, for instance) have concluded that PPP holds well in the long run.

DEVIATIONS FROM PPP

So far, the discussion has included several reasons why deviations from PPP occur. When discussing the role of arbitrage in goods markets, it was said that the law of one price would not apply to differentiated products or products that are not traded internationally. Furthermore, since international trade involves shipping goods across national borders, prices may differ because of shipping costs or tariffs. Relative price changes have been emphasized as a reason why PPP would hold better in the long run than the short run. Such relative price changes result from real economic events like changing tastes, bad weather, or government policy. As illustrated in Table 8.1, relative price changes cause deviations from PPP in terms of national price indexes. The law of one price could hold for individual goods, yet PPP could be violated for a price index. This, of course, just points out a problem in using price indexes rather than individual goods prices to measure PPP. Since consumers in different countries consume different goods, price indexes are not directly comparable internationally. We know that evaluating PPP between the United States and Japan using the U.S. and Japanese consumer price indexes is weakened by the fact that the typical Japanese consumer will buy a different basket of goods than the typical U.S. consumer. In this case, the law of one price could hold perfectly for individual goods, yet we would observe deviations from PPP using the consumer price index for Japan and the United States.

Recognizing that there are problems in using national price indexes to measure PPP might lead us to believe that PPP, or the law of one price, should hold well for individual goods. There is, however, evidence that PPP does not hold well for many individual goods traded internationally. There are several reasons why this may be true. First, it is important to realize that PPP is not a theory of exchange rate determination. In other words, inflation differentials do not *cause* exchange rate change. PPP is an equilibrium relationship between two endogenous variables. When we say that prices and exchange rates are *endogenous,* we mean that they are simultane-

ously determined by other factors. The other factors are called *exogenous* variables. Exogenous variables may change independently, as with bad weather or government policy. Given a change in an exogenous variable, as with poor weather and a consequent poor harvest, both prices and exchange rates will change. Deviations in measured PPP will occur if prices and exchange rates change at different speeds. Evidence suggests that, following some exogenous *shock*, changes in exchange rates precede changes in prices.

Such a finding can be explained by theorizing that the price indexes used for PPP calculations move slowly because commodity prices are not as flexible as financial asset prices (the exchange rate is the price of monies). We know that exchange rates vary throughout the day as the demand and supply for foreign exchange vary. But how often does the department store change the price of furniture, or how often does the auto parts store change the price of tires? Since the prices that enter into published price indexes are slower to adjust than are exchange rates, it is not surprising that exchange rate changes seem to lead price changes. Yet if exchange rates change faster than goods prices, then we have another reason why PPP should hold better in the long run than the short run. When economic *news* is received, both exchange rates and prices may change. For instance, suppose the Federal Reserve announces today that it will promote a 100 percent increase in the U.S. money supply over the next 12 months. Such a change would cause greater inflation, because more money in circulation leads to higher prices. The dollar would also fall in value relative to other currencies, because the supply of dollars rises relative to the demand.

Following the Fed's announcement, would you expect goods prices in the United States to rise before the dollar depreciates on the foreign exchange market? While there are some important issues in exchange rate determination that must wait until later chapters, we generally can say here that the dollar would depreciate immediately following the announcement. If traders believe that the dollar will be worth less in the future, they will attempt to sell dollars now, and this selling activity drives down the dollar's value today. There should be some similar forces at work in the goods market as traders expecting higher prices in the future buy more goods today. But for most goods, the immediate short-run result will be a depletion of inventories at constant prices. Only over time will most goods prices rise. Figure 8.2 illustrates how the exchange rate

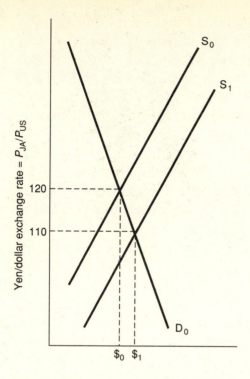

FIGURE 8.2 Shifts in the foreign exchange market and deviations from PPP.

will shift with news. The figure illustrates the quantity of dollars bought and sold on the horizontal axis and the yen price of the dollar on the vertical axis. Initially, the foreign exchange market equilibrium occurs where the demand curve D_0, intersects the supply curve S_0, at an exchange rate of 120 yen per dollar with quantity $\$_0$ of dollars being bought and sold. Suppose the Federal Reserve now issues a statement causing people to expect the U.S. money supply to grow more rapidly in the future. This causes foreign exchange traders to expect the dollar to depreciate in the future. As a result, they attempt to sell more dollars now, shifting the supply curve out to S_1 in Figure 8.2. This shift in supply, with constant demand, causes the dollar to depreciate now down to 110 yen per dollar. At this new exchange rate, a quantity $\$_1$ is traded.

Suppose initially PPP holds, so that $E = 120 = P_{JA}/P_{US}$. The announced change in monetary policy has an immediate effect on the exchange rate because currencies are traded continuously throughout the day. Prices of goods and services will change much

more slowly. In the short run, the ratio of the price level in Japan to the price level in the United States may remain unchanged at 120. So while E falls today to 110 in Figure 8.2, the ratio of the national price levels is still equal to the initial exchange rate of 120, and there is an apparent deviation from PPP.

Therefore, periods with important economic news will be periods where PPP deviations are large—the exchange rate adjusts while prices lag behind. In addition to the differential speed of adjustment between exchange rates and prices, periods dominated by news are likely to be periods involving much relative price change, so that PPP deviations would tend to appear even without exchange rates and prices changing at different speeds.

Another reason why deviations from PPP are likely is that international trade involves lags between order and delivery. Prices are often set by contract today for goods that are to be delivered several months later. If we compare goods prices and exchange rates today to evaluate PPP, we are using the exchange rate applicable to goods delivered today with prices that were set some time in the past. Ideally, we should compare contract prices in each country at the time contracts are signed with the exchange rate that is expected to prevail in the future period when goods are actually delivered and payment is made. If the exchange rate actually realized in the future period is the same as that expected when the goods prices were agreed upon, then there would be no problem in using today's exchange rate and today's delivered goods prices. The problem is that, realistically, exchange rates are very difficult to forecast, so that seldom would today's realized exchange rate be equal to the trader's forecast at some past period.

Let's consider a simple example. Suppose that on September 1, Mr. U.S. agrees to buy books from Ms. U.K. for £1 per book. At the time the contract is signed, books in the United States sell for $2, and the current exchange rate of $E_{\$/£} = 2$ ensures that the law of one price holds—a £1 book from the United Kingdom is selling for the dollar equivalent of $2 (the pound book price of 1 times the dollar price of the pound of $2). If the contract calls for delivery and payment on December 1 of £1 per book and Mr. U.S. expects the exchange rate and prices to be unchanged until December 1, he *expects* PPP to hold at the time the payment is due. Suppose that on December 1, the actual exchange rate is £1 = $1.50. An economist researching the law of one price for books would compare book

prices of £1 and $2 with the exchange rate of $E_{\$/£} = 1.50$, and examine if $E_{\$/£} = P_{US}/P_{UK}$. Since $\$1.50 \neq 2/1$, he would conclude that there are important deviations from PPP. Yet these deviations are *spurious*. At the time the prices were set, PPP was expected to hold. We generate the appearance of PPP deviations by comparing exchange rates today with prices that were set in the past.

The possible explanations for deviations from PPP include factors that would suggest permanent deviations (shipping costs and tariffs), factors that would produce temporary deviations (differential speed of adjustment between financial asset markets and goods markets or real relative price changes), and factors that cause the appearance of deviations where none may actually exist (comparing current exchange rates with prices set in the past or using national price indexes when countries consume different baskets of goods). Since PPP measurements convey information regarding the relative purchasing power of currencies, such measurements have served as a basis for economic policy discussions. The next section will provide an example of policy-related information contained in PPP measurement.

"OVERVALUED" AND "UNDERVALUED" CURRENCIES

If we observe E, P, and P^F over time, we find that the absolute PPP relationship does not hold very well for any pair of countries. If, over time, P^F rises faster than P, then we would expect E, the domestic currency price of the foreign currency, to fall. If E does not fall by the amount suggested by the lower P/P^F, then we could say that the domestic currency is undervalued or (the same thing) the foreign currency is overvalued.

In the early 1980s, there was much talk of an "overvalued" dollar. The foreign exchange value of the dollar appeared to be too high relative to the inflation differentials between the United States and the other developed countries. The term *overvalued* suggests that the exchange rate is not where it should be, yet if the free-market supply and demand factors are determining the exchange rate, then the "overvalued" exchange rate is actually the free-market equilibrium rate. In this case, the term *overvalued* might suggest that this equilibrium is but a temporary deviation from PPP, and over time the exchange rate will fall in line with the inflation differential.

In the early 1980s, the foreign exchange price of the dollar grew at a faster rate than the inflation differential between the other industrial nations and the United States. It appears then that, for more than four years, a dollar "overvaluation" developed. Not until 1985 did the exchange rate begin to return to a level consistent with PPP. Figure 8.3 illustrates what this pattern of percentage changes in exchange rates and price levels meant for the actual level of the mark/dollar exchange rate. Prior to 1981, the dollar appears to be undervalued in that the actual exchange rate is below that implied by PPP as measured by inflation differentials. In other words, the line labeled "PPP exchange rate" measures the values the exchange rate would take so that the percentage change in the exchange rate would equal the inflation differential between Germany and the United States. Figure 8.3 indicates that the actual exchange rate was below the PPP level—thus, the undervalued dollar. After 1981, the dollar appreciated against the mark at a faster rate than the inflation differential, so the dollar be-

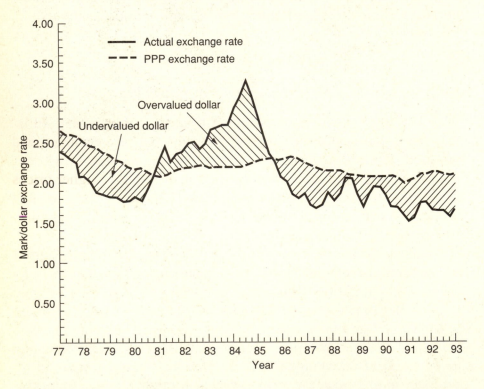

FIGURE 8.3
The actual mark/dollar exchange rate and the PPP implied exchange rate.

comes "overvalued." By 1985, the dollar begins to depreciate against the mark and move toward the PPP value of the exchange rate.

Since we know that PPP does not hold well for any pair of countries with moderate inflation in the short run, we must always have currencies that appear "overvalued" or "undervalued" in a PPP sense. The issue becomes important when the apparent over- or undervaluation persists for some time and has significant macroeconomic consequences. In the early 1980s, the U.S. political issue at the forefront of this apparent dilemma was that the "overvalued" dollar was hurting export-oriented industries. U.S. goods were rising in price to foreign buyers as the dollar appreciated. The problem was made visible by a large balance-of-trade deficit that became a major political issue. In 1985, coordinated intervention in the foreign exchange market (discussed in Chapter 1) contributed to a dollar depreciation that reduced the PPP-implied dollar overvaluation.

Besides the dollar overvaluation relative to the other developed countries' currencies, many developing countries have complained, from time to time, that their currencies are overvalued against the developed countries' currencies, and thus their balance of trade sustains a larger deficit than would otherwise occur. If PPP should only apply to internationally traded goods, then we can show how lower labor productivity in developing countries could contribute to the appearance of overvalued currencies. For nontraded goods we assume that production methods are similar worldwide. It may make more sense to think of the nontraded goods sector as being largely services. In this case the more productive countries tend to have higher wages and thus higher prices in the service sector than less productive, low-wage countries. We now have a situation in which the price indexes used to calculate PPP vary with productivity and hence with wages in each country. If we assume that exchange rates are determined by traded goods prices only (the idea being that if a good does not enter into international trade, there is no reason for its price to be equalized internationally and thus no reason for changes in its price to affect the exchange rate), then we can find how price indexes vary with service prices while exchange rates are unaffected. For instance, the price of a haircut in Paris should not be affected by an increase in Los Angeles haircut prices. So if the price of haircuts should rise in Los Angeles, other things equal, the average price level in the United

States increases. But this U.S. price increase should not have any impact on the dollar per franc exchange rate. If, instead, the price of an automobile rises in the United States relative to French auto prices, we would expect the dollar to depreciate relative to the franc, as demand for French autos, and thus francs, increases while demand for U.S. autos, and thus dollars, decreases.

If the world operates in the way just described, then we would expect that the greater the traded goods productivity differentials between countries are, the greater will be the wage differentials reflected in service prices, and thus the greater will be the deviations from absolute PPP over time. Suppose that developing countries, starting from lower absolute levels of productivity, have higher growth rates of productivity. If per capita income differences between countries give a reasonable measure of the productivity differences, then we would anticipate that, as developing country per capita income increases relative to developed country per capita income, the developing country price index will grow faster than that of the developed country. But at the same time, the depreciation of the developing country currency lags behind the inflation differentials, as measured by the average price levels in each country that include traded and nontraded goods prices. Thus over time the currency of the developing country will tend to appear overvalued (the foreign exchange value of developing country money has not depreciated as called for by the average price levels), whereas the developed country currency will appear undervalued (the exchange value of foreign money has not appreciated enough).

Does the preceding discussion describe the real world? Do you believe that labor-intensive services (domestic servants, haircuts, etc.) are cheaper in poorer countries than in wealthy countries? Researchers have provided evidence suggesting that the deviations from PPP as previously mentioned do indeed occur systematically with changes in per capita income.

What is the bottom line of the foregoing consideration? National price indexes are not particularly good indicators of the need for exchange rate adjustments. In this respect it is not surprising to find that many studies have shown that absolute PPP does not hold. The idea that currencies are undervalued or overvalued can be misleading if exchange rates are free to change with changing market conditions. Only if the central bank or

government intervention interrupts the free adjustment of the exchange rate to market clearing levels can we really talk about a currency as being overvalued or undervalued (and in many such instances black markets develop where the currency is traded at free-market prices). The fact that changes in PPP over time present the appearance of an undervalued currency in terms of the price indexes of two countries is perhaps more an indicator of the limitations of price indexes than of any real market phenomena.

SUMMARY

1. If the exchange rate is equal to the ratio of the price indexes, absolute PPP holds.
2. If the percentage change in the exchange rate is equal to the inflation differential between two countries, relative PPP holds.
3. PPP holds better for high-inflation countries or long time periods, when the movement of price levels overwhelms any relative price change.
4. Deviations from PPP may arise from the presence of nontraded goods prices in price indexes, differentiated goods, shipping costs, tariffs, relative price changes, different consumption bundles across countries (and thus different goods included in national price indexes), prices fixed by contract, or differential speeds of adjustment of exchange rates and goods prices.
5. Currencies are said to be overvalued (undervalued) if they have appreciated more (less) than the difference between the domestic and foreign inflation rate.

EXERCISES

1. Assume the U.S. price index is equal to 108 while the Japanese price index is equal to 14,000.
   a. What should the ¥/$ exchange rate be according to absolute purchasing power parity?
   b. If the actual exchange rate was equal to 120.0, would the dollar be considered undervalued or overvalued?
   c. Is purchasing power parity a good measure of what exchange rates should be?
2. Under what conditions is purchasing power parity most likely to hold best?
3. If nontradable goods prices rise faster in country A than in country B, and tradable goods prices remain unchanged, determine whether currency A will appear to be overvalued or undervalued.
4. Explain why relative purchasing power parity may hold when absolute purchasing power parity does not.

5. List four reasons why deviations from PPP might occur; then carefully explain how each causes such deviations.

REFERENCES

Frenkel, Jacob, "Purchasing Power Parity: Doctrinal Perspective and Evidence from the 1920s," *Journal of International Economics,* 8, May 1978.

Officer, L. H., *Purchasing Power Parity and Exchange Rates: Theory, Evidence, and Relevance.* Greenwich, Conn.: JAI Press, 1982.

Shapiro, A.C., "What Does Purchasing Power Parity Mean?" *Journal of International Money and Finance,* 2, December 1983.

chapter 9

Determinants of the Balance of Trade and Payments

Earlier chapters are full of discussions involving foreign exchange rates and the balance of payments. We now know the definitions and uses of these two important international finance terms, but have yet to consider what determines their values at any particular point in time. Why do some countries run a surplus balance of payments while others run deficits? How is it that some currencies appreciate in value during one period yet depreciate in another? These are important questions that are central to international monetary economics. It is worth noting that financial institutions, central banks, and governments invest many resources in trying to predict exchange rates and international trade and payments. The kinds of theories to be introduced in this chapter have shaped the way economists, investors, and politicians approach such problems.

ELASTICITIES APPROACH TO THE BALANCE OF TRADE

Economic behavior involves satisfying unlimited wants with limited resources. One implication of this fact of budget constraints is that consumers and business firms will substitute among goods as prices change to stretch their budgets as far as possible. For instance, if Italian-made shoes and U.S.-made shoes are good substitutes, then as the price of U.S. shoes rises relative to Italian shoes,

buyers will substitute the lower-priced Italian shoes for the higher-priced U.S. shoes. The crucial concept for determining consumption patterns is *relative price*—the price of one good relative to another.

Relative prices change as relative demand and supply for individual goods change. Such changes may result from changes in tastes, or production technology, or government taxes or subsidies, or many other possible sources. If the changes involve prices of goods at home changing relative to foreign goods, then international trade patterns may be altered. The elasticities approach to the balance of trade is concerned with how changing relative prices of domestic and foreign goods will change the balance of trade.

A change in the exchange rate will change the domestic currency price of foreign goods. Suppose, initially, a pair of shoes sells for $50 in the United States and Lit50,000 in Italy. At an exchange rate of Lit1000 = $1 (or Lit1 = $0.001), the shoes sell for the same price in each country when expressed in a common currency. If the lira is devalued to Lit1200 = $1, and shoe prices remain constant in the domestic currency of the producer, then shoes selling for Lit50,000 in Italy will now cost the U.S. buyer $41.67. After the devaluation, Lit1 = $0.00083, so Lit50,000 = $41.67, and the price of Italian shoes has fallen for U.S. buyers. Conversely, the price of $50 U.S. shoes to Italian buyers has risen from Lit50,000 to Lit60,000. The relative price effect of the lira devaluation should increase U.S. demand for Italian goods and decrease Italian demand for U.S. goods. How much quantity demanded changes in response to the relative price change is determined by the elasticity of demand.

In beginning economics courses, students learn that *elasticity* measures the responsiveness of quantity to changes in price. The *elasticities approach to the balance of trade* provides an analysis of how devaluations will affect the balance of trade depending on the elasticities of supply and demand for foreign exchange and foreign goods.

When demand or supply is elastic, it means that quantity demanded or supplied will be relatively responsive to the change in price. An inelastic demand or supply indicates that quantity is relatively unresponsive to price changes. We can make things more precise by using coefficients of elasticity. For instance, letting ϵ_d

represent the coefficient of elasticity of demand, we can write ϵ_d as

$$\epsilon_d = \% \, \Delta Q / \% \, \Delta P \tag{9.1}$$

This implies that the coefficient of elasticity of demand is equal to the percentage change in the quantity demanded, divided by the percentage change in price. If the price increases by 5 percent and the quantity demanded falls by more than 5 percent, then ϵ_d exceeds 1 (in absolute value), and we say that demand is elastic. If when the price increases by 5 percent the quantity demanded falls by less than 5 percent, we would say that demand is inelastic and ϵ_d would be less than 1.

Just as we can compute a coefficient of elasticity of demand ϵ_d, so we can compute a coefficient of elasticity of supply ϵ_s as the percentage change in the quantity supplied, divided by the percentage change in price. If ϵ_s exceeds 1, the quantity supplied is relatively responsive to price, and we say that supply is elastic. For ϵ_s less than 1, the quantity supplied is relatively unresponsive to price, so that the supply is inelastic.

Elasticity will determine what happens to total revenue (price times quantity) following a price change. With an elastic demand, quantity changes by a greater percentage amount than price, and thus total revenue will move in the opposite direction from the price change. Suppose the demand for black velvet paintings from Mexico is elastic. If the peso price rises 10 percent, the quantity demanded falls by more than 10 percent, so that the revenue received from sales will fall following the price change. If the demand for Colombian coffee is inelastic, then a 10 percent increase in price will result in a fall in the quantity demanded of less than 10 percent. The higher coffee price more than makes up for the lost sales and, therefore, coffee sales revenues rise following the price change. Obviously, elasticity of demand will be of great importance in determining export and import revenues as international prices change.

Now let us consider an example of supply and demand in the foreign exchange market. Figure 9.1 provides an example of the supply and demand for U.K. pounds. The demand curve labeled D is the demand for pounds, arising from the demand for British exports. The familiar downward slope indicates that, the higher the

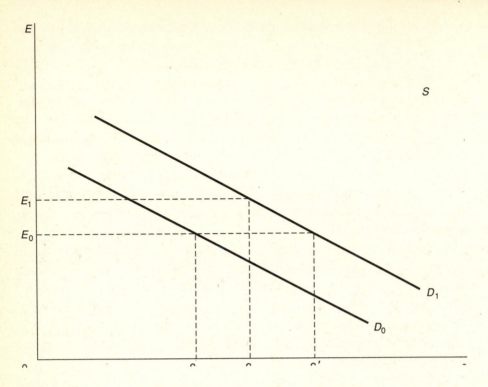

FIGURE 9.1 Supply and demand in the foreign exchange market.

price of pounds is, the fewer pounds will be demanded. The supply curve labeled S is the supply of pounds to the foreign exchange market. The upward slope indicates the positive relationship between the foreign exchange price of pounds and the quantity of pounds supplied. The point where the supply and demand curves intersect is the equilibrium point where the quantity of pounds demanded just equals the quantity supplied. Suppose initially we have an equilibrium at E_0 and $\pounds_0$; that is, $\pounds_0$ is the quantity of pounds bought and sold at the exchange rate E_0. Now suppose there is an increase in demand for pounds (say, because of an increase in demand for U.K. exports). There are several possible responses to this shift in demand:

1. The pound will appreciate, with freely floating exchange rates, so that the exchange rate rises to E_1, and $\pounds_1$ are bought and sold.

2. Central banks can peg the exchange rate at the old rate E_0 by providing $£'_1 - £_0$ from their reserves (and thereby artificially shifting the supply of pounds).
3. The supply and demand curves can be artificially shifted by imposing controls or quotas on the supply of, or demand for, pounds.
4. Quotas or tariffs could be imposed on foreign trade to maintain the old supply and demand for pounds.

The elasticities approach recognizes that the effect of an exchange rate change on the equilibrium quantity of currency being traded will depend on the elasticities of the supply and demand curves involved. It is important to remember that the elasticities approach is a theory of the balance of trade and can only be a theory of the balance of payments in a world without capital flows.

Suppose in Figure 9.1, E is the dollar price of pounds and the U.S. central bank decides to meet the increase in demand for pounds by supplying pounds to the market from U.S. reserves. Now the old exchange rate E_0 is maintained because of the central bank's addition of $£'_1 - £_0$ to the market supply. If it becomes apparent that the increase in demand is a permanent change, then the Federal Reserve will devalue the dollar, driving up the dollar price of pounds. This, of course, means that U.K. goods will be more expensive to the United States, whereas U.S. goods will be cheaper to the United Kingdom. Will this improve the U.S. trade balance? It all depends on the elasticities of supply and demand. With inelastic demands, it is possible to get what is called "J-curve effects," where at first the price of imports to the United States increases but the quantity of imports demanded changes little, so that total payments to the United Kingdom actually increase. Likewise, with an inelastic demand for U.S. exports in the United Kingdom, the price of imports from the United States could fall, yet few more are demanded. In this case the U.S. balance-of-trade deficit and the excess demand for pounds could actually increase following a devaluation. The *J-curve effect* refers to the pattern of the balance of trade following a devaluation. If the balance of trade is viewed over time, the initial decrease in the trade balance, because of inelastic demands followed by a growing trade balance, results in the time pattern of the trade balance, as shown in Figure 9.2. Note in the fig-

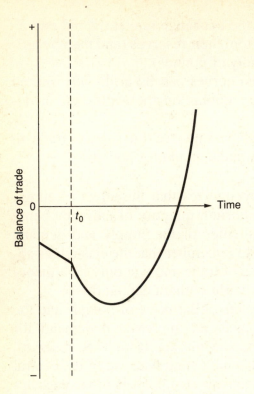

FIGURE 9.2 The J curve.

ure that the trade balance is initially negative, falling over time. The devaluation occurs at the point t_0. Following the devaluation, the balance of trade falls for a while before finally turning upward. The initial fall results from low elasticities in the short run. Over time, elasticities increase so that the balance of trade improves. This general pattern of the balance of trade falling before it increases traces a pattern that resembles the letter *J*.

ELASTICITIES AND J CURVES

Devaluation is conventionally believed to be a tool for increasing a country's balance of trade. Yet the J-curve effect indicates that, when the devaluation increases the price of foreign goods to the home country and decreases the price of domestic goods to foreign buyers, there is a short-run period when the balance of trade falls. Is this pattern to be expected, or is the J curve simply a theoretical

curiosity with no real-world importance? Before reviewing the evidence on this matter, let us investigate the factors that should be important in determining foreign trade elasticities in the short run, to see what the possible underlying reasons are for a J curve.

We can identify different periods following a devaluation in which the ability of traders to respond to the new set of prices is at first limited, but over time becomes complete.

CURRENCY CONTRACT PERIOD

Immediately following a devaluation, contracts negotiated prior to the exchange rate change become due. Let us refer to this as the *currency contract period*. The effects of such existing contracts on the balance of trade depend on the currency in which the contract is denominated. For instance, let us suppose that the United States devalues the dollar. Before the devaluation the exchange rate is $1 per unit of foreign currency (to simplify matters, we will assume only one foreign currency); afterward the rate jumps to $1.25. If a U.S. exporter has contracted to sell $1 worth of goods to a foreign firm payable in dollars, the exporter will still earn $1. However, if the export contract was written in terms of foreign currency (let FC stand for foreign currency), then the exporter expected to receive FC 1, which would be equal to $1. Instead, the devaluation leads to FC 1 = $1.25, so the U.S. exporter receives an unexpected gain from the dollar devaluation. On the other hand, consider an import contract where a U.S. importer contracts to buy from a foreign firm. If the contract calls for payment of $1, then the U.S. importer is unaffected by the devaluation. If the contract had been written in terms of foreign currency, so that the U.S. importer owes FC 1, then the importer would have to pay $1.25 to buy the FC 1 that the exporter receives. In this case the importer faces a loss because of the devaluation.

In the simple world under consideration here we would expect sellers to prefer a contract in the currency expected to appreciate, whereas buyers would prefer contracts written in terms of the currency expected to depreciate. Table 9.1 summarizes the possible trade balance effects during the currency contract period.

Table 9.1 divides the effects into four cells. Cell I represents the case in which U.S. export contracts are written in terms of for-

Table 9.1 U.S. TRADE BALANCE EFFECTS DURING CURRENCY CONTRACT PERIOD FOLLOWING A DEVALUATION

U.S. export contracts written in	U.S. import contracts written in	
	Dollars	**Foreign currency**
Foreign currency	I. Exports increase Imports constant Balance of trade increases	II. Exports increase Imports increase Initial surplus: balance of trade increases Initial deficit: balance of trade decreases
Dollars	III. Exports constant Imports constant Balance of trade unchanged	IV. Exports constant Imports increase Balance of trade decreases

eign currency although import contracts are denominated in dollars. In this case the dollar value of exports will increase since the foreign buyer must pay in foreign currency, which is worth more after the devaluation. Because imports are paid for with dollars, the devaluation will have no effect on the dollar value of U.S. imports. As a result, the balance of trade must increase.

Cell II indicates the trade balance effects when U.S. exports and imports are paid for with foreign currency. Since the dollar devaluation increases the value of foreign currency, the dollar values of both exports and imports will increase. The net effect on the U.S. trade balance depends on the magnitude of U.S. exports relative to imports. If exports exceed imports so that there is an initial trade surplus, then the increase in export values will exceed the increase in imports so that the balance of trade increases. Conversely, if there is an initial trade deficit so that imports exceed exports, then the increase in imports will exceed the increase in exports so that the balance of trade decreases.

If both exports and imports are payable in dollars, then the balance of trade is unaffected by a devaluation, as indicated in Cell III. But if exports are payable in dollars although imports require pay-

ment in foreign currency, the dollar value of exports will be unaffected by the devaluation while import values increase, so that the trade balance decreases as in Cell IV. Note that only in the case of Cell IV must there be a decline in the trade balance during the currency contract period following a devaluation. A decline could also occur in Cell II, although only if there is an initial trade deficit. The key feature of Table 9.1 is that foreign-currency-denominated imports provide a necessary condition for the U.S. trade balance to take the plunge observed in the J-curve phenomenon during the currency contract period.

PASS-THROUGH ANALYSIS

The *currency contract period* refers to that period following a devaluation when contracts negotiated prior to the devaluation come due. During this time it is assumed that goods prices do not adjust instantaneously to the change in currency values. Eventually, of course, as new trade contracts are negotiated, goods prices will tend toward the new equilibrium. The *pass-through* analysis considers the ability of prices to adjust in the short run. The kind of adjustment expected is an increase in the price of import goods in the devaluing country and a decrease in the price of this country's exports to the rest of the world. If goods prices do not adjust in this manner, then spending patterns will not be altered, so that the desirable balance-of-trade effects of devaluation do not appear.

Devaluation is normally a response to a persistent and growing balance-of-trade deficit. As import prices rise in the devaluing country, fewer imports should be demanded. At the same time the lower price of domestic exports to foreigners should increase the demand for exports. The combination of a higher demand for domestic exports and a lower domestic demand for imports should bring about an improvement in the trade balance. In the short run, however, if the response to the new prices is so slow that the quantities traded don't change much, then the new prices could contribute to the J curve. For instance, if the demand for imports is inelastic, then buyers will be relatively unresponsive to the higher price of imports, and thus the total import bill could rise rather than fall after the devaluation. Such behavior is not unreasonable since it takes time to find good substitutes for the now higher-priced import

goods. Eventually, such substitutions will occur, but in the short run buyers may continue to buy imports in large enough quantities so that the now higher price results in greater, rather than smaller, domestic imports after the devaluation. The same explanation could hold on the other side of the market if foreign demand for domestic exports is inelastic. In this case foreign buyers will not buy much more in the short run even though the price of domestic exports has fallen.

Table 9.2 summarizes the possible effects following a U.S. devaluation during the brief pass-through period before quantities adjust. The worst case is presented in Cell IV. With an inelastic demand for U.S. imports and an inelastic demand for U.S. exports, there will be a full pass-through of prices. To understand this effect fully, we should realize that the inelastic demands are in this case holding quantity fixed. Figure 9.3a illustrates the case of the perfectly inelastic demand for U.S. imports. The U.S. demand for imports is fixed at Q_0. This means that in the short run U.S. importers will buy Q_0 at any relevant price. After the devaluation the supply curve shifts to the left, representing the fact that foreign exporters now want to charge a higher dollar price for their exports to the United States because the dollar is worth less. The vertical distance between the old and new supply curves indicates how much more sellers wish to charge for any given quantity. Since the demand

Table 9.2 U.S. TRADE BALANCE EFFECTS DURING PASS-THROUGH PERIOD FOLLOWING A DEVALUATION

U.S. exports	U.S. imports	
	Inelastic supply	Inelastic demand
Inelastic supply	I. Exports increase Imports constant Balance of trade increases	II. Exports increase Imports increase Initial surplus: balance of trade increases Initial deficit: balance of trade decreases
Inelastic demand	III. Exports constant Imports constant Balance of trade constant	IV. Exports constant Imports increase Balance of trade decreases

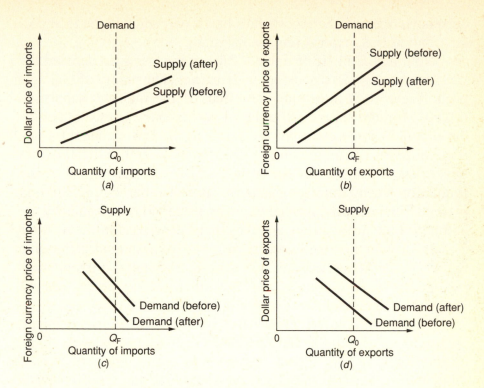

FIGURE 9.3 (*a*) Perfectly inelastic U.S. import demand; (*b*) perfectly inelastic demand for U.S. exports; (*c*) perfectly inelastic supply of U.S. imports; (*d*) perfectly inelastic supply of U.S. exports.

curve is a vertical line, fixed at Q_0, sellers will be able to pass through the full amount of the desired price increase to importers, so that importers will be buying Q_0 at a higher price than before, and the total dollar value of imports increases. This is the situation in Cell IV of Table 9.2, where the U.S. balance of trade decreases because of the full pass-through. Figure 9.3*b* shows why exports remain constant in Cell IV. Foreign buyers want to purchase Q_F amount of U.S. exports regardless of the price in the short run. Note that now the relevant price to foreign buyers is the foreign currency price. After the devaluation the supply curve shifts to the right to reflect the fact that U.S. exporters are willing to sell goods for less foreign currency because foreign currency is now worth more. However, with the perfectly inelastic demand curve, there is a full pass-through lowering the foreign currency price by the full amount of the devaluation. In other words, if the devaluation increased the value of foreign currency by 10 percent, the foreign

currency price of U.S. exports falls by 10 percent, and the total dollar value of U.S. exports remains constant.

Note that Cell III of Table 9.2 pairs the inelastic demand for U.S. exports, as just discussed, with an inelastic supply of U.S. imports. Figure 9.3c illustrates the effect of the inelastic supply. In this case foreign sellers will sell Q_F imports to the United States independent of price. After the devaluation, the U.S. demand for imports in terms of foreign currency shifts to the left, indicating that buyers are willing to pay fewer units of foreign currency than before for a given quantity of imports. Because the supply curve is perfectly inelastic, the foreign currency price of imports falls by the amount of the devaluation, and thus there is no pass-through. After a dollar devaluation we expect imports to become more expensive to the United States, and yet with a perfectly inelastic import supply curve, as in Figure 9.3c, U.S. dollar import prices are unchanged so that the dollar value of imports is also unchanged.

Cell II of Table 9.2 couples the inelastic U.S. import demand, as previously discussed and illustrated in Figure 9.3a, with an inelastic supply of U.S. exports. Figure 9.3d shows the supply effect. After the devaluation foreigners are willing to pay a higher dollar price for U.S. exports because dollars are cheaper. With the perfectly inelastic supply curve, the dollar price of exports rises by the full amount of the devaluation. Thus, rather than have a devaluation pass-through lower U.S. export prices to foreigners, the increase in dollar prices has foreign buyers paying the same price as before (because the foreign currency price is unchanged). But the higher dollar price results in an increase in the dollar value of U.S. exports. Since the inelastic demand for U.S. imports causes the dollar value of imports to increase also, the net result for the balance of trade depends on whether initially exports exceeded imports, in which case the increase in exports after the devaluation will be larger than the import increase. If imports initially exceed exports, then the devaluation will lower the trade balance.

Finally, we have the case of Cell I, where the balance of trade clearly increases during the pass-through period when quantities are fixed. The inelastic supply of U.S. exports leads to an increase in the dollar value of U.S. exports, whereas the inelastic supply of imports results in the value of imports holding constant.

The portrayal of perfectly inelastic supply and demand curves is made for illustrative purposes. We cannot argue that in the real

world there is absolutely no quantity response to changing prices in the short run. The important contribution of the pass-through analysis is to indicate how changing goods prices in the short run, when the quantity response is likely to be quite small, can affect the balance of trade. If it is more reasonable to expect producers to be less able to alter quantities supplied than buyers can alter quantity demanded, then Cell I of Table 9.2 is the most likely real-world case. In this instance the supplies of U.S. imports and exports are inelastic so that the U.S. trade balance should improve during the pass-through period.

THE EVIDENCE FROM DEVALUATIONS

The preceding discussion has shown the possible short-run effects of a devaluation on the trade balance through the currency contract and pass-through periods. What does the evidence of past devaluations have to offer regarding the *actual* effects? Unfortunately, the evidence available suggests that the effects of devaluation appear to differ across countries and time so that no strong generalizations are possible. We will briefly review the findings of a representative group of studies. For instance, Arthur Laffer investigated the time pattern of the trade balance for 15 countries that devalued their currency in the 1960s. Overall, the trade balance seems to improve in the year of a devaluation and the year after, before starting to fall again. Four of the 15 countries provided evidence of a J curve.

Marc Miles analyzed 16 devaluations for 14 countries and found little evidence that devaluation improves the balance of trade. However, he did find some evidence that devaluation improves the balance of payments. This implies that the capital account must have an increased surplus following a devaluation. This is a plausible result if we consider that, when investors expected the devaluation, there may have been a period of capital flight prior to the devaluation. Once the devaluation occurred, some of this flight capital then came back to the country, creating a larger surplus on the capital account.

Thorvaldur Gylfason and Ole Risager studied 15 highly indebted countries. Their analysis involves more than simply the effect of devaluation on trade flows, and one of their empirical questions deals with the responsiveness of the current account to

devaluation. They find that a devaluation should improve the current account for all but one country they studied.

Mohsen Bahmani-Oskooee specifically investigated whether a J curve exists for the balance of trade of Greece, India, Korea, and Thailand over the period from 1973 to 1980. He generally finds evidence of a J curve. However, he also presents evidence suggesting that exchange rate changes will have a different effect under fixed rates than floating rates. Basically, the conjecture is that devaluations are more likely expected when they occur in small steps instead of one large adjustment, and expected exchange rate changes should not have as great an effect as unexpected changes.

Michael Moffett analyzed the U.S. trade balance data for evidence of J-curve effects over the period from the late 1960s through the 1980s. Moffett shows that, following a depreciation of the dollar, the U.S. trade balance typically falls for about a year, after which there are about two years of a rising trade balance. This suggests a J-curve pattern for about three years following a fall in the value of the dollar. However, this rise in the trade balance is not sustained over time so that we should not believe that dollar devaluations would have the lasting effect of a smaller U.S. trade deficit.

The overview of the research on devaluation and the current account just provided should point out the lack of agreement among the studies. Some authors show that devaluation improves the trade account in the short run, while others disagree. The reasons for such disagreement come from different researchers using different sample periods and different statistical methodology. To show how crucial the latter can be, Daniel Himarios reworked the study originally completed by Miles. Using a different approach to analyzing the evidence, Himarios finds that a devaluation generally does improve the trade balance.

Peter Hooper and Jaime Marquez simulated the effects of a 10 percent depreciation of the yen and dollar on the trade balances of Japan and the United States. A J curve response was found in each case, with the initial decline in the trade balance being quite small for the United States relative to the Japanese case. The U.S. trade balance responded positively to the dollar depreciation after only six months had passed. However, the Japanese trade balance did not respond positively until almost two years after the yen depreci-

ation. The ultimate rise in the trade balance of a 10 percent depreciation of the domestic currency was much greater for the United
States than Japan. This result was due to the larger price elasticities
they found for U.S. imports and exports compared to Japan.

Several researchers have recently focused on the manner in
which producers in different countries adjust the profit margins on
exports to partially offset the effect of exchange rate changes. This
appears to be an important factor in explaining differences in the
pass-through effect across countries. For instance, if the Japanese
yen appreciates against the U.S. dollar, the yen appreciation would
tend to be passed through to U.S. importers as a higher dollar price
of Japanese exports. Japanese exporters could limit this pass
through of higher prices by reducing the profit margins on their
products and lowering the yen price to counter the effect of the yen
appreciation. This *pricing to market* behavior has been found to be
especially prevalent among Japanese and German exporters but is
much less common among U.S. exporters. For example, Joseph
Gagnon and Michael Knetter analyzed automobile trade and estimated that a 10 percent depreciation of the dollar against the yen
would result in Japanese auto firms reducing their prices so that the
dollar price to U.S. importers would rise by only 2.2 percent. There
was no similar evidence of U.S. auto firms reducing prices for exported autos in response to dollar appreciation. The Japanese resis-
tance to allowing pass-through effects is another reason why the
Japanese balance of trade may be less responsive to exchange rate
changes than the United States trade balance.

ABSORPTION APPROACH TO THE BALANCE OF TRADE

The elasticities approach showed that it is possible for a country to
improve its balance of trade through devaluation. Once the exchange rate effects pass through to import and export prices, imports should fall while exports increase, stimulating production of
goods and services and income at home. If a country is at the full
employment level of output prior to the devaluation, then it is producing all it can already, so that no further output is forthcoming.
What happens in this case following a devaluation? We now turn
to the absorption approach to the balance of trade to answer this
question.

The *absorption approach to the balance of trade* is a theory that emphasizes how domestic spending on domestic goods changes relative to domestic output. In other words, the balance of trade is viewed as the difference between what the economy produces and what it takes for domestic use or absorbs. As commonly treated in introductory economics classes, we can write total output, Y, as being equal to total expenditures, or

$$Y = C + I + G + (X - M) \qquad (9.2)$$

where C is consumption; I, investment; G, government spending; X, exports; and M, imports. We can define absorption, A, as being equal to $C + I + G$, and net exports as $(X - M)$. Thus we can write

$$Y = A + X - M$$

or

$$Y - A = X - M \qquad (9.3)$$

Absorption, A, is supposed to represent total domestic spending so that, if total domestic production, Y, exceeds absorption, the amount of the output consumed at home, then the nation will export the rest of its output and run a balance-of-trade surplus. On the other hand, if absorption exceeds domestic production, then $(Y - A)$ is negative; thus by Equation (9.3) we note that $(Y - M)$ will also be negative, which has the common-sense interpretation that the excess of domestic demand over domestic production will be met through imports.

The analysis of the absorption approach is really broken down into two categories depending on whether the economy is at full employment or has unemployed resources. If we have full employment, then all resources are being used so that the only way for net exports to increase is to have absorption fall. On the other hand, with unemployment, Y is not at its maximum possible value, and thus A could remain fixed and Y could increase because of increases in domestic sales to foreigners, X.

The absorption approach is generally concerned with the effects of a devaluation on the trade balance. If we begin from the case of unemployed resources, we know that domestic output, Y,

could increase, so that a devaluation would tend to increase net exports (if the elasticity conditions discussed in the last section are satisfied) and bring about an increase in output (given a constant absorption). If we start from full employment, then output, Y, is at the full employment level, and therefore it is not possible to produce more goods and services. If we devalue, then net exports will tend to increase, and the end result is strictly inflation. When foreigners try to spend more on our domestic production, and yet there is no increase in output forthcoming, the only result will be a bidding up of the prices of the goods and services currently being produced.

Of course, we must realize that the absorption approach is providing a theory of the balance of trade as did the elasticities approach before. The absorption approach can only be viewed as a theory of the balance of payments in a world without capital flows.

MONETARY APPROACH TO THE BALANCE OF PAYMENTS

The elasticities approach and the absorption approach are theories of the balance of trade that have been popular for over 30 years. As we have seen, these are theories that emphasize trade in real goods and have little to say about the capital account. For some purposes, these theories can still provide useful intuition. However, the world today is characterized by well-developed financial markets and large-scale international capital flows. To understand fully international economic linkages, we must look beyond merchandise trade and incorporate the important role of financial assets. It was in this spirit that the *monetary approach to the balance of payments* (MABP) came to popularity in the 1970s, and it emphasizes the monetary aspects of the balance of payments.

We may draw the line in the international accounts (see Chapter 2 for a review of balance-of-payments concepts) so that the current and capital accounts are above the line and only those items that directly affect the money supply are below the line [specifically, official holdings of gold, foreign exchange, special drawing rights (SDRs), and changes in reserves at the International Monetary Fund (IMF)—but do not worry about these terms now]. This allows us to concentrate on the monetary aspects of the balance of payments.

The basic premise of the MABP is that any balance-of-payments disequilibrium is based on a monetary disequilibrium—that is, differences existing between the amount of money people wish to hold and the amount supplied by the monetary authorities. In very simple terms, if people demand more money than is being supplied by the central bank, then the excess demand for money would be satisfied by inflows of money from abroad. On the other hand, if the central bank (the Federal Reserve in the United States) is supplying more money than is demanded, the excess supply of money is eliminated by outflows of money to other countries. Thus the MABP analysis emphasizes the determinants of money demand and money supply, since these will also determine the balance of payments.

The monetary approach has a long and distinguished history, so that the recent popularity of the approach can be viewed as a rediscovery rather than a modern innovation. In fact, the recent literature often makes use of a quote from *Of the Balance of Trade,* written by David Hume in 1752, to indicate the early understanding of the problem. Hume wrote:

> Suppose four-fifths of all the money in Great Britain to be annihilated in one night, and the nation reduced to the same condition, with regard to specie, as in the reigns of the Harrys and Edwards, what would be the consequence? Must not the price of all labour and commodities sink in proportion, and everything be sold as cheap as they were in these ages? What nation could then dispute with us in any foreign market, or pretend to navigate or to sell manufactures at the same price, which to us would afford sufficient profit? In how little time, therefore, must this bring back the money which we had lost, and raise us to the level of all the neighboring nations? Where after we have arrived, we immediately lose the advantage of the cheapness of labor and commodities; and the farther flowing in of money is stopped by our fullness and repletion.

Hume's analysis is a strict monetary approach to prices and the balance of payments. If England's money stock suddenly was reduced by four-fifths, we know from principles of economics that the price level would fall dramatically. The falling price level would give England a price advantage over its foreign competitors, so that its exports would rise and its imports fall. As the foreign money (gold in Hume's day) poured in, England's money supply would rise and its price level would follow. This process continues until England's prices reach the levels of its competitors, after which the system is back in equilibrium.

Thus far we have only discussed the monetary approach to the balance of payments, which is fine for a world with fixed exchange rates or a gold standard. For a world with flexible exchange rates, we have the *monetary approach to the exchange rate* (MAER). The dichotomy between fixed and floating exchange rates is an important one. When exchange rates are fixed between countries, we will observe money flowing between countries to adjust to disequilibrium. With floating exchange rates, the exchange rates are allowed to fluctuate with the free-market forces of supply and demand for each currency. The free-market equilibrium exchange rate occurs at a point where the flow of exports just equals the flow of imports so that no net international money flows are required. International economists refer to this choice of money flows or exchange rate changes as the choice of an international *adjustment mechanism.* With fixed exchange rates the adjustment to changes in international monetary conditions comes through international money flows, whereas with floating rates the adjustment comes through exchange rate changes. To organize our thoughts and provide a convenient framework for distinguishing the analysis under the MABP and MAER, we outline a simple economic model relating money demand, money supply, the balance of payments, and exchange rates.

Before turning to the model, we should consider some basic concepts and assumptions. In principles of macroeconomics we learn that the Federal Reserve controls the money supply by altering *base money* (currency plus commercial bank reserves held against deposits). As base money changes, the lending ability of commercial banks changes. Increases in base money tend to result in an expansion of the money supply, whereas decreases in base money tend to contract the money supply. For MABP purposes it is useful to divide base money into domestic and international components. The domestic component of base money we refer to as *domestic credit;* the remainder is made up of *international reserves* (money items that can be used to settle international debts, primarily foreign exchange). The international money flows that respond to excess demands or excess supplies at home affect base money and then the money supply. For instance, if a U.S. exporter receives payment in foreign currency, this payment will be presented to a U.S. commercial bank to be converted into dollars and deposited in the exporter's account. If

the commercial bank has no use for the foreign currency, the bank will exchange the foreign currency for dollars with the Federal Reserve (or Fed). The Fed creates new money to buy the foreign currency by increasing the commercial bank's reserve deposit with the Fed. Thus the Fed is accumulating international reserves, and this reserve accumulation brings about an expansion of base money. In the case of an excess supply of money at home, either domestic credit falls to reduce base money or else international reserves will fall to lower base money to the desired level.

Now we are ready to construct a simple model of the MABP. The usual assumption is that we are analyzing the situation of a *small open economy*. It is small because we want to assume that this country cannot affect the international price of goods or the interest rate it faces. Openness implies that this country is an active participant in international economic transactions. We could classify nations according to their degree of openness, or the degree to which they depend on international transactions. The United States would be relatively closed, considering the size of its GDP relative to the value of international trade, whereas Belgium would be relatively open.

We can begin our model by writing the demand for money as

$$L = kPY \tag{9.4}$$

where L is the demand for money, P is the domestic price level, Y is real income or wealth, and k is a constant fraction indicating how money demand will change given a change in P or Y. Equation (9.4) is often stated as "money demand is a function of prices and income" or "money demand depends on prices and income." The usual story is that the higher the income, the more money people will hold in order to buy more goods. The higher the price level, the more money is desired to buy any given quantity of goods. So the demand for money should rise with an increase in either P or Y.

A strong assumption of the monetary approach is that there is a stable demand for money. This means that the relationship among money demand, income, and prices does not change significantly over time. Without a stable demand for money, the monetary approach will not provide a useful framework for analysis.

Letting M stand for money supply, R for international reserves, and D for domestic credit (we assume that base money equals the money supply to simplify matters), we can write the money supply relationship as

$$M = R + D \qquad (9.5)$$

Letting P stand for the domestic price level, E for the domestic currency price of foreign currency, and P^F for the foreign price level, we can write the law of one price as

$$P = EP^F \qquad (9.6)$$

Finally, we need the assumption that equilibrium in the money market holds so that money demand equals money supply, or

$$L = M \qquad (9.7)$$

The adjustment mechanism that ensures equilibrium in Equation (9.7) will vary with the exchange rate regime. With fixed exchange rates, money supply adjusts to money demand through international flows of money via balance-of-payments imbalances. With flexible exchange rates, money demand will be adjusted to a money supply set by the central bank via exchange rate changes. In the case of a dirty or managed float, where theoretically we have floating exchange rates but the central banks intervene to keep exchange rates at desired levels, we have both international money flows and exchange rate changes. All three cases will be analyzed subsequently.

Now we develop the model in a manner that will allow us to analyze the balance of payments and exchange rates in a monetary framework. We begin by substituting Equation (9.6) into Equation (9.4):

$$L = kEP^FY \qquad (9.8)$$

Substituting Equations (9.8) and (9.5) into (9.7), we obtain

$$kEP^FY = R + D \qquad (9.9)$$

Finally, we want to discuss Equation (9.9), money demand and money supply, in terms of percentage changes. Since k is a constant,

the change is zero, and thus k drops out of the analysis and we are left with[1]

$$\hat{E} + \hat{P}^F + \hat{Y} = \hat{R} + \hat{D} \tag{9.10}$$

where the hat ($\,\hat{}\,$) over a variable indicates percentage change in.

Since the goal of this analysis is to be able to explain changes in the exchange rate or balance of payments, we should have $\hat{R}$ and $\hat{E}$ on the left-hand side of the equation. Rearranging Equation (9.10) in this manner gives

$$\hat{R} - \hat{E} = \hat{P}^F + \hat{Y} - \hat{D} \tag{9.11}$$

This indicates that the change in reserves (the balance of payments) minus the percentage change in exchange rates is equal to the foreign inflation rate plus the percentage growth of real income minus the change in domestic credit. With fixed exchange rates, $\hat{E} = 0$, and we have the monetary approach to the balance of payments:

$$\hat{R} = \hat{P}^F + \hat{Y} - \hat{D} \tag{9.12}$$

Therefore, with fixed exchange rates, an increase in domestic credit with constant prices and income (and thus constant money demand) will lead to a decrease in international reserves. This means that, if the central bank expands domestic credit, creating an excess supply of money, reserves will flow out or there will be a balance-of-payments deficit as people spend to lower the excess cash balances. Conversely, a decrease in domestic credit would lead to an excess demand for money since money demand is unchanged for a given $\hat{P}^F$ and $\hat{Y}$; yet D is falling so that R will increase to bring money supply equal to money demand.

In the case of flexible exchange rates with no central bank intervention, we assume reserve flows, $\hat{R}$, are equal to zero, whereas

---

[1]If $a = bc$, the percentage change in a is equal to the sum of the percentage change in b plus the percentage change in c: $\hat{a} = \hat{b} + \hat{c}$. In Equation (9.10), $\hat{R} + \hat{D}$ is actually the change in $R + D$ as a fraction of the money supply, or the change in reserves plus the change in domestic credit divided by the money supply. So $\hat{R} = \Delta R/M$ and $\hat{D} = \Delta D/M$.

exchange rate changes are nonzero. The general Equation (9.11) is now written for the monetary approach to the exchange rate as

$$-\hat{E} = \hat{P}^F + \hat{Y} - \hat{D} \qquad (9.13)$$

With the MAER, an increase in domestic credit, given a constant $\hat{P}^F$ and $\hat{Y}$ (so that money demand is constant), will result in a depreciation of the domestic currency. Examining Equation (9.13), we see that $\hat{D}$ and $\hat{E}$ both have a negative sign; thus if $\hat{D}$ increases, $\hat{E}$ will also increase. Since E is domestic currency units per foreign currency unit, an increase in E means that foreign currency is becoming more expensive or appreciating in value, whereas the domestic currency is depreciating. Under the MAER domestic monetary policy will not cause flows of money internationally but will lead to exchange rate changes.

The fact that $\hat{P}^F$ and $\hat{Y}$ have signs opposite that of $\hat{E}$ in Equation (9.13) indicates that changes in inflation and income growth will cause changes in exchange rates in the opposite direction. For instance, if $\hat{P}^F$ or $\hat{Y}$ increase, we know that money demand increases. With constant domestic credit, we have an excess demand for money. As individuals try to increase their money balances, we observe a decrease in E or an appreciation of the domestic currency.

So far we have discussed the case of fixed or flexible exchange rates, but what is the framework for analysis of a managed float? Remember that a managed float means that, although exchange rates are theoretically flexible and determined by the market forces of supply and demand, central banks intervene at times to peg the rates at some desired level. Thus the managed float has the attributes of both a fixed and a floating exchange rate regime since changing supply and demand will affect exchange rates, but the actions of the central bank will also allow international reserves to change. To allow for reserve changes as well as for exchange rate changes, we can simply return to the initial Equation (9.11). Therefore we see that, given money demand or money supply changes, the central bank can choose to let $\hat{E}$ adjust to the free-market level, or by holding E at some disequilibrium level, it will allow $\hat{R}$ to adjust.

Given the framework just developed, we can now consider some of the implications and extensions of the monetary approach.

First, the assumption of purchasing power parity implies that the central bank must make a policy choice between an exchange rate or a domestic price level. Since $P = EP^F$, under fixed exchange rates, E is constant, so that maintaining the pegged value of E implies that the domestic price level will correspond to that of the rest of the world. This is the case in which people discuss imported inflation. If the foreign price level is increasing rapidly, then our price must follow if we are to maintain the fixed E. On the other hand, with flexible rates, E is free to vary to whatever level is necessary to clear the foreign exchange market, and so we can choose our domestic rate of inflation independent of the rest of the world. If we select a lower rate of inflation than foreigners do, then PPP suggests that our currency will tend to appreciate. This issue of choosing either the domestic inflation rate or a preferred exchange rate has important economic as well as political implications and is not made without much thought and consultation among central bankers.

We might mention at this point that there are two views of how PPP operates in the short run, and these two views imply a different mechanism of adjustment to a change in the world economy, like a change in the foreign price level. One view is that PPP holds strictly, even in the short run. In this case a change in the foreign price induces an immediate change in the domestic price and a corresponding change in money demand or money supply. The other view is along the lines of the Hume quote mentioned previously. The idea here is that prices adjust slowly through the balance-of-payments effects on the money supply. Thus if foreign prices rise relative to domestic prices, we tend to sell more to foreigners and run a larger balance-of-trade surplus. Since we gain international reserves from these goods sales, over time our money supply rises and our prices increase until PPP is restored. We find that the two approaches differ primarily with regard to timing. The first case assumes that PPP holds in the short run because international reserves flow quickly in response to new events and prices adjust quickly to new equilibrium levels. This fast adjustment is supposedly due to an emphasis on the role of financial assets that are bought and sold, resulting in international capital flows. Since financial assets are easily bought and sold, it is easy to understand why many believe that PPP should hold in

the short run (ignoring any relative price effects, which we are not discussing in this section). The second case also assumes that PPP holds, but only in the long run. This approach emphasizes the role of goods markets in international adjustment. Since goods prices are supposedly slow to adjust, short-run deviations from PPP will occur that give rise to the balance-of-trade effects previously discussed. The truth most likely lies between these two extremes. It is reasonable to expect goods prices to adjust slowly over time to changing economic conditions, so that it may be reasonable to doubt that PPP holds well in the short run. On the other hand, PPP is not strictly dependent on goods markets. To ignore international capital flows is to miss the potential for a faster adjustment than is possible strictly through goods markets.

We can summarize the policy implications of the monetary approach as follows:

1. Balance-of-payments disequilibria are essentially monetary phenomena. Thus countries would not run long-term (or structural, as they are called) deficits if they did not rely so heavily on inflationary money supply growth to finance government spending.
2. Balance-of-payments disequilibria must be transitory. If the exchange rate remains fixed, eventually the country must run out of reserves by trying to support a continuing deficit.
3. Balance-of-payments disequilibria can be handled with domestic monetary policy rather than with adjustments in the exchange rate. Devaluation of the currency exchange rate is a substitute for reducing the growth of domestic credit in that devaluation lowers the value of a country's money to the rest of the world (conversely, an appreciation of the currency is a substitute for increasing domestic credit growth). Following any devaluation, if the underlying monetary cause of the devaluation is not corrected, then future devaluations will be required to offset the continued excess supply of the country's money.
4. Domestic balance of payments will be improved by an increase in domestic income via an increase in money demand, if not offset by an increase in domestic credit.

SUMMARY

1. Consumption decisions respond to changes in relative prices.
2. The elasticity of supply or demand measures the responsiveness of quantity to changes in price.
3. A devaluation of the domestic currency should raise the price of foreign goods relative to domestic.
4. The J curve describes the pattern of the balance of trade following a devaluation in which the trade balance first falls before rising.
5. Immediately following a devaluation, the invoicing currency used for contracts written prior to the devaluation becomes an important determinant of the value of the trade account.
6. The pass-through of devaluation to domestic and foreign prices depends on elasticities of supply and demand for international trade.
7. The evidence regarding the effects of devaluation on the balance of trade indicates no standard pattern.
8. The balance of trade can only improve if income increases relative to absorption.
9. The monetary approach analyzes the balance of payments and exchange rates in terms of money supply and money demand.
10. With fixed exchange rates, money supply adjusts to money demand through international reserve flows.
11. With floating exchange rates, money demand adjusts to money supply through exchange rate changes.
12. With a managed float, monetary disequilibrium is eliminated through exchange rate changes and balance-of-payments flows.

EXERCISES

1. What does a J curve refer to?
2. Explain the necessary conditions for a devaluation to improve the balance of trade for each of the following:
    a. Elasticities approach
    b. Absorption approach
    c. Contract period
    d. Pass-through period
3. According to the monetary approach to the balance of payments, what type of economic policies would help a country resolve a balance-of-payments deficit?
4. Using the monetary approach to exchange rates model developed in the text, explain how the following events would affect the value of the U.S. dollar:
    a. The Japanese inflation rate falls.
    b. The Federal Reserve implements restrictive monetary policy.
    c. The United States increases tariffs against Japan.
    d. The German economy suffers a recession.

REFERENCES

Bahmani-Oskooee, Mohsen, "Devaluation and the J-Curve: Some Evidence from LDCs," *Review of Economics and Statistics,* August 1985.

Gagnon, Joseph E., and Michael M. Knetter, "Markup Adjustment and Exchange Rate Fluctuations: Evidence from Panel Data on Automobile Exports," *Journal of International Money and Finance,* forthcoming.

Goldstein, Morris, and Mohsin S. Khan, "Income and Price Effects in Foreign Trade," in Ronald W. Jones and Peter B. Kenen, eds., *Handbook of International Economics, Volume II.* Amsterdam: North-Holland, 1985.

Gylfason, Thorvaldur, and Ole Risager, "Does Devaluation Improve the Current Account?" *European Economic Review,* June 1984.

Himarios, Daniel, "The Effects of Devaluation on the Trade Balance: A Critical View and Reexamination of Miles's New Results," *Journal of International Money and Finance,* December 1985.

Hooper, Peter, and Jaime Marquez, "Exchange Rates, Prices, and External Adjustment in the United States and Japan," International Finance Discussion Papers, No. 456, Federal Reserve Board, October 1993.

Laffer, Arthur B., "Exchange Rates, the Terms of Trade, and the Trade Balance," in Peter B. Clark, Dennis E. Logue, and Richard James Sweeney, eds., *The Effects of Exchange Rate Adjustments.* Washington, D.C.: U.S. Department of the Treasury, 1974.

Magee, Stephen P., "Currency Contracts, Pass-Through, and Devaluation," *Brookings Papers on Economic Activity,* 1, 1973.

Miles, Marc A., "The Effect of Devaluation on the Trade Balance and the Balance of Payments: Some New Results," *Journal of Political Economy,* June 1979.

Moffett, Michael, "The J-Curve Revisited: An Empirical Examination for the United States," *Journal of International Money and Finance,* September 1989.

chapter 10

Exchange Rate Determination

An exchange rate is a financial asset price. It is the price of one money in terms of another. It would seem straightforward to analyze exchange rate determination by considering the supply and demand for each money. In Chapter 9, the monetary approach to the exchange rate was just such an analysis. Prior to the monetary approach, it was common to emphasize international trade flows as primary determinants of exchange rates. The traditional approach emphasized the role of exchange rate changes in eliminating international trade imbalances. In this context, we should expect countries with current trade surpluses to have an appreciating currency, while countries with trade deficits should have depreciating currencies. Such exchange rate changes would lead to changes in international relative prices that would work to eliminate the trade imbalance.

In recent years it became clear that the world did not work in the simple way just considered. We have seen some instances when countries with trade surpluses have depreciating currencies, while countries with trade deficits have appreciating currencies. Economists have responded to the real-world events by devising several alternative views of exchange rate determination. This chapter considers some of the recent advances in exchange rate theory.

THE ASSET APPROACH

Modern exchange rate models emphasize financial asset markets. Rather than the traditional view of exchange rates adjusting to equilibrate international trade in goods, the exchange rate is viewed as adjusting to equilibrate international trade in financial assets. Since goods prices adjust slowly relative to financial asset prices, and financial assets are traded continuously each business day, the shift in emphasis from goods markets to asset markets has important implications. Exchange rates will change every day or even every minute as supplies and demands for financial assets of different nations change.

An implication of the asset approach is that exchange rates should be much more variable than goods prices. This seems to be an empirical fact. Table 10.1 lists the standard deviation of the percentage changes in prices and exchange rates calculated for three countries. Over the period covered in the table, we observe that spot exchange rates for the three countries studied were much more volatile than prices. Comparing the prices with the exchange rates, we find that the volatility of exchange rates averaged from 3.2 to 11 times the volatility of prices. Such figures are consistent with the fact that exchange rates respond to changing conditions in financial asset markets and are not simply reacting to changes in international goods trade.

Exchange rate models emphasizing financial asset markets typically assume perfect capital mobility. *Perfect capital mobility* means that capital will flow freely between nations because there are no significant transactions costs or capital controls to serve as barriers to investment. In such a world, covered interest arbitrage will ensure covered interest rate parity:

Table 10.1 STANDARD DEVIATIONS OF PRICES AND EXCHANGE RATES

Country	Price	Exchange rate
France	.003	.029
Germany	.003	.033
United Kingdom	.009	.029

Note: The table reports the standard deviations of the percentage changes in the consumer price index and the spot exchange rate of each country's currency against the U.S. dollar for the period January 1974 to December 1992.

$$\frac{i - i_f}{1 + i_f} = \frac{F - E}{E}$$

where i is the domestic interest rate and i_f is the foreign interest rate. Since this relationship will hold continuously, spot and forward exchange rates as well as interest rates will adjust instantaneously to changing financial market conditions.

Within the family of asset approach models, there are two basic groups: the monetary approach and the portfolio-balance approach. The monetary approach to the exchange rate was introduced in Chapter 9. As stated there, in the monetary approach the exchange rate for any two currencies is determined by relative money demand and money supply between the two countries. Relative supplies of domestic and foreign bonds are unimportant. The *portfolio-balance approach* allows relative bond supplies and demands as well as relative money market conditions to determine the exchange rate.

The essential difference is that monetary approach (MA) models assume domestic and foreign bonds to be perfect substitutes, while portfolio-balance (PB) models assume imperfect substitutability. If domestic and foreign bonds are perfect substitutes, then demanders are indifferent between the currencies of denomination of the bond as long as the expected return is the same. In this case, bond holders do not require a premium to hold foreign bonds—they would just as soon hold foreign bonds as domestic—so there is no risk premium and uncovered interest rate parity holds in MA models.

With imperfect substitutability, demanders have preferences for distributing their portfolio over different countries' assets. They have a desired portfolio share for any particular countries' assets. If the supply of one country's assets increases, they will hold a greater proportion of that country's assets only if they are compensated. This requires a premium to be paid on these assets. In general, then, PB models have risk premiums that are a function of relative asset supplies. As the supply of country A's financial assets rises relative to B's, there will be a higher premium paid on A's assets. An implication of this premium is that uncovered interest rate parity will not hold, since there will exist risk premiums in the forward market. This premium is missing in the MA model because there it is assumed that investors don't care whether they hold country A or country B bonds, or in what mix they are held.

We might guess that the PB approach is more relevant if we doubt the MA assumption of perfect substitutability of assets internationally. In such cases we would view the exchange rate as being determined by relative supplies of domestic and foreign bonds as well as domestic and foreign money. We may then modify the monetary approach to the exchange rate equation found in Chapter 9 to incorporate this additional effect. The basic MA equation presented in Chapter 9 is

$$- \hat{E} = \hat{P}^F + \hat{Y} - \hat{D} \tag{10.1}$$

where $\hat{E}$ is the percentage change in the exchange rate, $\hat{P}^F$ is the foreign inflation rate, $\hat{Y}$ is the percentage change in domestic income, and $\hat{D}$ is the percentage change in domestic credit. Equation (10.1) has the appreciation of the exchange rate as a function of money supply $(\hat{D})$ and money demand $(\hat{P}^F + \hat{Y})$ variables. If domestic and foreign bonds are perfect substitutes, then Equation (10.1) is a useful MA description of exchange rate determination. The PB approach assumes that assets are imperfect substitutes internationally because investors perceive foreign exchange risk to be attached to foreign-currency-denominated bonds. As the supply of domestic bonds rises relative to foreign bonds, there will be an increased risk premium on the domestic bonds that will cause the domestic currency to depreciate in the spot market. If the spot exchange rate depreciates today, and if the expected future spot rate is unchanged, the expected rate of appreciation over the future increases.

For instance, if the dollar/pound spot rate is initially $E_{\$/£} = 2.00$, and the expected spot rate in 1 year is $E_{\$/£} = 1.90$, then the expected rate of dollar appreciation is 5 percent $[(1.90 - 2.00)/2.00]$. Now suppose an increase in the outstanding stock of dollar-denominated bonds results in a depreciation of the spot rate today to $E_{\$/£} = 2.05$, The expected rate of dollar appreciation is now approximately 7.3 percent $[(1.90 - 2.05)/2.05]$.

If the spot exchange rate is a function of relative asset supplies, then the MA equation (10.1) should be modified to include the percentage change in the supply of domestic bonds $(\hat{B})$ relative to the percentage change in the supply of foreign bonds $(\hat{B}^F)$:

$$- \hat{E} = \hat{P}^F + \hat{Y} - \hat{D} - \hat{B} + \hat{B}^F \tag{10.2}$$

This broader PB view might be expected to explain exchange rate changes better than the MA equation. However, the empirical evi-

dence is not at all clear on this matter. One potential problem for analyzing the MA and PB models of exchange rate determination is central bank activities aimed at insulating the domestic money supply from international events. The next section discusses the importance of this issue.

STERILIZATION

In recent years an important topic of debate has emerged from the literature on the monetary approach regarding the ability of central banks to sterilize reserve flows. *Sterilization* is the offsetting of international reserve flows by central banks that wish to follow an independent monetary policy. Under the monetary approach to the balance of payments (with fixed exchange rates), if a country had an excess supply of money, this country would tend to lose international reserves or run a deficit until money supply equals money demand. If the central bank for some reason desires this higher money supply and reacts to the deficit by further increasing the money supply, then the deficit will increase and persist as long as the central bank tries to maintain a money supply in excess of money demand. With an excess demand for money, the concept is reversed. The excess demand results in reserve inflows to equate money supply to money demand. If the central bank tries to decrease the money supply so that the excess demand still exists, its efforts will be thwarted by further reserve inflows, which will persist as long as the central bank tries to maintain the policy of a money supply less than money demand.

If sterilization is possible, then the monetary authorities may in fact be able to determine the money supply in the short run without having reserve flows offset their goals. This would be possible if the forces that lead to international arbitrage are slow to operate. For instance, if there are barriers to international capital mobility, then we might expect international asset return differentials to persist following a change in economic conditions. In this case, if the central bank wants to increase the growth of the money supply in the short run, it can do so regardless of money demand and reserve flows. In the long run, when complete adjustment of asset prices is possible, the money supply must grow at a rate consistent with money demand. In the short run, however, the central bank can exercise some discretion.

The actual use of the word *sterilization* derives from the fact that the central bank must be able to neutralize or sterilize any reserve flows induced by monetary policy if the policy is to achieve the central bank's money supply goals. For instance, if the central bank is following some money supply growth path, and then money demand increases leading to reserve inflows, the central bank must be able to sterilize these reserve inflows to keep the money supply from rising to what it considers undesirable levels. This is done by decreasing domestic credit by an amount equal to the growth of international reserves, thus keeping base money and the money supply constant.

In Chapter 9, the fixed exchange rate monetary approach to the balance-of-payments equation was

$$\hat{R} = \hat{P}^F + \hat{Y} - \hat{D} \tag{10.3}$$

where $\hat{R}$ is the percentage change in international reserves. Given money demand, an increase in domestic credit would be reflected in a fall in $\hat{R}$ or lower growth of reserves. If sterilization occurs, then the causality implied in Equation (10.3) is no longer true.

Instead of the monetary approach equation previously written, where changes in domestic credit ($\hat{D}$, on the right-hand side of the equation) lead to changes in reserves ($\hat{R}$, on the left-hand side) with sterilization, we also have changes in reserves inducing changes in domestic credit in order to offset the reserve flows. With sterilization, the causality implied in Equation (10.3), where domestic credit causes reserve changes, must be reconsidered. Sterilization means that there is also a causality flowing from reserve changes to domestic credit, as in

$$\hat{D} = \alpha - \beta\hat{R} \tag{10.4}$$

where β is the sterilization coefficient, ranging in value from 0 (when there is no sterilization) to 1 (complete sterilization). Equation (10.4) states that the percentage change in domestic credit will be equal to some constant amount (α) determined by the central bank's domestic policy goals minus some number (β)times the percentage change in reserves. β will reflect the central bank's ability to use domestic credit to offset reserve flows. Of course, it is possible that the central bank cannot fully offset international reserve flows, and yet some sterilization is possible, in which case β

will lie between 0 and 1. Evidence has in fact suggested both extremes as well as an intermediate value for β. It is reasonable to interpret the evidence regarding sterilization as indicating that central banks are able to sterilize a significant fraction of reserve flows in the short run. This means that the monetary authorities can likely choose the growth rate of the money supply in the short run, although long-run money growth must be consistent with money demand requirements.

We have, so far, discussed sterilization in the context of fixed exchange rates. Now let's consider how a sterilization operation might occur in a floating exchange rate system. Suppose the Japanese yen is appreciating against the dollar, and the Bank of Japan decides to intervene in the foreign exchange market to increase the value of the dollar and stop the yen appreciation. The Bank of Japan increases domestic credit in order to purchase U.S. dollar-denominated bonds. The increased demand for dollar bonds will mean an increase in the demand for dollars in the foreign exchange market. This results in the higher foreign exchange value of the dollar. Now suppose that the Bank of Japan has a target level of the Japanese money supply that requires the increase in domestic credit to be offset. The central bank will sell yen-denominated bonds in Japan to reduce the domestic money supply. The domestic Japanese money supply was originally increased by the growth in domestic credit used to buy dollar bonds. The money supply ultimately returns to its initial level since the Bank of Japan uses a domestic open market operation (the formal term for central bank purchases and sales of domestic bonds) to reduce domestic credit. In this case of managed floating exchange rates, the Bank of Japan uses sterilized intervention to achieve its goal of slowing the appreciation of the yen while keeping the Japanese money supply unchanged. *Sterilized intervention* is ultimately an exchange of domestic bonds for foreign bonds. We may well ask how sterilized intervention could cause a change in the exchange rate if money supplies are unchanged. It is difficult to explain in terms of a monetary approach model but not a portfolio-balance approach. Equation (10.2) showed that the exchange rate will be a function of relative asset supplies. When the Bank of Japan buys dollar assets, this reduces the supply of dollar assets relative to yen assets available to private market participants. This should cause the yen to de-

preciate. This effect is reinforced by the open market sale of yen securities by the Bank of Japan.

Even in a monetary approach setting, it is possible for sterilized intervention, with unchanged money supplies, to have an effect on the spot exchange rate if money demand changes. The intervention activity could alter the private market view of what to expect in the future. If the intervention changes expectations in a manner that changes money demand (for instance, money demand in Japan falls because the intervention leads people to expect higher Japanese inflation), then the spot rate could change.

EXCHANGE RATES AND THE TRADE BALANCE

The introduction to this chapter discussed the modern shift in emphasis away from exchange rate models that rely on international trade in goods to exchange rate models based on financial assets. However, there is still a useful role for trade flows in asset approach models, since trade flows have implications for financial asset flows.

If balance-of-trade deficits are financed by depleting domestic stocks of foreign currency and trade surpluses are associated with increases in domestic holdings of foreign money, we can see the role for the trade account. If the exchange rate adjusts so that the stocks of domestic and foreign money are willingly held, then the country with a trade surplus will be accumulating foreign currency. As holdings of foreign money increase relative to domestic, the relative value of foreign money will fall or the foreign currency will depreciate.

Although realized trade flows and the consequent changes in currency holdings will determine the current spot exchange rate, the expected future change in the spot rate will be affected by expectations regarding the future balance of trade and its implied currency holdings. An important aspect of this analysis is that changes in the future expected value of a currency can have an immediate impact on current spot rates. For instance, if there is suddenly a change in the world economy that leads to expectations of a larger trade deficit in the future, say, an international oil cartel may develop, so that the domestic economy will have to pay much more for oil imports. In this case forward-looking individuals will antici-

pate a decrease in domestic holdings of foreign money over time. This will, in turn, cause expectations of a higher rate of appreciation in the value of foreign currency in the future, or a faster expected depreciation of the domestic currency. This higher expected rate of depreciation of the domestic currency leads to an immediate attempt by individuals and firms to shift from domestic into foreign money. Because at this moment the total stocks of foreign and domestic money are constant, the attempt to exchange domestic for foreign money will cause an immediate appreciation of the foreign currency to maintain equilibrium, and so the existing supplies of domestic and foreign money are willingly held.

We note that current spot exchange rates are affected by changes in expectations concerning future trade flows, as well as by current international trade flows. As is often the case in economic phenomena, the short-run effect of some new event determining the balance of trade can differ from the long-run result. Suppose the long-run equilibrium under floating exchange rates is balanced trade, where exports equal imports. If we are initially in equilibrium and then experience a disturbance like an oil cartel formation, in the short run we expect large balance-of-trade deficits, but in the long run as all prices and quantities adjust to the situation, we return to the long-run equilibrium of balanced trade. The new long-run equilibrium exchange rate will be higher than the old rate, since foreigners will have larger stocks of domestic currency while domestic residents hold less foreign currency as a result of the period of the trade deficit. The exchange rate need not move to the new equilibrium immediately. In the short run during which trade deficits are experienced, the exchange rate will tend to be below the new equilibrium rate. Thus, as the outflow of money from the domestic economy proceeds with the deficits, there is a steady depreciation of the domestic currency to maintain the short-run equilibrium where quantities demanded and supplied of monies are equal. Figure 10.1 illustrates the effects just discussed. Some unexpected event occurs at time t_0 that causes a balance-of-trade deficit. The initial exchange rate is E_0. With the deficit, and consequent outflow of money from home to abroad, the domestic currency will depreciate. Eventually, as prices and quantities adjust to the changes in the structure of trade, a new long-run equilibrium is reached at E_1

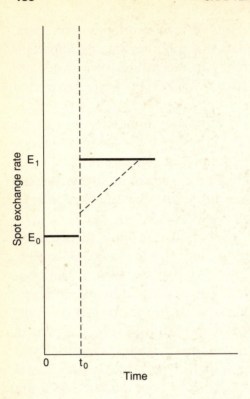

FIGURE 10.1 The path of the exchange rate following a new event that causes balance-of-trade deficits.

where trade balance is restored. This move to the new long-run exchange rate E_1 does not have to come instantaneously, because the deficit will persist for some time. However, the forward rate could jump to E_1 at time t_0 as the market now expects E_1 to be the long-run equilibrium exchange rate. The dashed line in Figure 10.1 represents the path taken by the spot exchange rate in the short run. At t_0 there is an instantaneous jump in the exchange rate even before any trade deficits are realized, because individuals try to exchange domestic money for foreign in anticipation of the domestic currency depreciation. Over time, as the trade deficits occur, there is a steady depreciation of the domestic currency with the exchange rate approaching its new long-run steady-state value E_1 as the trade deficit approaches zero.

The inclusion of the balance of trade as a determinant of exchange rates is particularly useful since the popular press often emphasizes the trade account in explanations of exchange rate behavior. As previously shown, it is possible to make sense of

balance-of-trade flows in a model where the exchange rate is determined by desired and actual financial asset flows, so that the role of trade flows in exchange rate determination may be consistent with the modern asset approach to the exchange rate.

OVERSHOOTING EXCHANGE RATES

Figure 10.1 indicates that, with news regarding a higher trade deficit for the domestic country, the spot exchange rate will jump immediately above E_0 with the news and will then rise steadily until the new long-run equilibrium E_1 is reached. It is possible that the exchange rate may not always move in such an orderly fashion to the new long-run equilibrium following a disturbance.

We know that purchasing power parity does not hold well under flexible exchange rates. Exchange rates exhibit much more volatile behavior than do prices. We might expect that in the short run, following some disturbance to equilibrium, prices will adjust slowly to the new equilibrium level, whereas exchange rates and interest rates adjust quickly. This different speed of adjustment to equilibrium allows for some interesting behavior regarding exchange rates and prices.

At times it appears that spot exchange rates move too much given some economic disturbance. Moreover, we have observed instances when country A has a higher inflation rate than country B, yet A's currency appreciates relative to B's. Such anomalies can be explained in the context of an "overshooting" exchange rate model. We assume that financial markets adjust instantaneously to an exogenous shock, whereas goods markets adjust slowly over time. With this setting, we analyze what happens when country A increases its money supply.

For equilibrium in the money market, money demand must equal money supply. Thus if the money supply increases, something must happen to increase money demand. We assume money demand depends on income and the interest rate, so that we can write a money demand function like

$$M^d = aY + bi \tag{10.5}$$

where M^d is the real stock of money demanded (the nominal stock of money divided by the price level), Y is income, and i is the interest rate. Money demand is positively related to income, so a

exceeds zero. As Y increases, people tend to demand more of everything, including money. Since the interest rate is the opportunity cost of holding money, there is an inverse relation between money demand and i, or b is negative. It is commonly believed that in the short run following an increase in the money supply both income and the price level are relatively constant. As a result, interest rates must drop to equate money demand to money supply.

The interest rate parity relation for countries A and B may be written as

$$i_A = i_B + (F - E)/E \qquad (10.6)$$

Thus, if i_A falls, given the foreign interest rate i_B, $(F - E)/E$ or the expected depreciation of currency A must fall. When the money supply in country A increases, we expect that eventually prices there will rise, since we have more A currency chasing the limited quantity of goods available for purchase. This higher future price in A will imply a higher future exchange rate to achieve purchasing power parity:

$$E = P_A/P_B \qquad (10.7)$$

Since P_A is expected to rise over time, given P_B, E will also rise. This higher expected future spot rate will be reflected in a higher forward rate now. But if F rises, while at the same time $(F - E)$ must fall to maintain interest rate parity, E will have to increase more than F. Then once prices start rising, real money balances fall so that the domestic interest rate rises. Over time, as the interest rate increases, E will fall to maintain interest rate parity. Therefore, the initial rise in E will be in excess of the long-run E, or E will overshoot its long-run value.

If the discussion seems overwhelming at this point, the reader will be relieved to know that a concise summary can be given graphically. Figure 10.2 summarizes the discussion thus far. The initial equilibrium is given by E_0, F_0, P_0, and i_0. When the money supply increases at time t_0, the domestic interest rate falls, and the spot and forward exchange rates increase while the price level remains fixed. The eventual equilibrium price and exchange rate will rise in proportion to the increase in the money supply. Although the forward rate will move immediately to its new equilibrium, F_1, the spot rate will increase above the eventual equilib-

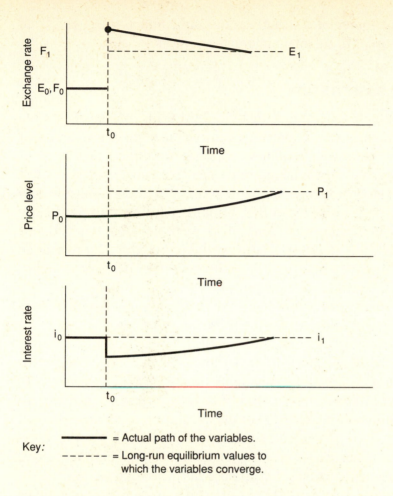

FIGURE 10.2 The time path of the forward and spot exchange rate, interest rate, and price level following an increase in the domestic money supply at time t_0.

rium E_1 because of the need to maintain interest parity (remember i has fallen in the short run). Over time, as prices start rising, the interest rate increases and the exchange rate converges to the new equilibrium E_1.

As a result of the overshooting E, we observe a period where country A has rising prices relative to the fixed price of country B, yet A's currency appreciates along the solid line converging to E_1. We might explain this period as one when prices increase, lowering real money balances and raising interest rates. Country A experiences capital inflows in response to the higher interest rates, so that

A's currency appreciates steadily at the same rate as the interest rate increase in order to maintain interest rate parity.

CURRENCY SUBSTITUTION

Economists have long argued that one of the advantages of flexible exchange rates is that countries become independent in terms of their ability to formulate domestic monetary policy. This is obviously not true when exchange rates are fixed. If country A must maintain a fixed exchange rate with country B, then A must follow a monetary policy similar to B's. Should A follow an inflationary policy in which prices are rising 20 percent per year while B follows a policy aimed at price stability, then a fixed rate of exchange between the money of A and B will prove very difficult to maintain. Yet with flexible exchange rates, A and B can each choose any monetary policy they like, and the exchange rate will simply change over time to adjust for the inflation differentials.

This independence of domestic policy under flexible exchange rates may be reduced if there is an international demand for monies. Suppose country B residents desire to hold currency *A* to use for future transactions or simply to hold as part of their investment portfolio. As demand for money shifts between currencies *A* and *B*, the exchange rate will shift as well. In a region with substitutable currencies, shifts in money demand between currencies will add an additional element of exchange rate variability.

With fixed exchange rates, central banks make currencies perfect substitutes on the supply side. They alter the supplies of currency to maintain the exchange rate peg. The issue of currency substitution deals with the substitutability among currencies on the demand side of the market. If currencies were perfect substitutes to money demanders, then all currencies would have to have the same inflation rates, or demand for the high-inflation currency would fall to zero (since the inflation rate determines the loss of purchasing power of a money). Perfectly substitutable monies indicate that demanders are indifferent between the use of one currency or another. If the cost of holding currency *A* rises relative to the cost of holding *B*, say because of a higher inflation rate for currency *A*, then demand will shift away from *A* to *B* if *A* and *B* are substitutes. This would cause the *A* currency to depreciate even

more than was initially called for by the inflation differential between *A* and *B*.

For instance, suppose Italy has a 10 percent annual inflation rate while Germany has a 5 percent rate. With no currency substitution, we would expect the mark to appreciate against the lira on purchasing power parity grounds. Now suppose that Italian citizens hold stocks of mark currency, and these marks are good substitutes for lira. The higher inflation rate on the lira means that stocks of lira held will lose value more rapidly than marks, so there is an increased demand for mark currency. This attempt to exchange lira currency for marks results in a further depreciation of the lira. Such shifts in demand between currencies can result in volatile exchange rates and can be very unsettling to central banks desiring exchange rate stability. Therefore, one implication of a high degree of currency substitution is a need for international coordination of monetary policy. If money demanders substitute between currencies to force each currency to follow a similar inflation rate, then the supposed independence of monetary policy under flexible exchange rates is largely illusory. Although central banks may attempt to follow independent monetary policies, money demanders will adjust their portfolio holdings away from high-inflation currencies to low-inflation currencies. This currency substitution leads to more volatile exchange rates, since not only does the exchange rate adjust to compensate for the original inflation differential, but it also adjusts as currency portfolios are altered.

We should expect currency substitution to be most important in a regional setting where there is a relatively high degree of mobility of resources between countries. For instance, the European Monetary System in Western Europe is a European currency union and may be evidence of a high degree of currency substitution existing among European currencies. Alternatively, there is evidence of a high degree of currency substitution existing between the U.S. dollar and Latin American currencies. In many Latin American countries, dollars serve as an important substitute currency, both as a store of value (the dollar being more stable than the typical Latin American currency) and as a medium of exchange used for transactions. This latter effect is particularly pronounced in border areas. Aside from regional settings, it is not clear that currency substitution should be a potentially important source of exchange rate vari-

ability. Even at the regional level, economists disagree on the practical importance of currency substitution. Much of the disagreement among researchers has to do with differences in methodology and countries studied. At this point it is probably safe to treat currency substitution as a potentially important source of exchange rate variability that may not be relevant to all country pairs.

THE ROLE OF NEWS

Considering the theories of exchange rate determination discussed so far, we might believe that with all this knowledge experts should be quite adept at forecasting future exchange rates. In fact, forecasting future spot exchange rates is very difficult. Although researchers have shown the theories we have covered to be relevant in terms of explaining systematic patterns of exchange rate behavior, the usefulness of these theories for predicting future exchange rates is limited by the propensity for the unexpected to occur. The real world is characterized by unpredictable shocks or surprises. When some unexpected event takes place, we refer to this as *news*. Since interest rates, prices, and incomes are often affected by news, it follows that exchange rates will also be affected by news. By definition, the exchange rate changes linked to news will be unexpected. Thus we find the great difficulty in predicting future spot rates, because we know the exchange rate will be, in part, determined by events that cannot be foreseen.

The fact that the predicted change in the spot rate, as measured by the forward premium, varies less over time than does the actual change indicates how much of the change in spot rates is unexpected. Periods dominated by unexpected announcements or realizations of economic policy changes will have great fluctuations in spot and forward exchange rates as expectations are revised subject to the news.

The news also has implications for purchasing power parity. Since exchange rates are financial asset prices that respond quickly to new information, news will have an immediate impact on exchange rates. Prices of goods and services, however, will not be affected by the news in such a rapid manner. One reason is that goods and services are often contracted for in advance, so that prices are inflexible for the duration of the contract. A more basic and general

reason is that financial assets, like foreign exchange, have long lives relative to the goods and services that are incorporated in national price indexes. This is important because longer-lived, or durable, goods prices are more sensitive to changes in expectations than are nondurable, or relatively short-lived, assets. For this reason, during periods dominated by news we will observe exchange rates varying a great deal relative to prices, and thus large deviations from purchasing power parity are realized. The differences between prices and exchange rates are illustrated in Table 10.1. As was discussed earlier, in the context of asset models of exchange rate determination, exchange rates change much more than do goods prices. Periods like the 1970s and 1980s, when many unexpected economic events occurred (oil price shocks and international debt problems are two of the more obvious surprises), will be times of large unexpected exchange rate changes and also of large deviations from PPP.

It is important to realize that the variability of the exchange rate is a result of new developments. Volatile exchange rates simply reflect turbulent times. Even with a good knowledge of the determinants of exchange rates as discussed in this chapter, without perfect foresight, exchange rates will always prove to be difficult to forecast in a dynamic world full of surprises.

SUMMARY

1. Modern exchange rate models emphasize financial asset markets.
2. Asset approach models may be divided into monetary approach models, assuming perfect substitutability of assets internationally, and portfolio-balance models, assuming imperfect substitutability.
3. Portfolio-balance models of exchange rate determination add relative asset supplies as a determinant.
4. Central bank sterilization occurs when domestic credit is changed to offset international reserve flows.
5. Since balance-of-trade flows are balanced by financial asset flows, changes in the trade balance have a role in asset approach views of exchange rate determination.
6. If financial asset markets clear fast relative to goods markets, then the exchange rate may overshoot the new long-run equilibrium following some shock to the system.
7. International currency substitution will add an additional source of exchange rate variability.

8. A high degree of currency substitution breeds currency union.
9. Exchange rates are difficult to forecast because the market is continually reacting to unexpected events or news.

EXERCISES

1. Suppose Japan discovers a new technology that will result in doubling Japanese exports. As a result, Japan moves from a position of balance-of-trade deficits to expected long-term surpluses. How should the foreign exchange value of Japanese yen be affected? Do you expect any difference between the long run and the short run?

2. A major complaint regarding flexible exchange rates is that they are too volatile when they float. Explain how each of the topics considered in this chapter—the trade balance, currency substitution, differential speed of adjustment of asset markets versus goods markets, and news—contributes to exchange rate volatility.

3. Suppose the German central bank unexpectedly lowers the German money supply. In a world of exchange rate overshooting, how would the mark/dollar spot rate, forward rate, German interest rate, and German price level change in response? Draw graphs representing the expected time paths. Why does your exchange rate path have the shape that it does?

4. Carefully monitor the local newspaper (better still, the *Wall Street Journal*) for news that should have an impact on the foreign exchange market. Keep a list of each news event, the effect on the value of the domestic currency you would expect (and why), and the actual effect. If you find the market moving in a different way than you expected, why do you suppose this happened?

5. Suppose the Federal Reserve in the United States wants to decrease the value of the Japanese yen against the dollar. How might the Fed intervene in the foreign exchange market to accomplish this? If the Fed wants to leave the U.S. money supply unchanged by the foreign exchange market intervention, how will it conduct a sterilized intervention?

REFERENCES

Aivazian, Varouj A., Jeffrey L. Callen, Itzhak Krinsky, and Clarence C. Y. Kwan, "International Exchange Risk and Asset Substitutability," *Journal of International Money and Finance*, December 1986.

Dominguez, Kathryn M., and Jeffrey A. Frankel, *Does Foreign Exchange Intervention Work?* Washington: Institute for International Economics, 1993.

Frankel, Jeffrey, "Monetary and Portfolio-Balance Models of Exchange Rate Determination," in J. Bhandari and B. Putnam, eds., *Economic Interdependence and Flexible Exchange Rates*. Cambridge, Mass.: MIT Press, 1982.

Hoffman, Dennis L., and Don E. Schlagenhauf, "The Impact of News and Alternative Theories of Exchange Rate Determination," *Journal of Money, Credit, and Banking*, August 1985.

Levin, Jay H., "Trade Flow Lags, Monetary and Fiscal Policy, and Exchange Rate Overshooting," *Journal of International Money and Finance*, December 1986.

Mussa, Michael, "The Theory of Exchange Rate Determination," in John F. O. Bilson and Richard C. Marston, eds., *Exchange Rate Theory and Practice*. Chicago: University of Chicago Press, 1984.

Rodriguez, Carlos Alfredo, "The Role of Trade Flows in Exchange Rate Determination: A Rational Expectations Approach," *Journal of Political Economy*, December 1980.

chapter 11

Import and Export Financing

International trade, like domestic trade, is not carried out strictly on a cash basis. Trade across national borders involves loans, advances, and guarantees of payment that bring third parties, like banks, into a trade transaction. Besides commercial banks, governments are involved since often low-cost financing is used as a means of stimulating exports.

Banks and governments are not the only institutions that finance international trade. Banks account for the major share of trade finance, but they specialize in short-term unsecured loans. Other institutions specialize in higher-risk loans that must be secured by a pledge of the borrower's assets as collateral. We begin this chapter with a discussion of the institutions involved in financing trade. Then we examine exactly how trade transactions are arranged and the various alternatives available for financing.

INSTITUTIONS

Let us now consider in more detail the major institutions involved in financing world trade.

Commercial Banks

Commercial banks dominate world trade financing. Banks have a varied assortment of financing alternatives available that allow them

to compete for almost any type of financing deal. These alternatives include short-term unsecured loans with a borrowing period of up to 1 year; "letters of credit," guaranteeing that an importer will make payment to an exporter; foreign receivables financing, wherein exporters receive financing by pledging the money to be received from importers as collateral; and longer-term loans, wherein repayment is to be made in installments over time. We will consider these alternative financing arrangements in more detail later.

Factors

Factors are firms that buy accounts receivable from a trading firm and then assume responsibility for collecting the receivables. For instance, suppose Motorola sells $500,000 worth of computer chips to a French manufacturer with payment due in 90 days. Motorola could sell the right to collect the $500,000 to a factor. The factor will pay Motorola less than $500,000 for this right, and then the factor must collect from the French buyer. Should the French firm default on the contract, it is the factor's loss.

  A factor is not a bank, although it could be a subsidiary of a bank. The factor is a specialized combination of lender and collection agency. In fact, Motorola could use the factor's collection services and not sell the receivables. In this case, the factor would collect the money owed from the French manufacturer and turn the funds over to Motorola after deducting a service charge.

  To overcome the lack of credit information on foreign firms, domestic factors have foreign affiliates or cooperative agreements with foreign factors, under which the U.S. factor provides credit expertise on U.S. firms in exchange for the foreign factor's information on foreign firms.

  Exporters benefit from selling their accounts receivable to a factor by transferring credit and collection problems to the factor, reducing administrative expenses related to carrying accounts receivable, and eliminating foreign exchange risk if the receivables were denominated in foreign currency. The exporter receives payment now, rather than when the importer pays, and is free to concentrate on sales and product development, allowing the financial expertise of the factor to deal with credit issues.

  The price that the exporter receives from the factor for receivables will be lower the longer the time until importer payment is

due, the poorer the credit rating of the importer, and the greater the foreign exchange risk associated with the transaction.

Commercial Finance Companies

Loans too risky or unsuitable for banks may be made by commercial finance companies. These are secured loans—secured by other than the accounts receivable handled by factors.

For instance, suppose a small, financially unstable U.S. exporter, Tex's Trading Company, receives a large order for cowboy boots from a German buyer backed by a letter of credit guaranteeing importer payment from a large commercial bank. Tex's Trading Company must first buy the boots from Acme Boot Company in El Paso, Texas. The problem is that Tex's Trading Company does not have sufficient credit to cover its purchase from Acme. In fact, Acme wants a letter of credit in its favor against Tex's Trading Company. Commercial banks are not generally willing to open a letter of credit for weak exporters, so Tex's turns to a finance company. The finance company will require Tex's to assign the German buyer's letter of credit to it. Then the finance company issues a letter of credit to Acme.

Finance companies specialize in such "back-to-back" letters of credit for firms lacking the financial strength required to deal with commercial banks. In addition, finance companies may provide exporter financing to allow production or acquisition of goods to be traded by stipulating that goods must be stored in an independent warehouse prior to export, so that the exporter cannot have access to them. Alternatively, the finance company may require that the export contract and accounts receivable be pledged as collateral for the loan. The finance company does not collect the receivables without recourse as a factor would; it will pursue payment from the exporter should the importer default.

Finance companies generally deal with riskier loans. As a result, they charge a higher rate of interest than a bank. The example of the boot exporter could have been reversed, with a finance company providing importer financing. The weak importer can arrange for the finance company to obtain a letter of credit from a major international bank by using the assets and credit of the finance company to back up the resources of the importer.

Government Institutions

International trade financing can involve government agencies as well as private lenders. The role of government is generally one of stimulating exports. In the United States, there are a few institutions of the federal government that aid the efforts of U.S. exporters.

The *Export-Import Bank,* or *Eximbank,* was established as an independent government agency in 1945. The role of the Eximbank is to provide export financing for U.S. firms that is competitive with the financing available in the other major industrial countries. The Eximbank is not in competition with other firms. Its role is that of supplementing private credit to allow U.S. firms to compete with foreign firms receiving subsidies from their governments.

The Eximbank offers several different programs to meet the financing needs of U.S. exporters and foreign importers. For large purchases requiring a long period for repayment, direct loans are made to foreign importers. In some cases, commercial banks would provide a direct loan to a foreign buyer, except when the buyer is in a high-risk region of the world or lacks sufficient credit strength to qualify for the loan. The Eximbank may guarantee the loan for either a U.S. or a foreign bank. There are several additional Eximbank programs that offer various combinations of loans and guarantees. In addition, the Eximbank provides financing for export feasibility studies, shares credit information with U.S. banks, and offers counseling and training for U.S. export firms.

The *Commodity Credit Corporation* (CCC) operates in the U.S. Department of Agriculture to support the export of U.S. agricultural products. As part of CCC support operations, loans to foreign buyers are made at longer terms than private lenders will provide. Since agricultural products are usually consumed in a short time, private lenders are only willing to offer short-term loans to buyers of agricultural output. The CCC has a program of up to 36-month financing to stimulate exports from the United States. These loans are supposed to be available only when necessary to meet certain criteria, like matching credit terms offered by competing countries.

The *Overseas Private Investment Corporation* (OPIC) is operated by the U.S. Treasury to assist U.S. investments in friendly developing countries. OPIC is not principally engaged in financing trade, although there may be some impact on international trade flows of direct investment subsidized by OPIC.

The discussion of government institutions has focused on U.S. operations, but other countries also have agencies for stimulating exports. The typical arrangement is that of the Eximbank in providing competitive financing to importers.

EXECUTING TRANSACTIONS

Once the importer has agreed to buy goods from an exporter, a sales contract must be written. The *sales contract* explicitly lists the obligations of each party and will generally include a description of the goods sold, price, method of payment, shipping date, and who must be responsible for shipping charges, insurance, and taxes. A crucial issue in a sales contract is when possession of the goods is transferred from seller to buyer. The following are some of the common delivery terms used:

Ex factory: The goods are transferred to the buyer at the point of origin, the seller's factory. The seller is responsible for all costs of making the goods available at the factory. The buyer assumes all further expenses.

Free on board (FOB): The title to the goods passes to the buyer when the goods are loaded aboard ship (or airplane, or however the goods are being shipped). The seller is responsible for all costs until the goods are on board; the buyer then pays all further costs.

Free alongside (FAS): The seller delivers the goods alongside the ship that will transport the goods, within reach of the ship's loading apparatus. The buyer is responsible for the goods beyond this point.

Cost and freight (C&F): The seller pays for transportation to the destination point. This could be combined with an "on board" instruction specifying when title to the goods changes hands.

Cost, insurance, and freight (CIF): This is similar to C&F, except the seller must also pay for insurance. Generally this means ocean marine insurance in case the ship sinks or the goods are otherwise damaged by an event other than war. War risk insurance may also be available and is generally paid for by the buyer.

> *Ex dock:* The seller is responsible for all costs required to deliver the goods at the port of destination. Title to the goods passes to the buyer at the dock of the port of importation.

In addition to the sales contract, a few other key documents are involved in international trade. One of the most important documents is the bill of lading, which is illustrated in Figure 11.1. A *bill of lading* is issued by the shipping company to the exporter and states the agreement to carry the goods to the destination port. This document serves as a receipt for the goods and can be negotiable and used to transfer the title to the goods. This function of a bill of lading as a negotiable instrument is important in trade finance, since the exporter can endorse the bill of lading to a bank to obtain financing for the shipping costs using the goods as collateral.

For goods shipped by air, the bill of lading is called an *airbill*. Airbills are rarely negotiable because the goods are received by the importer very quickly, and the exporter or bank would control the goods for only a short period.

Once the goods are received at the port of importation, a *dock receipt* is issued by the shipping company and given to the truck or railroad firm that picks up the goods at the dock. The dock receipt lists the quantity and condition of goods delivered.

LETTERS OF CREDIT

A *letter of credit* (LOC) is a written instrument issued by a bank at the request of an importer obligating the bank to pay a specific amount of money to an exporter. The time at which payment is due is specified, along with conditions regarding necessary documents to be presented by the exporter prior to payment.

The LOC may stipulate that a bill of lading be presented that evidences no damaged goods. Perhaps some minimal level of damage (like 2 percent of the boxes or crates) is stipulated. In any case, such conditions in a LOC allow the importer to retain some quality control prior to payment.

Figure 11.2 illustrates a simple letter of credit. Note that this is an *irrevocable* LOC. This means that the agreement cannot be modified without the express permission of all parties. Most letters of credit are of this type. A *revocable* LOC may be altered by the account party—the importer buying the goods. Since the importer is free to alter the LOC, we might wonder why any exporter would

BILL OF LADING

Shipper/Exporter	Document No.
	Export References
Consignee	Forwarding Agent
	Point and Country of Origin
Notify Party	Domestic Routing Export Instructions
Pier or Airport	
Exporting Carrier Port of Loading	Onward Inland Routing
Port of Discharge For Transshipment To	

Particulars Furnished by Shipper

Marks and Numbers	No. of Pkgs.	Description of Packages and Goods	Gross Weight	Measurement

Freight Charges Payable At   By

	Prepaid	Collect	
Land Origin Charges			Signed at (location):
Port Charges			
			Name of Carrier:
Subtotal			
Ocean Freight			
			Mo./Day/Year: Signature:
Subtotal			
Port Charges			
and Destination Charges			
Subtotal			
Grand Total			

FIGURE 11.1 Bill of lading.

ever accept a revocable LOC. The exporter may interpret the issuance of the LOC as a favorable credit report on the buyer. The exporter will call the issuing bank prior to shipment to make sure that the LOC has not been altered or revoked, and then present the necessary documents and collect payment as soon as possible. The

[Bank Letterhead (Name & Address
of Importer's Bank)]

LETTER OF CREDIT NO.   ACCOUNT PARTY
DATE: (Buyer's Name & Address)

                                                         BENEFICIARY
                                                         (Seller's Name & Address)

TO: *(Seller's Bank & Address)*

WE HAVE OPENED AN IRREVOCABLE LETTER OF CREDIT IN FAVOR OF: *(Seller's Name)*
FOR THE AMOUNT OF: $ _____
                                (Dollar amount is written in words here)

AVAILABLE WITH US AGAINST THE FOLLOWING DOCUMENTS:
                        (Required documents are listed here)

TRANSHIPMENTS: *(Permitted or not)*
PARTIAL SHIPMENTS: *(Permitted or not)*

THIS CREDIT IS VALID UNTIL *(Date)* FOR PRESENTATION OF DOCUMENTS TO US.
DOCUMENTS ARE TO BE PRESENTED WITHIN *(Number)* DAYS AFTER DATE OF
ISSUANCE OF BILLS OF LADING.
PLEASE ADVISE THE BENEFICIARY OF YOUR CONFIRMATION.

THIS CREDIT IS SUBJECT TO THE UNIFORM CUSTOMS AND PRACTICE FOR
DOCUMENTARY CREDITS. INTERNATIONAL CHAMBER OF COMMERCE
PUBLICATION NO. 400.
THIS CREDIT IS IRREVOCABLE AND WE HEREBY ENGAGE WITH THE DRAWERS THAT
DRAWINGS IN ACCORD WITH THE TERMS OF THIS CREDIT WILL BE DULY HONORED BY US.

                                        Yours truly,

                                        (Signature)

                                        International Department

FIGURE 11.2 Letter of credit.

revocable LOC is still safer than shipping goods based on the importer's promise to pay, with no bank credit backing up the transaction. Still, revocable letters of credit are primarily used only when
there is no question of revocation. This form of LOC may save

bank fees, which are higher with irrevocable LOCs, so if there is no chance of revocation, it may pay to use the revocable LOC.

The sales contract stipulates the method of payment. The use of LOCs is widespread, so let us assume the contract calls for payment by LOC. The importer must then apply for an LOC from a bank. The importer requests that the LOC stipulate no payment until appropriate documents are presented by the exporter to the bank. These document stipulations cannot violate the sales contract since the bank is at risk to ensure that the documents are in order at the time of payment.

If the bank considers the importer an acceptable credit risk, the letter of credit is issued and sent to the exporter. The exporter then examines the LOC to ensure that it conforms to the sales contract. If it does not, then modifications must be made before the goods are shipped. Once the exporter fulfills all obligations in delivering the goods, the documentary proof is presented to the bank for examination. If the documents conform to the LOC, payment is made by the bank's collecting from the importer and then paying the exporter.

If the importer does not pay the bank, the bank is still obligated to pay the exporter. The exporter is then satisfied, and any problems must be settled between the importer and the bank.

Banks may or may not require that the underlying goods serve as collateral for the LOC. If the bank does require an interest in the goods, then the bill of lading is consigned to the bank. With an unsecured LOC, the bank assumes the credit risk of a buyer default. With a secured LOC, the bank assumes the risk of changes in the value of the goods and the cost of disposal. Even if the importer is a sound credit risk, the bank assumes the risk that it misses a document discrepancy and that the importer refuses to pay as a result.

What are the risks of the buyer and seller? The exporter faces the risk of shipping goods without being able to meet all terms listed in the LOC. If the goods are shipped and a document discrepancy exists, then the seller will not be paid. The buyer risks fraud from the seller. The goods may not meet the specifications ordered, but the seller fraudulently prepares documents stating otherwise. The bank is not responsible for such fraudulent documents, so the risk is the buyer's.

Banks charge a flat fee for issuing and amending letters of credit. A percentage of the amount paid is also charged at the time

payment is made. These charges generally apply to the importer unless the parties agree otherwise.

BANKERS' ACCEPTANCES

In the discussion of the institutions involved in financing trade, it was apparent that there exist many alternatives for trade finance arrangements. Suppose an exporter needs funds now to purchase and produce goods for shipment, or to meet its obligations until payment is received from the importer. The exporter may have several alternatives for obtaining the funds. Similarly, an importer may need funds now to meet current obligations or its financial needs until the goods are received and sold. The importer may also face several financing alternatives. Often international trade will require the use of bankers' acceptances. A *bankers' acceptance* (BA) is a time draft drawn on and accepted by a particular bank to be paid at maturity.

A bank creates a BA by approving a line of credit for a customer, let's assume an importer, and then creating a bank draft payable to the exporter's bank at a future date. The bank then may pay the exporter some amount less than the face value of the draft prior to maturity. Once the draft is accepted by the bank, the BA is sold in the acceptance market to an investor. The investor will pay less than the face value of the draft, but more than the amount the bank paid the importer. At maturity, the BA is settled by the bank's receiving the full face value of the draft from the importer and paying the full value to the investor holding the BA.

Suppose an importer requires acceptance financing to meet the terms of a sales contract. The importer will agree to provide the funds needed to pay for the acceptance at least one day prior to maturity of the acceptance. The importer will use the goods purchased as security for the bank, in the event that the importer does not perform its obligation to fund the acceptance one day prior to maturity.

The Federal Reserve in the United States permits bankers' acceptances only for financing international trade in readily marketable staple products. U.S. banks issue acceptances for trade between the United States and other countries as well as trade between two foreign countries.

BAs are generally created only by major banks. This allows a market for safe short-term investments for other investors. Banks will not always sell their acceptances, preferring at times to retain

BAs in their own portfolio. When acceptances are sold, usually large dollar amounts are involved, so only wealthy individuals participate and the market is dominated by institutional buyers.

The total cost of the acceptance includes the discount from the face value already mentioned. This discount is determined by the interest rate on other short-term instruments like Treasury bills or certificates of deposit. In addition to the discount, there is an acceptance fee (usually 1.5 percent of the value of the draft) charged to customers seeking acceptances. Finally, some customers may be required to hold demand deposits at the bank before a BA is created. In these cases, the forgone interest on such deposits is another cost of creating the BA.

Why use acceptance financing for international trade? During times of tight credit conditions, the acceptance market may be the only way to channel short-term funds to trade financing. The active investor market for acceptances can supplement the squeeze on loanable funds facing banks. Furthermore, bankers often prefer BAs for trade financing since the transaction requiring the loan is clearly specified, as is the source of the loan payback.

AN EXAMPLE OF TRADE FINANCING

Let's consider an example that applies some of the issues covered so far. Suppose a U.S. firm, New York Wine Importers, wants to import wine from a French firm, Paris Wine Exporters. Figure 11.3 illustrates the steps involved in the transaction. First, the importer and exporter must agree on the basics of the transaction. The sales contract will stipulate the amount and kind of wine, price, shipping date, and payment method.

Following the sales contract, the importer requests a letter of credit from its bank, New York First Bank. The bank issues an LOC that authorizes Paris Wine Exporters to draw a bank draft on New York First Bank for payment. The bank draft is like a check except that it is dated for maturity at some time in the future when payment will be made. Paris Wine Exporters ships the wine and gives its bank, Paris First Bank, the bank draft along with the necessary shipping documents for the wine. Paris First Bank then sends the bank draft, shipping documents, and LOC to New York First Bank.

When New York First Bank accepts the bank draft, a bankers' acceptance is created. At this point, Paris Wine Exporters may receive payment of a discounted value of the BA. New York First

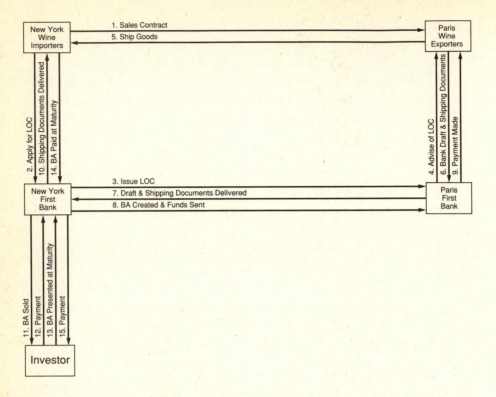

FIGURE 11.3 Steps involved in a U.S. import transaction.

Bank discounts the BA and sends the funds to Paris First Bank for the account of Paris Wine Exporters. New York First Bank delivers the shipping documents to New York Wine Importers, and the importer takes possession of the wine.

New York First Bank is now holding the BA after paying a discounted value to Paris First Bank. Instead of holding the BA until maturity, New York First Bank sells it to an investor. Upon maturity, the investor will receive the face value of the BA from New York First Bank and New York First Bank will receive the face value from New York Wine Importers.

SUMMARY

1. Commercial banks account for most of international trade financing.
2. Factors buy accounts receivable from exporters and then are responsible for collection.
3. Commercial finance companies specialize in high-risk secured loans.
4. The Eximbank provides export financing for U.S. firms that matches the terms offered by foreign competitors.

5. The CCC provides long-term financing for U.S. agricultural exports.
6. The sales contract is the basic document of international trade.
7. A bill of lading documents the shipper's receipt and the shipment of goods.
8. A bankers' acceptance is a draft drawn on a firm and accepted by a bank as payable at maturity.
9. A letter of credit guarantees that the bank will pay the exporter the amount of money owed by the importer.
10. The letter of credit stipulates that payment will be made only upon presentation of required documents.

EXERCISES

1. Why would an export firm want to sell its accounts receivable to a factor?
2. Why should U.S. taxpayers fund agencies like the Eximbank that provide subsidized loans to foreign buyers? What are the costs and benefits of such agencies?
3. If you were importing toy guns from a Korean exporter, what delivery terms would you choose (FOB, C&F, and so on) if the price you paid would not be changed by your choice?
4. What is a bankers' acceptance, and why is it traded among third parties?
5. What is a letter of credit? What risks do the parties to a letter of credit take?

REFERENCES

Kingman-Brundage, Jane, and Susan Schulz, *The Fundamentals of Trade Finance.* New York: Wiley, 1986.

Official Export Guide. Philadelphia: North American Publishing Co., 1986.

Venedikian, Harry M., and Gerald A. Warfield, *Export-Import Financing.* New York: Wiley, 1986.

chapter *12*

Financial Management of the Multinational Firm

Since multinational firms are involved in payables and receivables denominated in different currencies, product shipments across national borders, and subsidiaries operating in different political jurisdictions, they face a different set of problems than the firm with a purely domestic operation. The corporate treasurer and other financial decision makers of the multinational firm operate in a cosmopolitan setting that offers profit and loss opportunities never considered by the executives of the purely domestic firm. This chapter looks at the unique attributes of financial management in the multinational firm. The basic issues—control, cash management, intrafirm transfers, and capital budgeting—face all firms. The problems particular to the internationally oriented firm are the ones addressed.

FINANCIAL CONTROL

Any business firm must evaluate its operations periodically to better allocate resources and increase income. The financial management of a multinational firm involves exercising control over foreign operations. The responsible individuals at the parent office or headquarters review financial reports from foreign subsidiaries with a view toward modifying operations and assessing the performance of foreign managers.

Typical control systems are based on setting standards with regard to sales, profits, inventory, or other specific variables and then examining financial statements and reports to evaluate the achievement of such goals. There is no "correct" system of control. Methods vary across industries and even across firms in a single industry. All methods have the common goal of providing management a means of monitoring the performance of the firm's operations, new strategies, and goals as conditions change. However, establishing a useful control system is more difficult for a multinational firm than for a purely domestic firm. For instance, should foreign subsidiary profits be measured and evaluated in foreign currency or the domestic currency of the parent firm? The answer to this question depends on whether foreign managers are to be held responsible for currency translation gains or losses.

If top management wants foreign managers to be involved in currency management and international financing issues, then the domestic currency of the parent would be a reasonable choice. On the other hand, if top management wants foreign managers to concern themselves with production operations and behave as other managers (managers not themselves a part of a foreign multinational) in the foreign country would, then the foreign currency would be the appropriate currency for evaluation.

Some multinational firms prefer a decentralized management structure in which each subsidiary has a great deal of autonomy and makes most financing and production decisions subject only to general parent-company guidelines. In this management setting, the foreign manager may be expected to operate and think as the stockholders of the parent firm would want, so the foreign manager makes decisions aimed at increasing the parent's domestic currency value of the subsidiary. The control mechanism in such firms is to evaluate foreign managers based on their ability to increase that value.

Other firms prefer more centralized management in which financial managers at the parent make most of the decisions. They choose to move funds among divisions based on a systemwide view rather than what is best for a single subsidiary. A highly centralized system would have foreign managers evaluated on their ability to meet goals established by the parent for key variables like sales or labor costs. The parent-firm managers assume responsibility for maximizing the value of the firm, with foreign managers ba-

sically responding to directives from the top. We see then that the appropriate control system is largely determined by the management style of the parent.

Considering the discussion to this point, it is clear that managers at foreign subsidiaries should be evaluated only on the basis of things they control. Foreign managers may often be asked by the parent to follow policies and relations with other subsidiaries of the firm that the managers would never follow if they sought solely to maximize their subsidiary's profit. Actions of the parent that lower a subsidiary's profit should not result in a negative view of the foreign manager. In addition, other actions beyond the foreign manager's control—changing tax laws, foreign exchange controls, or inflation rates—could result in reducing foreign profits through no fault of the foreign manager. The message to parent-company managers is to place blame fairly where the blame lies. In a dynamic world, corporate fortunes may rise and fall because of events entirely beyond any manager's control.

CASH MANAGEMENT

Cash management involves utilizing the firm's cash as efficiently as possible. Given the daily uncertainties of business, firms must maintain some liquid resources. *Liquid assets* are those that are readily spent. Cash is the most liquid asset. But since cash (and traditional checking accounts) earns no interest, the firm has a strong incentive to minimize its holdings of cash. There are highly liquid short-term securities that serve as good substitutes for actual cash balances and yet pay interest. The corporate treasurer is concerned with maintaining the correct level of liquidity at the minimum possible cost.

The multinational treasurer faces the challenge of managing liquid assets denominated in different currencies. The challenge is compounded by the problem that subsidiaries operate in foreign countries where financial market regulations and institutions differ.

When a subsidiary receives a payment and the funds are not needed immediately by this subsidiary, the managers at the parent headquarters must decide what to do with the funds. For instance, suppose a U.S. multinational's Mexican subsidiary receives 500 million pesos. Should the pesos be converted to dollars and invested in the United States, or placed in Mexican peso investments,

or converted into any other currency in the world? The answer depends on the current needs of the firm as well as the current regulations in Mexico. If Mexico has strict foreign exchange controls in place, the 500 million pesos may have to be kept in Mexico and invested there until a future time when the Mexican subsidiary will need them to make a payment.

Even without legal restrictions on foreign exchange movements, we might invest the pesos in Mexico for 30 days if the subsidiary faces a large payment in 30 days, if we have no need for the funds in another area of the firm, and if the return on the Mexican investment is comparable to what we could earn in another country on a similar investment (which interest rate parity would suggest). By leaving the funds in pesos, we do not incur any transaction costs by converting pesos to another currency now and then going back to pesos in 30 days. In any case, we would never let the funds sit idly in the bank for 30 days.

There are times when the political or economic situation in a country is so unstable that we keep only the minimum possible level of assets in that country. Even when we will need pesos in 30 days for the Mexican subsidiary's payable, if there exists a significant threat that the government could confiscate or freeze bank deposits or other financial assets, we would incur the transaction costs of currency conversion to avoid the political risk associated with leaving the money in Mexico.

Multinational cash management involves centralized management. Subsidiaries and liquid assets may be spread around the world, but they are managed from the home office of the parent firm. Through such centralized coordination, the overall cash needs of the firm are lower. This occurs because subsidiaries do not all have the same pattern of cash flows. When one subsidiary receives a dollar payment, for instance, and now has surplus cash, another subsidiary faces a dollar payment and must obtain dollars. If each subsidiary operated independently, there would be more cash held in the multinational family of foreign units than if the parent headquarters directed the surplus funds of one subsidiary to the subsidiary facing the payable.

Centralization of cash management allows the parent to offset subsidiary payments and receivables with a process called *netting*. Netting involves the consolidation of payables and receivables in a currency so that only the difference between them must be bought

or sold. For example, suppose Oklahoma Instruments in the United States sells Can$2 million worth of car phones to its Canadian sales subsidiary and buys Can$3 million worth of computer frames from its Canadian manufacturing subsidiary. If the payment and receivable both are due on the same day, then the Can$2 million receivable can be used to fund the Can$3 million payable, and only Can$1 million must be bought in the foreign exchange market. Rather than buy Can$3 million to settle the payable and sell the Can$2 million to convert the receivable into dollars, incurring transaction costs twice on the full Can$5 million, the firm has one foreign exchange transaction for Can$1 million.

Had the two Canadian operations not been subsidiaries, the financial managers would still practice netting but on a corporatewide basis, buying or selling only the net amount of any currency required after aggregating the receivables and payables of all subsidiaries over all currencies. Effective netting requires accurate and timely reporting of transactions by all divisions of the firm.

As an example of intrafirm netting, let us consider a U.S. parent firm with subsidiaries in Canada, the United Kingdom, Germany, and Mexico. Table 12.1 sets up the report for the week of January 15. We assume that netting occurs weekly. Each division's scheduled payments and receipts are converted to dollars so that aggregation across all units can occur. Table 12.1 indicates that the Canadian subsidiary will pay $0.7 million and receive $3.2 million, so it will have a cash surplus of $2.5 million. The U.K. subsidiary will pay $1.3 million and receive $1.2 million, so it will have a cash shortage of $0.1 million. The German subsidiary will pay $3.1

Table 12.1 INTRAFIRM PAYMENTS FOR NETTING MILLION-DOLLAR VALUES, WEEK OF JANUARY 15

Receipts	Payments				
	Canada	United Kingdom	Germany	Mexico	Total
Canada	—	1.2	2.0	0.0	3.2
United Kingdom	0.0	—	1.1	0.1	1.2
Germany	0.5	0.0	—	0.0	0.5
Mexico	0.2	0.1	0.0	—	0.3
Total	0.7	1.3	3.1	0.1	5.2

million and receive $0.5 million, so it has a shortage of $2.6 million and, finally, the Mexican subsidiary will pay $0.1 million and receive $0.3 million, so it has a surplus of $0.2 million. The parent financial managers determine the net payer or receiver position of each subsidiary for the weekly netting. Only these net amounts are transferred within the firm. The firm does not have to change $0.7 million worth of Canadian dollars into the currencies of Germany and Mexico to settle the payable of the Canadian subsidiary and then convert $3.2 million worth of pounds, marks, and pesos into Canadian dollars. Only the net cash surplus flowing to the Canadian subsidiary of $2.5 million must be converted into Canadian dollars.

So far we have considered netting when the currency flows occur at the same time. What if the payments and receipts are not for the same date? Suppose in our Oklahoma Instruments example that the Can$3 million payable is due on October 1, and the Can$2 million receivable is due September 1. Netting could still occur by *leading* or *lagging* currency flows. The sales subsidiary could lag its Can$2 million payment by 1 month, or the Can$3 million could lead 1 month and be paid on September 1. Leads and lags increase the flexibility of parent financial managers, but require excellent information flows between all divisions and headquarters.

INTRAFIRM TRANSFERS

Since the multinational firm is made up of subsidiaries located in different political jurisdictions, transferring funds among divisions of the firm often depends on what governments will allow. Beyond the transfer of cash, as covered in the last section, the firm will have goods and services moving between subsidiaries. The price that one subsidiary charges another subsidiary for internal goods transfers is called a *transfer price*. The choice of transfer prices can be a sensitive internal corporate issue because it helps to determine how total firm profits are allocated across divisions. Governments are also interested in transfer pricing since the prices at which goods are transferred will determine tariff and tax revenues.

The parent firm always has an incentive to minimize taxes by pricing transfers in order to keep profits low in high-tax countries and by shifting profits to subsidiaries in low-tax countries. This is

done by having intrafirm purchases by the high-tax subsidiary made at artificially high prices, while intrafirm sales by the high-tax subsidiary are made at artificially low prices.

Governments often restrict the ability of multinationals to use transfer pricing to minimize taxes. The U.S. Internal Revenue Code requires *arm's-length pricing* between subsidiaries—charging prices that an unrelated buyer and seller would willingly pay. When tariffs are collected on the value of trade, the multinational has the incentive to assign artificially low prices on goods moving between subsidiaries. Customs officials may determine that a shipment is being "underinvoiced" and may assign a value that more truly reflects the market value of the goods.

Transfer pricing may also be used for "window-dressing"—that is, to improve the apparent profitability of a subsidiary. This may be done to allow the subsidiary to borrow at more favorable terms since its credit rating will be revised with the increased profitability. The higher profits can be created by paying the subsidiary artificially high prices for its products in intrafirm transactions.

The firm that uses transfer pricing to shift profits from one subsidiary to another introduces an additional problem for financial control. It is important that the firm be able to evaluate each subsidiary on the basis of its contribution to corporate income. Any artificial distortion of profits should be accounted for so that corporate resources are efficiently allocated.

CAPITAL BUDGETING

Capital budgeting refers to the evaluation of prospective investment alternatives and the commitment of funds to preferred projects. Such long-term commitments of funds expected to provide cash flows extending beyond 1 year are called *capital expenditures*. Capital expenditures are made to acquire *capital assets*, like machines or factories or whole companies. Since such long-term commitments often involve large sums of money, careful planning is required to determine which capital assets to acquire. Plans for capital expenditures are usually summarized in a *capital budget*.

The multinational firm considering foreign investment opportunities faces a more complex problem than the domestic firm. Foreign projects involve foreign exchange risk, political risk, and

foreign tax regulations. Comparing projects in different countries requires a consideration of how all factors will change over countries.

There are several alternative approaches to capital budgeting. A useful approach for multinational firms is the adjusted present value approach. We work with *present value* because the value of a dollar to be received today is worth more than a dollar to be received in the future, say 1 year from now. As a result, we must discount future cash flows to reflect the fact that the present value today will fall according to how long it takes before the cash flows are realized. The appendix to this chapter reviews present value calculations for those readers unfamiliar with the concept.

For multinational firms, the adjusted present value approach of Donald Lessard is presented here as an appropriate tool for capital budgeting decisions. The *adjusted present value* (APV) measures total present value as the sum of the present values of the basic cash flows estimated to result from the investment (operations flows) plus all financial effects related to the investment. Or

$$\text{APV} = -I + \sum_{t=1}^{T} \frac{\text{CF}_t}{(1+d)^t} + \sum_{t=1}^{T} \frac{\text{FIN}_t}{(1+df)^t} \tag{12.1}$$

where $-I$ is the initial investment or cash outlay, Σ is the summation operator, t indicates time or year when cash flows are realized (t extends from year 1 to year T, where T is the final year), CF_t represents estimated basic cash flows in year t resulting from project operations, d is the discount rate on those cash flows, FIN_t is any additional financial effect on cash flows in year t (these will be discussed shortly), and df is the discount rate applied to the financial effects.

CF_t should be estimated on an after-tax basis. Problems of estimation include deciding whether cash flows should be those directed to the subsidiary housing the project, or only those flows remitted to the parent company. The appropriate combination of cash flows can reduce the taxes of the parent and subsidiary.

Several possible financing effects should be included in FIN_t. These may include depreciation charges arising from the capital expenditure, financial subsidies or concessionary credit terms extended to the subsidiary by a government or official agency, deferred or reduced taxes given as incentive to undertake the expendi-

ture, or a new ability to circumvent exchange controls on remittances.

Each of the flows in Equation (12.1) is discounted to the present. The appropriate discount rate should reflect the uncertainty associated with the flow. CF_t is not known with certainty and could fluctuate over the life of the project. Furthermore, the nominal cash flows from operations will change over time as inflation changes. One approach is to estimate CF_t in *real* terms, removing the effect of inflation. Then a real interest rate can be used to discount the flows. The discount rate could be the risk-free rate plus a risk premium that reflects the systematic risk of the project.

The financial terms in FIN_t are likely to be fixed in nominal terms over time. In this case, current market interest rates may be acceptable as discount rates.

Consider this example to illustrate the APV approach to capital budgeting decisions. Suppose Midas Gold Extractors has an opportunity to enter a small developing country and apply its new gold recovery technique to some old mines that no longer yield profitable amounts of ore under conventional mining. Midas estimates that the cost of establishing the foreign operation will be $10 million. The project is expected to last for two years, during which the operating cash flows from the new gold extracted will be $7.5 million per year. In addition, the new operating unit will allow Midas to repatriate an additional $1 million per year in funds that have been tied up in the developing country by capital controls. If Midas applies a discount rate of 6 percent to operating cash flows and 10 percent to the funds that will be freed from controls, then the APV is:

$$\text{APV} = -10 + 7.5/(1.06) + 7.5/(1.06)^2 + 1/(1.10) + 1/(1.10)^2$$
$$= -10 + 15.49 = 5.49$$

So the adjusted present value of the gold recovery project equals $5.49 million. The firm can compare this value to the APV of other projects it is considering in order to budget its capital expenditures in the optimum manner.

Capital budgeting is an imprecise science, and forecasting future cash flows is sometimes viewed as more art than science. The typical firm experiments with several alternative scenarios to test the sensitivity of the budgeting decision to different assumptions.

One of the key assumptions in projects considered for unstable countries is the level of political risk that must be accounted for. Cash flows should be adjusted for the threat of loss resulting from government expropriation or regulation. Chapter 13 will consider the issue of political risk in detail.

SUMMARY

1. Financial control is used to monitor the firm's operations.
2. The choice of a financial control system is determined by the management style of the firm.
3. Cash management aims to utilize the firm's liquid assets efficiently.
4. Netting is the consolidation of payables and receivables in a currency so that only the difference between them must be bought or sold.
5. A transfer price is the price paid by one subsidiary to another for goods transfers within the firm.
6. Transfer prices may be used to shift profits among subsidiaries or lower tariffs.
7. Plans for capital expenditures are summarized in a capital budget.
8. Adjusted present value is a project evaluation approach that separates operations cash flows from financing effects on cash flow.

EXERCISES

1. Suppose that the Japanese firm Sanpo will receive from its U.S. sales subsidiary $1.5 million on June 3. Moreover, on June 3, a U.S. bank is due a $2.3 million repayment of a loan from Sanpo. Explain how netting by Sanpo would apply to this example, and what the advantages are.
2. What could be done if question 1 is modified so that Sanpo owes the $2.3 million on June 13, but the $1.5 million receivable is still scheduled for June 3?
3. Give an example of how transfer pricing can be used to
   a. Shift profits to a low-tax subsidiary in Ireland.
   b. Reduce the tariff on a shipment of computer parts from a subsidiary in Taiwan to a subsidiary in Brazil.
   c. Increase profits in a French subsidiary that is applying for a loan soon.
4. What is arm's-length pricing?
5. Why are capital budgeting decisions made using present values when the cash flows will not be realized until future periods?
6. Suppose that a U.S. multinational firm estimates that a $150 million capital expenditure in a new plant in an unstable developing country will have a life of 2 years before it is confiscated by the foreign government. During this 2-year period, the operating cash flows will be $100 million each year. In addition, the firm will be able to use the new facility to repatriate $10 million each year in funds that have been held in the country involuntarily. If the discount rate for the operations cash flows is 10 percent and the discount rate for the exchange control avoidance is 8 percent, what is the adjusted present value of the project?

REFERENCES

Lessard, Donald R., "Evaluating Foreign Projects: An Adjusted Present Value Approach," in Donald R. Lessard, ed., *International Financial Management.* New York: Wiley, 1985.

Oppenheim, Peter K., *International Banking,* Washington: American Bankers Association, 1991.

Rao, Ramesh K. S., *Financial Management.* New York: Macmillan, 1987.

Rodriguez, Rita M., and E. Eugene Carter, *International Financial Management.* Englewood Cliffs, N.J.: Prentice-Hall, 1984.

APPENDIX: PRESENT VALUE

What would you pay today to receive $1000 in 1 year? The answer will vary from individual to individual, but we would all want to pay less than $1000 today. How much less depends on the *discount rate*—a measure, like an interest rate or rate of return, that we would use to discount to the present the $1000 to be received in 1 year.

Suppose that I require a 10 percent return on all my investments. Then one way of viewing present value is as the principal amount today that when invested at 10 percent simple interest would be worth $1000 when the principal and interest are summed after 1 year. To find the required principal amount, we divide the future value (FV) of $1000 by 1 plus the discount rate (d) of 10 percent, or the present value (PV) formula, which is

$$PV = \frac{FV}{1 + d} = \frac{\$1000}{1.10} = \$909.09 \qquad (12A.1)$$

I would pay $909.09 for the right to receive $1000 in 1 year. Another way of stating this is to say that the present value of $1000 to be received in 1 year is $909.09.

For amounts to be received at some year *n* in the future, the formula is modified to

$$PV = \frac{FV}{(1 + d)^n} \qquad (12A.2)$$

In the example just used, the $1000 is received in 1 year, so *n* equals 1. What if the $1000 is to be received in 2 years? Then the formula gives us

$$PV = \frac{1000}{(1 + 0.1)^2} = \frac{\$1000}{(1.10)(1.10)} \tag{12A.3}$$

$$= \frac{\$1000}{1.21} = \$826.45$$

The present value of $1000 to be received in 2 years is $826.45. The farther into the future we go, the lower the present value of any future value. Furthermore, the higher the discount rate, the lower the present value of any future value to be received.

If a capital outlay will generate a stream of earnings to be received over many years, we simply sum the present value of each individual year to obtain the present value of the future cash flows associated with the expenditure. Then we subtract the initial investment or cash outflow to find the present value of the project. If Σ is the summation operator and t denotes time (like years), then the present value of an investment of I dollars today yielding cash flows of CF_t over each year t in the future for T years is

$$PV = -I + \sum_{t=1}^{T} \frac{CF_t}{(1 + d)^t} \tag{12A.4}$$

If we can estimate the after-tax cash flows (CF_t) associated with a capital expenditure (I) today, and we can choose an appropriate discount rate (d), then the present value of the project is indicated by Equation (12A.4).

chapter 13

The International
Money Market

The foreign exchange market is a market in which monies are traded. Money serves as a means of paying for goods and services, and the foreign exchange market exists to facilitate international payments. Just as there exists a need for international money payments, there also is a need for international credit or deposits and loans denominated in different currencies. The international deposit and loan market is often called the *Eurocurrency market,* and banks that accept these deposits and make loans are often called *Eurobanks.*

The use of the prefix *Euro,* as in Eurocurrency or Eurobank, is misleading since the activity described is related to *offshore banking* (providing foreign currency borrowing and lending services) in general and is in no way limited to Europe. For instance, the Eurodollar market originally referred to dollar banking outside the United States. But now Eurodollar banking also occurs in the United States. The Euroyen market involves yen-denominated bank deposits and loans outside Japan. Similarly, there are Euromarks, Eurosterling, and Eurofrancs.

The distinguishing feature of the Eurocurrency market is that the currency used in the banking transaction generally differs from the domestic currency of the country in which the bank is located. This is not strictly true, as there may exist some international bank-

ing activity in domestic currency. Where such international banking occurs, it is segregated from other domestic currency banking activities in regard to regulations applied to such transactions. As we learn in the next section, offshore banking activities have grown rapidly because of a lack of regulation, which allows greater efficiency in providing banking services.

ORIGINS OF OFFSHORE BANKING

The Eurodollar market began in the late 1950s. Why and how the market originated have been subjects of debate, but it appears that certain elements are agreed upon. Given the reserve currency status of the dollar, it was only reasonable that the first external money market to develop would be for dollars. Some argue that the Communist countries were the source of early dollar balances held in Europe, since these countries needed dollars from time to time but did not want to hold these dollars in U.S. banks for fear of reprisal should hostilities flare up. Thus, the dollar deposits in U.K. and French banks owned by the Communists would represent the first Eurodollar deposits.

Aside from political considerations, the Eurobanks developed as a result of profit considerations. Since costly regulations are imposed on U.S. banks, banks located outside the United States could offer higher interest rates on deposits and lower interest rates on loans than their U.S. competitors. For instance, U.S. banks are forced to hold a fraction of their deposits in the form of non-interest-bearing reserves. Because Eurobanks are essentially unregulated and hold much smaller reserves than their U.S. counterparts, they can offer narrower spreads on dollars. The *spread* is the difference between the deposit and loan interest rate. Besides reserve requirements, Eurobanks also benefit from having no government-mandated interest rate controls, no deposit insurance, no government-mandated credit allocations, no restrictions on entry of new banks (thus encouraging greater competition and efficiency), and low taxes. This does not mean that the countries hosting the Eurobanks do not use such regulations. What we observe in these countries are two sets of banking rules: various regulations and restrictions apply to banking in the domestic currency,

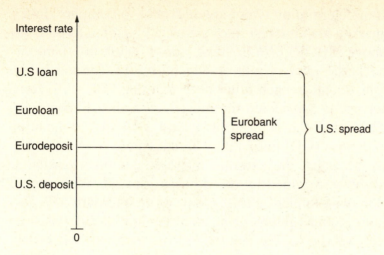

FIGURE 13.1 Comparison of U.S. and Eurodollar spreads.

whereas offshore banking activities in foreign currencies go largely unregulated.

Figure 13.1 portrays the standard relationship between the U.S. domestic loan and deposit rates and the Euroloan and Eurodeposit rates. The figure illustrates that U.S. spreads exceed Eurobank spreads. Eurobanks are able to offer a lower rate on dollar loans and a higher rate on dollar deposits than their U.S. competitors. Without these differences, the Eurodollar market would not likely exist, since Eurodollar transactions, lacking deposit insurance and government supervision, are considered to be riskier than are domestic dollar transactions in the United States. This means that, with respect to the supply of deposits to Eurobanks, the U.S. deposit rate provides an interest rate floor for the Eurodeposit rate, since the supply of deposits to Eurobanks is perfectly elastic at the U.S. deposit rate (this means that if the Eurodeposit rate fell below this rate, Eurobanks would have no dollar deposit). With respect to the demand for loans from Eurobanks, U.S. loan rates provide a ceiling for Euroloan rates because the demand for dollar loans from Eurobanks is perfectly elastic at the U.S. loan rate (any Eurobank charging more than this would find the demand for its loans falling to zero).

When making comparisons of actual loan and deposit interest rates in the United States with those in the Eurobank market, there

is a problem of determining which interest rates to compare. In the Eurodollar market, loan interest rates are usually quoted as percentage points above LIBOR. *LIBOR* stands for "London interbank offer rate" and is the interest rate at which six big London banks would deposit or lend to each other each morning. The U.S. commercial paper rate is considered the most comparable domestic interest rate. The Eurodollar deposit rate is best compared to the large certificate of deposit (CD) rate in the United States.

We have seen that the external interest rates on a particular currency will be constrained by the domestic spread. With capital controls this may no longer be true. Controls on international capital flows could include quotas on foreign lending and deposits or taxes on international capital flows. For instance, if Switzerland limits inflows of foreign money, then we could have a situation where the domestic Swiss deposit interest rate exceeds the external rate on Swiss franc deposits in other nations. Although foreigners would prefer to have their Swiss franc deposits in Swiss banks in order to earn the higher interest, the legal restrictions on capital flows prohibit such a response.

It is also possible that a perceived threat to private property rights could lead to seemingly perverse interest rate relations. If the United States threatens to confiscate foreign deposits, the funds would tend to leave the United States and shift to the external dollar market. This could result in the Eurodollar deposit rate falling below the U.S. deposit rate.

In general, risk contributes to the domestic spread exceeding the external spread. In domestic markets government agencies help ensure the sound performance of domestic financial institutions, whereas the Eurocurrency markets are largely unregulated, with no central bank ready to come to the rescue. There is an additional risk in international transactions in that investment funds are subject to control by the country of currency denomination (when it is time for repayment) as well as the country of the deposit bank. For instance, if a U.S. firm has a U.S. dollar bank deposit in Hong Kong, when the firm wants to withdraw those dollars—say, to pay a debt in Taiwan—not only is the transaction subject to control in Hong Kong (the government may not let foreign exchange leave the country freely), but the United States may control outflows of dollars from the United States, so that the Hong Kong bank may have

difficulty paying back the dollars. It should be recognized that, even though domestic and external deposit and loan rates differ primarily because of risk, all interest rates tend to move together. When the domestic dollar interest rate is rising, the external rate will also tend to rise.

The growth of the Eurodollar market is the result of the narrower spreads offered by Eurobanks. We would expect the size of the market to grow as the total demand for dollar-denominated credit increases and as dollar banking moves from the United States to the external market. The shift of dollar intermediation would occur as the Eurodollar spread narrows relative to the domestic spread or as individual responsiveness to the spread differential changes.

Over time, important external markets have developed for the other major international currencies (mark, franc, pound, yen, Canadian dollar, Swiss franc, and lira). But the value of activity in Eurodollars (which refers to offshore banking in U.S. dollars) dwarfs the rest.

Figure 13.2 illustrates the foreign assets held by banks of different nations. The major role of the United Kingdom, Japan, and the United States in international banking is obvious. Note that the figure distinguishes between bank assets, including interbank claims and credit extended to nonbanks. Interbank claims are deposits held in banks in other countries. If we want to know the actual amount of credit extended to nonbank borrowers, we must remove the interbank activity. Figure 13.2 illustrates the huge size of the interbank market in international finance. An example of interbank deposits versus credit extended to nonbanks is provided later in the chapter.

INTERNATIONAL BANKING FACILITIES

In December 1981, the Federal Reserve permitted U.S. banks to engage in Eurobanking activity on U.S. soil. Prior to this time, U.S. banks engaged in international banking by processing loans and deposits through their offshore branches. Many "shell" bank branches in places like the Cayman Islands or the Bahamas really amounted to nothing more than a small office and a telephone. Yet by using these locations for booking loans and deposits, U.S. banks could

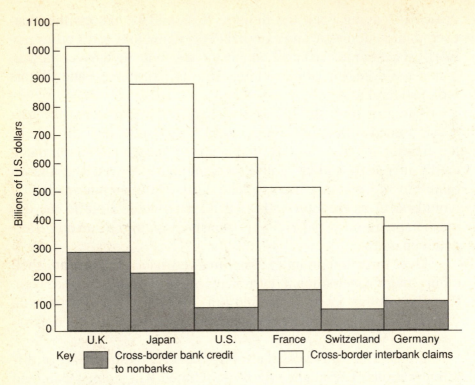

FIGURE 13.2 Deposit banks' foreign assets, by country. (Data are from International Monetary Fund, *International Financial Statistics,* October 1993.)

avoid the reserve requirements and interest rate regulations that applied to normal U.S. banking.

In December 1981, international banking facilities, or *IBFs,* were legalized. IBFs did not involve any new physical presence in U.S. bank offices. Instead, they simply required a different set of books for an existing bank office to record the deposits and loans permitted under the IBF proposal. IBFs are allowed to receive deposits from, and make loans to, nonresidents of the United States or other IBFs. These loans and deposits are kept separate from the rest of the bank's business because IBFs are not subject to reserve requirements, interest rate regulations, or Federal Deposit Insurance Corporation deposit insurance premiums applicable to normal U.S. banking.

The goal of the IBF plan was to allow banking offices in the United States to compete with offshore banks without having to use

an offshore banking office. The location of IBFs reflects the location of banking activity in general. It is not surprising that New York State, as the financial center of the country, has over 75 percent of IBF deposits. Aside from New York, California and Illinois are the only states with a significant IBF business. After IBFs were permitted, several states encouraged their formation by granting low or no taxes on IBF business. The volume of IBF business that resulted mirrored the preexisting volume of international banking activity, with New York dominating the level of activity found in other states.

Since IBFs grew very rapidly following their creation, we may ask where the growth came from. Rather than new business that was stimulated by the existence of IBFs, it appears that much of the growth was a result of shifting business from Caribbean shell branches to IBFs. After the first month of IBF operation, $29.1 billion in claims on foreign residents existed. During this same period, the claims existing at Caribbean branches of U.S. banks fell $23.3 billion. Since this time, IBF growth has continued with growth of Eurodollar banking in general. U.S. IBFs have emerged as a major source of "offshore banking" activity.

OFFSHORE BANKING PRACTICES

The Eurocurrency market handles a tremendous volume of funds. Because of the importance of interbank transactions, the gross measure overstates the actual amount of activity regarding total intermediation of funds between nonbank savers and nonbank borrowers as Figure 13.2 shows. To measure the amount of credit actually extended through the Eurobanks, we use the net size of the market—subtracting interbank activity from total deposits or total loans existing. To understand the difference between the gross and net volume of Eurodollar activity, consider the following example.

Suppose that a U.S. firm, company X, shifts $1 million from its U.S. bank to a Eurobank in order to receive a higher return on its deposits. Table 13.1 shows the T accounts recording this transaction. The U.S. bank now has a liability (recorded on the right-hand side of its balance sheet) of $1 million owed to Eurobank A, since the ownership of a $1 million deposit has shifted from company X to Eurobank A. Eurobank A records the transaction as a $1 million

Table 13.1 COMPANY X DEPOSITS $1 MILLION IN EUROBANK A

U.S. Bank	
Assets	**Liabilities**
	$1 million due Eurobank A

Eurobank A	
Assets	**Liabilities**
$1 million deposit in U.S. bank	$1 million Eurodollar deposit due company X

asset in the form of a deposit it owns in a U.S. bank, plus a $1 million liability from the deposit it has accepted from company X. Now suppose that Eurobank A does not have a borrower waiting for $1 million (U.S.), but another Eurobank, Eurobank B, does have a borrower. Eurobank A will deposit the $1 million with Eurobank B, earning a fraction of a percent greater than it must pay company X for the $1 million. Table 13.2 shows that after Eurobank A deposits in B, the U.S. bank now owes the U.S. dollar deposit to B, which is shown as an asset of Eurobank B matched by the deposit liability of $1 million from B to A.

Finally, in Table 13.3, Eurobank B makes a loan to company Y. Now the U.S. bank has transferred the ownership of its deposit liability to company Y. (Whenever dollars are actually spent following a Eurodollar transaction, the actual dollars must come from the United States—only the United States creates U.S. dollars; the Eurodollar banks simply act as intermediaries.) The gross size of the market is measured as total deposits in Eurobanks, or $2 million ($1 million in Eurobank A and $1 million in B). The net size of the market is found by subtracting interbank deposits, and thus is a measure of the actual credit extended to nonbank users of dollars. In the example, Eurobank A deposited $1 million in Eurobank B. If we subtract this interbank deposit of $1 million from the total Eurobank deposits of $2 million, we find the net size of the market to be $1 million. This $1 million is the value of credit actually intermediated to nonbank borrowers.

Since the Eurodollar market deals with such large magnitudes, it is understandable that economists and politicians are concerned about the effects the Eurodollar market can have on domestic markets. In the United States, overnight Eurodollar deposits are

Table 13.2 EUROBANK A DEPOSITS $1 MILLION IN EUROBANK B

U.S. Bank

Assets	Liabilities
	$1 million due Eurobank B

Eurobank A

Assets	Liabilities
$1 million Eurodollar deposit in Eurobank B	$1 million Eurodollar due company X

Eurobank B

Assets	Liabilities
$1 million deposit in U.S. bank	$1 million Eurodollar deposit due Eurobank A

counted in the M2 definition of the money supply. Longer-term Eurodollar deposits are counted in the M3 definition of the money supply. These alternative measures of the U.S. money supply are used to evaluate the resources available to the public for spending. Eurodollars are not spendable money but, instead, are money substitutes like time deposits in a domestic bank. Because Eurodollars do not serve as a means of payment, Eurobanks are not able to create money as banks can in a domestic setting. Eurobanks are essentially intermediaries; they accept deposits and then loan these deposits.

Even though Eurodollars do not provide a means of payment, they still may have implications for domestic monetary practice. For countries without efficient money markets, access to the very efficient and competitive Eurodollar market may reduce the demand for domestic money.

The efficiency of the Eurodollar market may also have encouraged international capital flows and thus led to a greater need for sterilization on the part of central banks. In Chapter 10 we defined sterilization as a change in the domestic component of base money aimed at offsetting a change in the foreign reserve component. Thus, if international reserve flows are greater due to the international capital flows encouraged by Eurodollar market efficiency, then central banks must engage in larger and more frequent sterilization operations to achieve a given domestic money growth policy.

All banks are interested in maximizing the spread between their deposit and loan interest rates. In this regard, Eurobanks are no different from domestic banks. All banks are also concerned with managing risk, the risk associated with their assets and liabilities. Concerning risk management, we find interesting differences between Eurobanks and domestic banks. In the Eurodollar market there was a period in the 1970s when the great bulk of deposits came from the Organization of Petroleum Exporting Countries (OPEC), the oil-exporting nations. If one of these countries withdrew a large amount of funds from the market, there would be large costs for Eurobanks that did not have their assets and liabilities matched on a term basis. Like all intermediaries, Eurobanks tend to borrow short term and lend long term. Thus, if the deposit liabilities were reduced greatly, we would see deposit interest rates rise very rapidly in the short run. The advantage of matching the term

structures of deposits and loans is that deposits and loans are maturing at the same time so that the bank is better able to respond to a change in demand for deposits or loans.

Deposits in the Eurocurrency market are for fixed terms, ranging from days to years, although most are for less than 6 months. Certificates of deposit are considered to be the closest domestic counterpart to a Eurocurrency deposit. Loans in the Eurocurrency market can range up to 10 or more years. The interest rate on a Eurocurrency loan is usually stated as some spread over LIBOR and is adjusted at fixed intervals, like every 3 months. These adjustable interest rates serve to minimize the interest rate risk to the bank. Although LIBOR is the dominant pricing tool, the second-most popular pricing mechanism is the U.S. prime rate; at this rate, the borrower pays according to the lower of the two rates at the time interest is due.

Large loans are generally made by syndicates of Eurobanks. The syndicate will be headed by a lead or managing bank; other banks wishing to participate in the loan will join the syndicate and help fund the loan. By allowing banks to reduce their level of participation in any loan, syndicates can participate in more loans so that such diversification reduces their risk of loss.

INTERNATIONAL DEBT

During the 1970s banks were flush with *petrodollars,* since the OPEC nations deposited huge sums of dollars in the Eurobanks. The banks, in turn, lent these dollars, generated by the OPEC balance-of-payments surplus, to deficit nations; this is often referred to as *petrodollar recycling.* By 1982 many of these loans began to sour because the developing countries found themselves overextended. Table 13.4 presents estimates of the burden this external debt placed on the major LDC (less developed country) borrowers.

Recalling that exports provide the foreign exchange earnings needed to repay the debt, we note, upon examining the columns of Table 13.4 on debt as a percent of exports, the predicaments into which many of these countries had fallen. The only way that Argentina or Brazil could service their existing debt was to borrow more until their export earnings increased or interest rates fell, lowering their interest payments (remember, these are vari-

Table 13.4 EXTERNAL DEBT-TO-EXPORT RATIOS: AVERAGE GROSS EXTERNAL DEBT AS PERCENT OF EXPORTS OF GOODS, SERVICES, AND PRIVATE TRANSFERS

	1982	1984	1986	1988	1991	Commercial bank claims outstanding, end of 1988 (billion dollars)
Argentina	405	482	561	480	433	30.4
Brazil	339	331	425	305	325	67.6
Chile	333	409	370	217	154	11.0
Colombia	191	223	214	232	168	6.0
Ecuador	239	271	337	395	363	5.5
Mexico	299	284	406	302	224	63.4
Nigeria	84	149	336	397	257	6.7
Peru	269	311	441	477	484	5.3
Philippines	269	289	308	256	216	10.8
Venezuela	84	195	291	270	187	26.6

Source: World Debt Tables, 1989–90, First Supplement. Washington, D.C.: The World Bank, 1990; and *World Development Report 1993,* New York: Oxford, 1993

able interest rate loans). In cases where the debt is simply too burdensome to repay, the debt is rescheduled. (It seems that no country defaults anymore; they reschedule the repayment of the debt instead.)

One of the most important arenas for debt rescheduling in recent years has been the Paris Club, which is not an official organization with a continuous life. The term *Paris Club* refers to irregular meetings of creditor governments (typically the Western developed countries) with debtor nations. When creditor countries will extend no further loans so that a nation is in danger of default on existing debt, the debtor may contact the French government and request a meeting with the debtor's official creditors. There appears no special reason for holding such meetings in Paris beyond the tradition of meeting there because of the French willingness to host such activities. The debtor must apply for a standby credit arrangement with the IMF before the meeting is held. The Paris Club meeting involves negotiations between the debtor and creditor governments for rescheduling repayment in terms of both timing and costs. Table 13.5 provides an example of the Paris Club reschedulings that occurred in the midst of the debt crisis. Since

Table 13.5 PARIS CLUB DEBT RESCHEDULINGS IN 1984

Country	Agreement signed	Repayment period	Amount of debt rescheduled ($)
Sierra Leone	2/8/84	12/31/89–12/31/94	10 million
Madagascar	3/23/84	9/30/89–3/31/95	170 million
Sudan	5/3/84	1/1/91–7/1/00	260 million
Ivory Coast	5/4/84	12/31/88–6/30/93	310 million
Yugoslavia	5/22/84	12/31/88–6/30/91	750 million
Peru	6/5/84	6/15/90–12/15/93	600 million
Togo	6/6/84	2/28/90–8/31/94	140 million
Jamaica	7/16/84	2/15/89–8/15/93	100 million
Cuba	7/19/84	7/1/89–7/1/93	200 million
Zambia	7/20/84	12/31/89–6/30/94	200 million
Ecuador	7/28/84	5/31/87–11/30/91	180 million
Mozambique	10/25/84	6/30/90–12/31/95	350 million
Niger	11/30/84	11/1/90–5/1/95	25 million
Liberia	12/17/84	6/30/90–12/31/94	15 million
Philippines	12/20/84	3/15/91–9/15/95	1280 million

Source: Alexis Rieffel, "The Role of the Paris Club in Managing Debt Problems," *Princeton Essays in International Finance,* No. 161, December 1985.

1980, 55 countries have rescheduled debts through the Paris Club totaling $209 billion.

Aside from Paris Club reschedulings of debts owed to governments, debts owned to commercial banks have also been rescheduled. In these cases, commercial banks form committees to negotiate with the debtor. In addition to extending debt repayment and revising loan terms, commercial banks have also become involved in exchanging developing country debt for equity in commercial projects in these debtor countries. *Debt-equity swaps* involve an exchange of debt for the debtor's domestic currency, which is then used to purchase an ownership position in a debtor country business.

The existence of debt-equity swaps has stimulated the growth of a secondary market in which creditor commercial banks may sell their developing country debt. The buyers in this market can then trade this debt for an equity position in the debtor country. This market has remained quite small, accounting for as little as 1 or 2 percent of total developing country debt held by commercial banks. The "thinness" of the market can result in a single buyer or seller

"moving the market"—that is, with a relatively small market size, a single large order to buy debt could increase the price of the debt. According to one broker cited in *Euromoney,* Citibank once bought $62 million of Mexican debt for Nissan to swap for an auto manufacturing plant in Mexico. The purchase of this quantity of debt moved the market price of the debt more than 3 percent.

Debt-equity swaps rarely occur at the face value of the debt. The secondary market price of developing country debt is discounted from the face value. Table 13.6 provides an indication of the range of the prices at which debt was traded in 1992. Peruvian debt sold for 15 to 17 cents on the dollar because Peru had decided arbitrarily to stop (without negotiation) repaying its debt. The prices in

Table 13.6 SECONDARY MARKET LDC SOVEREIGN DEBT PRICES

Country	Bid	Offer
Algeria	87.00	90.00
Argentina	49.63	49.88
Bolivia	12.00	14.00
Brazil	33.75	33.88
Bulgaria	17.00	19.00
Chile	90.00	92.00
Colombia	75.00	85.00
Costa Rica	58.50	59.38
Cote d'Ivoire	7.88	8.50
Ecuador	31.25	31.75
Honduras	27.00	28.00
Jamaica	74.00	75.00
Mexico	84.25	84.50
Morocco	47.63	47.88
Nigeria	40.75	41.13
Panama	30.50	31.50
Peru	15.00	17.00
Philippines	58.75	59.00
Poland	23.00	23.25
Sudan	1.00	4.00
Uruguay	70.00	75.00
Venezuela	71.00	73.00
Yugoslavia	22.00	25.00
Zaire	9.00	11.00

Source: LDC Debt Report, June 29, 1992, p. 2.

Table 13.6 reflect the risk of nonpayment. The higher the probability of the debt not being repaid, the lower the value of the debt. Even if commercial bank willingness to sell developing country debt increased, the size of the debt-equity swap market is likely to remain small unless investment opportunities in these countries increase.

IMF CONDITIONALITY

The IMF has been an important source of funding for debtor nations experiencing repayment problems. Earlier we saw that debtors cannot approach a Paris Club rescheduling without a standby loan agreement with the IMF. The importance of an IMF loan is more than simply the IMF "bailing out" commercial bank and government creditors. The IMF requires borrowers to adjust their economic policies to reduce balance-of-payments deficits and improve the chance for debt repayment. Such IMF-required adjustment programs are known as *IMF conditionality*.

Part of the process of developing a loan package includes a visit to the borrowing country by an IMF "mission." The mission comprises economists who review the causes of the country's economic problems and recommend solutions. Through negotiation with the borrower, a program of conditions attached to the loan is agreed to. The conditions usually involve targets for macroeconomic variables, such as money supply growth or the government deficit. The loan is disbursed at intervals with a possible cutoff of new disbursements if the conditions have not been met.

The importance of IMF conditionality to creditors can now be understood. Loans to sovereign governments involve risk management from the lenders' point of view just as loans to private entities do. Although countries cannot go out of business, they can have revolutions or political upheaval leading to a repudiation of the debts incurred by the previous regime. Even without such drastic political change, countries may not be able or willing to service their debt due to adverse economic conditions. International lending adds a new dimension to risk since there is neither an international court of law to enforce contracts nor a loan collateral aside from assets that the borrowing country may have in the lending country. The IMF serves as an overseer that can offer debtors new loans if they agree to conditions. Sovereign governments may be offended if a foreign creditor government or commercial bank

suggests changes in the debtor's domestic policy, but the IMF is a multinational organization of 178 countries. The members of the IMF mission to the debtor nation will be of many different nationalities, and their advice will be nonpolitical. However, the IMF is still criticized at times as being dominated by the interests of the advanced industrial countries. In terms of voting power, this is true.

Votes in the IMF determine policy, and voting power is determined by a country's "quota." The quota is the financial contribution of a country to the IMF and it entitles membership. Table 13.7 lists the quotas of countries. Each country receives 250 votes plus one additional vote for each SDR100,000 of its quota. (At least 75 percent of the quota may be contributed in domestic currency with less than 25 percent paid in reserve currencies or SDRs.) Table 13.7 indicates that the United States has the most votes, since the U.S. quota accounts for almost 20 percent of the total fund. Then come Japan and Germany with 5.7 percent of the total, followed by the U.K. and France with 5.1 percent of the total. These five developed countries contribute more than 40 percent of the IMF quotas and dominate voting accordingly.

The IMF has been criticized for imposing conditions that restrict economic growth and lower living standards in borrowing countries. The typical conditionality involves reducing government spending, raising taxes, and restricting money growth. For example, in July 1986, Mexico signed a $1.6 billion loan agreement with the IMF that included the following conditions: the budget deficit would fall by 3 percentage points over the next 18 months, monetary growth should be restricted to reduce capital flight, nominal interest rates should exceed the inflation rate, and the deductibility of business expenses should fall to increase the tax base. Such policies may be interpreted as austerity imposed by the IMF, but the austerity is intended for the borrowing government in order to permit the productive private sector to play a larger role in the economy.

The view of the IMF is that adjustment programs are unavoidable in debtor countries facing repayment difficulties. The adjustments required are those that promote long-run growth. While there may indeed be short-run costs of adjusting to a smaller role for government and fewer and smaller government subsidies in the long run, the required adjustments should stimulate growth to allow debt repayment.

Table 13.7 IMF QUOTAS[1]

Member	Quota (million SDRs)	Member	Quota (million SDRs)	Member	Quota (million SDRs)
Afghanistan, Islamic		Czech Republic	589.6	Kiribati	4.0
State of	120.4	Denmark	1,069.9	Korea	799.6
Albania	35.3	Djibouti	11.5	Kuwait	995.2
Algeria	914.4	Dominica	6.0	Kyrgyz Republic	64.5
Angola	207.3	Dominican Republic	158.8		
Antigua and				Lao People's	
Barbuda	8.5	Ecuador	219.2	Dem. Rep.	39.1
		Egypt	678.4	Latvia	91.5
Argentina	1,537.1	El Salvador	125.6	Lebanon	78.7
Armenia	67.5	Equatorial Guinea	24.3	Lesotho	23.9
Australia	2,333.2	Estonia	46.5	Liberia	71.3
Austria	1,188.3				
Azerbaijan	117.0	Ethiopia	98.3	Libya	817.6
		Fiji	51.1	Lithuania	103.5
Bahamas, The	94.9	Finland	861.8	Luxembourg	135.5
Bahrain	82.8	France	7,414.6	Macedonia,	
Bangladesh	392.5	Gabon	110.3	former Yugoslav	
Barbados	48.9			Republic of	49.6
Belarus	280.4	Gambia, The	22.9	Madagascar	90.4
		Georgia	111.0		
Belgium	3,102.3	Germany	8,241.5	Malawi	50.9
Belize	13.5	Ghana	274.0	Malaysia	832.7
Benin	45.3	Greece	587.6	Maldives	5.5
Bhutan	4.5			Mali	68.9
Bolivia	126.2	Grenada	8.5	Malta	67.5
		Guatemala	153.8		
Botswana	36.6	Guinea	78.7	Marshall Islands	2.5
Brazil	2,170.8	Guinea-Bissau	10.5	Mauritania	47.5
Bulgaria	464.9	Guyana	67.2	Mauritius	73.3
Burkina Faso	44.2			Mexico	1,753.3
Burundi	57.2	Haiti	44.1	Micronesia,	
		Honduras	95.0		
Cambodia	25.0	Hungary	754.8	Moldova	90.0
Cameroon	135.1	Iceland	85.3	Mongolia	37.1
Canada	4,320.3	India	3,055.5	Morocco	427.7
Cape Verde	7.0			Mozambique	84.0
Central African Rep.	41.2	Indonesia	1,497.6	Myanmar	184.9
		Iran, Islamic			
Chad	41.3	Rep. of	1,078.5	Namibia	99.6
Chile	621.7	Iraq	504.0	Nepal	52.0
China	3,385.2	Ireland	525.0	Netherlands	3,444.2
Colombia	561.3	Israel	666.2	New Zealand	650.1
Comoros	6.5			Nicaragua	96.1
		Italy	4,590.7		
Congo,		Jamaica	200.9	Niger	48.3
People's Republic of	57.9	Japan	8,241.5	Nigeria	1,281.6
Costa Rica	119.0	Jordan	121.7	Norway	1,104.6
Côte d'Ivoire	238.2	Kazakhstan	247.5	Oman	119.4
Croatia	261.6			Pakistan	758.2
Cyprus	100.0	Kenya	199.4		

Table 13.7 IMF (Continued)

Member	Quota (million SDRs)	Member	Quota (million SDRs)	Member	Quota (million SDRs)
Panama	149.6	Singapore	357.6	Tunisia	206.0
Papua New Guinea	95.3	Slovak Republic	257.4	Turkey	642.0
Paraguay	72.1	Slovenia	150.5	Turkmenistan	48.0
Peru	466.1	Solomon Islands	7.5	Uganda	133.9
Philippines	633.4	Somalia	44.2	Ukraine	997.3
Poland	988.5	South Africa	1,365.4	United Arab Emirates	392.1
Portugal	557.6	Spain	1,935.4	United Kingdom	7,414.6
Qatar	190.5	Sri Lanka	303.6	United States	26,526.8
Romania	754.1	Sudan	169.7	Uruguay	225.3
Russian Federation	4,313.1	Suriname	67.6	Uzbekistan	199.5
Rwanda	59.5	Swaziland	36.5	Vanuatu	12.5
St. Kitts and Nevis	6.5	Sweden	1,614.0	Venezuela	1,951.3
St. Lucia	11.0	Switzerland	2,470.4	Viet Nam	241.6
St. Vincent and		Syrian Arab Republic	209.9	Western Samoa	8.5
the Grenadines	6.0	Tajikistan	40.0	Yemen,	
San Marino	10.0			Republic of	176.5
		Tanzania	146.9		
Sao Tome and Principe	5.5	Thailand	573.9	Zaïre	291.0
Saudi Arabia	5,130.6	Togo	54.3	Zambia	270.3
Senegal	118.9	Tonga	5.0	Zimbabwe	261.3
Seychelles	6.0	Trinidad and Tobago	246.8		
Sierra Leone	57.9				

Quotas are those in effect on October 13, 1993. As of this date, 10 members had not yet paid for their quota increases under the Ninth General Review of Quotas; the quotas listed for these members are those determined under the Eigth General Review. These members (with their Ninth Review quotas, in millions of SDRs, appearing in parentheses) are as follows: Haiti (60.7), Iraq (864.8), Lebanon (146.0) Liberia (96.2), Sierra Leone (77.2), Somolia (60.9), Sudan (233.1), Tajikstan (60.0), Zaïre (394.8), and Zambia (363.5).

COUNTRY RISK ANALYSIS

International financial activity involves risks that are missing in domestic transactions. There are no international courts to enforce contracts and a bank cannot repossess a nation's collateral, because typically no collateral is pledged. Problem loans to sovereign governments have received most of the "debt problem" publicity, but it is important to realize that loans to private firms can also become nonperforming because of capital controls or exchange rate policies. In this regard, even operating subsidiary units in foreign countries may not be able to transfer funds to the parent multinational firm if foreign exchange controls block the transfer of funds.

It is important for commercial banks and multinational firms to be able to assess the risks involved in international deals. Country risk analysis has become an important part of international

business. *Country risk analysis* refers to the evaluation of the overall political and financial situation in a country and the extent to which these conditions may affect the country's ability to repay its debts. In determining the degree of risk associated with a particular country, we should consider both qualitative and quantitative factors. The qualitative factors include the political stability of the country. Certain key features may indicate political uncertainty:

1. Splits between different language, ethnic, and religious groups that threaten to undermine stability.
2. Extreme nationalism and aversion to foreigners that may lead to preferential treatment of local interests and nationalization of foreign holdings.
3. Unfavorable social conditions, including extremes of wealth.
4. Conflicts in society evidenced by frequency of demonstrations, violence, and guerrilla war.
5. The strength and organization of radical groups.

Besides the qualitative or political factors, we also want to consider the financial factors that allow an evaluation of a country's ability to repay its debts. Country risk analysts examine factors such as these:

1. *External debt.* Specifically, this is the debt owed to foreigners as a fraction of GDP or foreign exchange earnings. If a country's debts appear to be relatively large, then the country may have future repayment problems.
2. *International reserve holdings.* These reserves indicate the ability of a country to meet its short-term international trade needs should its export earnings fall. The ratio of international reserves to imports is used to rank countries according to their liquidity.
3. *Exports.* Exports are looked at in terms of the foreign exchange earned as well as the diversity of the products exported. Countries that depend largely on one or two products to earn foreign exchange may be more susceptible to

wide swings in export earnings than countries with a diversified group of export products.

4. *Economic growth.* Measured by the growth of real GDP or real per capita GDP, economic growth may serve as an indicator of general economic conditions within a country.

Although no method of assessing country risk is foolproof, by evaluating and comparing countries on the basis of some structured approach international lenders have a base on which they can build their subjective evaluations of whether to extend credit to a particular country.

Institutional Investor magazine surveys international bankers twice a year seeking their evaluation of country creditworthiness. The bankers are asked to rank each country on a scale from zero (for least creditworthy) to 100 (for most creditworthy). Bankers are not permitted to rank their home countries. Table 13.8 provides the results from a recent survey. It is interesting that the United States had always been the top-ranked country until the September 1986 survey when Japan passed the United States. Bankers argued that the persistent large budget deficit and trade deficit of the United States lowered its standing. Still, all of the countries at the top of the list are good risks to which banks readily extend new credit. Those countries at the bottom would find new commercial bank lending practically impossible to attract.

SUMMARY

1. The international bank deposit and loan market is called the Eurocurrency market.
2. Eurobanking grew because it is less regulated and permits greater efficiency.
3. International banking facilities (IBFs) are departments of U.S. banks that are permitted to engage in Eurocurrency banking.
4. The net size of the Eurodollar market measures the amount of credit actually extended to nonbanks.
5. Large Eurocurrency loans are made by bank syndicates.
6. Sovereign loans are rescheduled with creditor governments in the Paris Club.
7. A secondary market in developing country debt has encouraged the development of debt-equity swaps in debtor countries.
8. IMF loans come with conditions that require the debtor country to adjust its economy to increase the likelihood of repayment.
9. Country risk analysis involves a consideration of both economic and political factors.

TABLE 13.8 INSTITUTIONAL INVESTOR'S 1993 COUNTRY CREDIT RATINGS

Rank March 1993	Rank Sept. 1993	Country	Institutional Investor Credit Rating	Six-month Change	One-year Change	Rank March 1993	Rank Sept. 1993	Country	Institutional Investor Credit Rating	Six-month Change	One-year Change
1	1	Switzerland	92.0	0.0	0.2	62	69	Algeria	27.1	-1.0	-1.7
2	2	Japan	91.7	0.7	1.0	66	70	Zimbabwe	26.9	-0.8	0.8
3	3	Germany	89.8	-0.5	0.0	71	71	Costa Rica	26.8	2.0	3.1
5	4	United States	89.2	0.6	2.1	74	72	Ghana	26.0	1.8	5.7
4	5	Netherlands	88.8	-0.4	0.7	70	73	Sri Lanka	25.5	0.0	1.4
6	6	France	88.2	0.6	2.4	77	74	Swaziland	24.5	2.3	5.2
8	7	United Kingdom	85.4	0.7	0.8	73	75	Romania	24.4	0.2	-0.4
7	8	Austria	85.3	0.0	1.0	72	76	Kenya	23.0	-1.7	-1.3
9	9	Luxembourg	84.6	0.1	1.4	76	77	Syria	22.7	0.2	2.9
10	10	Canada	82.0	-0.1	0.4	80	78	Nepal	22.1	0.4	0.3
12	11	Singapore	80.9	0.7	2.7	78	79	Jamaica	21.9	0.0	1.9
11	12	Belgium	79.8	-0.6	0.1	84	80	Seychelles	21.4	0.7	6.0
14	13*	Norway	78.1	0.9	2.1	79	81*	Cameroon	21.3	-0.4	-0.3
13		Taiwan	78.1	-0.4	0.5	83		Ecuador	21.3	0.5	1.0
16	15	Denmark	76.7	1.4	3.3	82	83	Jordan	21.1	0.1	0.4
15	16	Spain	75.2	-0.7	-0.7	81	84†	Estonia	20.9	-0.5	-1.2
17	17	Sweden	74.4	-0.7	-1.4	85	85†	Panama	20.9	0.5	2.7
18	18	Italy	73.5	-1.5	-2.5	88	86	Senegal	20.1	0.1	2.4
20	19	Ireland	70.0	0.7	1.4	89	87	Latvia	20.0	0.5	-1.4
19	20	Finland	69.4	-0.2	-0.6	97	88†	Vietnam	19.5	2.1	2.6
21	21	South Korea	68.9	0.4	1.3	91	89†	Bulgaria	19.5	0.6	-0.4
22	22	Australia	68.1	0.3	1.2	94	90	Dominican Republic	19.2	0.7	2.1
23	23	Portugal	66.7	0.6	1.7	86	91	Nigeria	19.1	-1.2	-0.5
24	24	Hongkong	66.1	0.5	1.5	87	92†	Russia	19.0	-1.2	-4.6

(continued)

Table 13.8 (Continued)

Rank March 1993	Rank Sept. 1993	Country	Institutional Investor Credit Rating	Six-month Change	One-year Change		Rank March 1993	Rank Sept. 1993	Country	Institutional Investor Credit Rating	Six-month Change	One-year Change
25	25	Malaysia	64.8	0.9	1.9		91	93†	Lithuania	19.0	0.1	-1.7
26	26	New Zealand	64.7	0.9	2.5		96	94†	Bolivia	18.7	0.6	1.8
27	27	Thailand	60.8	0.8	-0.5		90	95†	Bangladesh	18.7	-0.6	1.6
29	28	United Arab Emirates	58.3	0.4	1.0		95	96	Ukraine	18.2	0.0	-2.9
28	29	Saudi Arabia	57.9	-0.1	0.6		93	97	Guatemala	18.1	-0.7	1.4
30	30	China	57.3	1.0	2.5		101	98	Kazakhstan	17.6	1.8	-1.1
31	31	Iceland	54.9	-0.2	1.6		—	99†	Burkina Faso	17.5	—	—
32	32	Qatar	52.9	0.7	1.2		98	100†	Belarus	17.5	0.1	-3.6
34	33	Bahrain	51.6	0.6	2.1		100	101	Malawi	17.3	1.0	1.9
36	34†	Chile	51.5	2.6	5.6		107	102	Lebanon	17.1	3.0	5.0
33	35†	Indonesia	51.5	0.4	1.0		—	103	Benin	16.9	—	—
35	36	Oman	50.7	-0.1	1.3		99	104	Côte d'Ivoire	16.2	-0.5	-0.3
37	37	Kuwait	49.2	0.4	1.9		103	105	Congo	15.8	0.6	1.8
38	38	Cyprus	48.8	0.0	1.8		102	106	Honduras	15.6	-0.1	1.9
39	39	Greece	48.6	0.7	1.9		104	107*	El Salvador	15.3	0.2	3.6
42	40	Czech Republic	46.6	2.0	—		—		Mali	15.3		
41	41	Mexico	45.6	0.4	3.0		108	109	Peru	15.0	1.1	1.8
40	42	Turkey	45.1	-0.2	1.2		105	110	Uzbekistan	14.4	-0.1	-2.1
43	43	Hungary	44.8	0.5	2.5		—	111*	Guinea	14.0	—	—
44	44	Botswana	44.7	3.6	9.4		110		Tanzania	14.0	1.1	2.2
51	45	Mauritius	41.0	2.6	5.3		106	113	Croatia	13.6	-0.6	-2.9
46	46	Israel	40.5	0.9	5.4		111	114	Myanmar	13.0	0.6	0.5
48	47	Colombia	40.4	1.6	3.2		109	115	Angola	12.6	-1.1	-1.4
47	48	Tunisia	40.3	1.5	3.5		112	116	Zambia	12.4	0.7	3.0

(continued)

Table 13.8 (Continued)

Rank March 1993	Rank Sept. 1993	Country	Institutional Investor Credit Rating	Six-month Change	One-year Change
49	49	India	38.4	-0.3	0.9
45	50	South Africa	38.2	-1.6	-1.6
50	51	Venezuela	37.6	-1.0	-1.5
52	52	Barbados	35.2	-0.7	-1.3
53	53	Uruguay	34.2	0.5	2.2
55	54	Morocco	33.4	1.2	3.4
58	55	Argentina	32.6	2.1	6.5
54	56	Papua New Guinea	32.4	-0.1	1.3
57	57	Slovakia	30.6	-0.4	—
59	58†	Trinidad & Tobago	29.4	-0.1	1.6
56	59†	Iran	29.4	-2.7	2.9
61	60	Libya	28.8	0.2	2.8
75	61†	Slovenia	28.6	6.1	8.3
69	62†	Poland	28.6	1.7	3.9
63	63	Gabon	28.2	0.2	1.8
68	64	Philippines	28.0	0.9	2.8
65	65	Brazil	27.8	0.1	0.7
60	66	Pakistan	27.7	-1.3	0.0
67	67	Egypt	27.5	0.4	0.7
64	68	Paraguay	27.2	-0.6	1.0

Country	Institutional Investor Credit Rating	Six-month Change	One-year Change	Rank March 1993	Rank Sept. 1993
Georgia	11.7	—	—	—	117
Albania	10.5	0.6	1.3	113	118
Afghanistan	10.3	—	—	—	119
Ethiopia	9.8	1.3	2.9	116	120
Mozambique	9.7	1.3	2.2	117	121
Nicaragua	8.7	0.4	0.8	118	122
Uganda	8.4	1.1	3.2	121	123
Yugoslavia	8.3	-1.7	-4.2	114	124
Haiti	8.0	0.8	1.5	122	125
Zaire	7.7	-1.1	-1.4	115	126†
Cuba	7.7	-0.6	-0.1	119	127†
Grenada	7.5	0.2	0.4	124	128
Iraq	7.2	-0.2	-0.4	120	129
Sierra Leone	6.6	-0.1	0.8	126	130
North Korea	6.3	-0.9	-1.3	123	131
Liberia	6.0	0.0	-0.1	127	132
Sudan	5.7	-1.3	0.4	125	133
Global average rating	36.1	-0.7	0.2		

*Actual tie
†Order determined by actual results before rounding.
Source: Institutional Investor, September 1993.

247

EXERCISES

1. Why must Eurobanks operate with narrower spreads than domestic banks? What would happen if the spreads were equal in both markets?
2. Use T accounts to explain the difference between the gross and net size of the Eurodollar market.
3. Why would a debtor nation prefer to borrow from a bank rather than the IMF, other things equal? Can "other things" ever be equal between commercial bank and IMF loans?
4. Pick three developing countries and create a country risk index for them. Rank them ordinally in terms of factors that you can observe (like exports, GNP growth, reserves, etc.) by looking at *International Financial Statistics* published by the IMF. Based on your evaluation, which country appears to be the best credit risk? How does your ranking compare to that found in the most recent *Institutional Investor* survey?
5. Why would the founding of IBFs hurt the Eurodollar business in the Caribbean?

REFERENCES

Clark, Jack, and Eliot Kalter, "Recent Innovations in Debt Restructuring" *Financial Development,* September 1992, 6–8.

Gutman, Peter, "Assessing Country Risk," *National Westminster Bank Quarterly Review,* May 1980, 58–68.

Hogan, W., and I. Pearce, *The Incredible Eurodollar.* London: Allen & Unwin, 1983.

Lipin, Steven, "Banks Escape the Latin Debt Crisis With Little Damage," the *Wall Street Journal,* July 10, 1992, B4.

Mills, Rodney, H., "Foreign Lending by Banks: A Guide to International and U.S. Statistics," *Federal Reserve Bulletin,* October 1986.

chapter *14*

Macroeconomic Policy in the Open Economy

An economy open to international trade and payments will face different problems than an economy closed to the rest of the world. The typical introductory economics presentation of macroeconomic equilibrium and policy is a closed-economy view. Discussions of economic adjustments required to combat unemployment or inflation do not consider the rest of the world. Clearly, this is no longer an acceptable approach in an increasingly integrated world.

In the open economy, we can summarize the desirable economic goals as being the attainment of internal and external balance. *Internal balance* means a steady growth of the domestic economy consistent with a low unemployment rate. *External balance* is the achievement of a desired trade balance or desired international capital flows. In principles of economics classes, the emphasis is on internal balance. By concentrating solely on internal goals like inflation, unemployment, and economic growth, simpler-model economies may be used for analysis. A consideration of the joint pursuit of internal and external balance calls for a more detailed view of the economy. The slight increase in complexity yields a big payoff in terms of a more realistic view of the problems facing the modern policymaker. It is no longer a question of changing policy to change unemployment or inflation at home. Now the

authorities must also consider the impact on the balance of trade, capital flows, and exchange rates.

INTERNAL AND EXTERNAL MACROECONOMIC EQUILIBRIUM

The major tools of macroeconomic policy are fiscal policy (government spending and taxation) and monetary policy (central bank control of the money supply). These tools are used to achieve macroeconomic equilibrium. We assume that macroeconomic equilibrium requires equilibrium in three major sectors of the economy:

> *Goods market equilibrium:* The quantity of goods and services supplied is equal to the quantity demanded. This is represented by the IS curve.
> *Money market equilibrium:* The quantity of money supplied is equal to the quantity demanded. This is represented by the LM curve.
> *Balance-of-payments equilibrium:* The current account deficit is equal to the capital account surplus so that the official settlements definition of the balance of payments equals zero. This is represented by the BP curve.

We will analyze the macroeconomic equilibrium with a graph that summarizes equilibrium in each market. Figure 14.1 displays the IS-LM-BP diagram. This graph illustrates various combinations of the domestic interest rate (i) and domestic national income (Y) that yield equilibrium in the three markets considered here.

THE IS CURVE

First, let's look at the *IS curve* representing combinations of i and Y that provide equilibrium in the goods market holding everything else (like the price level) constant. Equilibrium occurs when the output of goods and services is equal to the quantity of goods and services demanded. In principles of economics classes, macroeconomic equilibrium is said to exist when the "leakages equal the injections" of spending in the economy. More precisely, domestic saving (S), taxes (T), and imports (IM) represent income received that is not spent on domestic goods and services—the leakages

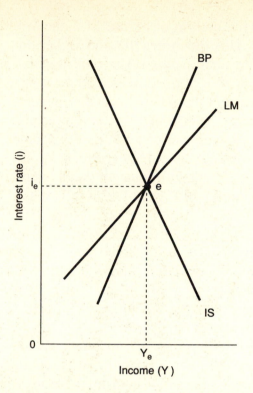

FIGURE 14.1 Equilibrium in the goods market (IS), in the money market (LM), and in the balance of payments (BP).

from spending. The offsetting injections of spending are represented by investment spending (I), government spending (G), and exports (X). Investment spending is the spending of business firms for new plants and equipment.

Equilibrium occurs when

$$S + T + IM = I + G + X \qquad (14.1)$$

When the leakages from spending equal the injections, then the value of income received from producing goods and services will be equal to total spending or the quantity of output demanded. The IS curve in Figure 14.1 depicts the various combinations of i and Y that yield the equality in Equation (14.1). We now consider why the IS curve is downward sloping.

We assume that S and IM are both functions of income and taxes are set by governments independent of income. The higher domestic income, the more domestic residents want to save and the

more they spend on imports. In the bottom of Figure 14.2, the $S + T + IM$ line is upward sloping. This illustrates that the higher domestic income rises, the greater saving plus taxes plus imports. Investment is assumed to be a function of the domestic interest rate and so does not change as current domestic income changes. Similarly, exports are assumed to be determined by foreign income (they are foreign imports) and so do not change as domestic income changes. Finally, government spending is set independent of income. Since I, G, and X are all independent of current domestic income, the $I + G + X$ line in the bottom of Figure 14.2 is drawn as a horizontal line.

Equation (14.1) indicated that equilibrium occurs at that income level where $S + T + IM = I + G + X$. In the bottom panel of Figure 14.2, point A represents an equilibrium point with an equilibrium level of income Y_A. In the upper panel of the figure, Y_A is shown to be consistent with point A on the IS curve. This point is also associated with a particular interest rate i_A.

To understand why the IS curve slopes downward, consider what happens as the interest rate varies. Suppose the interest rate falls. At the lower interest rate, more potential investment projects become profitable (firms will not require as high a return on investment as the cost of borrowed funds falls), so investment increases as illustrated in the move from $I + G + X$ to $I' + G + X$ in Figure 14.2. At this higher level of investment spending, equilibrium income increases to Y_B. Point B on the IS curve depicts this new goods market equilibrium, with a lower equilibrium interest rate i_B and higher equilibrium income Y_B.

Finally, consider what happens when the interest rate rises. Investment spending will fall, as fewer potential projects are profitable as the cost of borrowed funds rises. At the lower level of investment spending, the $I + G + X$ curve shifts down to $I'' + G + X$ in Figure 14.2. The new equilibrium point C is consistent with the level of income Y_C. In the IS diagram in the upper panel we see that point C is consistent with equilibrium income level Y_C and equilibrium interest rate i_C. The other points on the IS curve are consistent with alternative combinations of income and interest rate that yield equilibrium in the goods market.

We must remember that the IS curve is drawn holding the domestic price level constant. A change in the domestic price level will change the price of domestic goods relative to foreign. If the

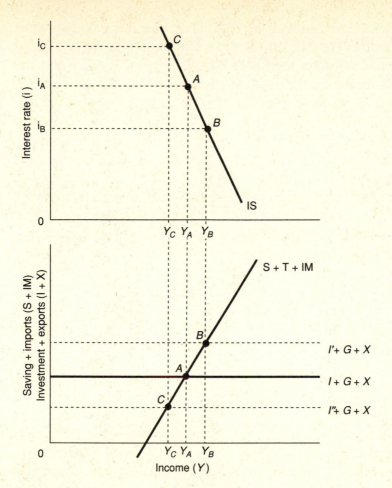

FIGURE 14.2 Derivation of the IS curve.

domestic price level falls with a given interest rate, then investment, government spending, taxes, and saving don't change but, since domestic goods are now cheaper relative to foreign, exports increase and imports fall. The rise in the $I + G + X$ curve and the fall in the $S + T + IM$ curve would both increase income. Because income increases with a constant interest rate, the IS curve shifts right. A rise in the domestic price level would cause the IS curve to shift left.

THE LM CURVE

The *LM curve* in Figure 14.1 displays the alternative combinations of i and Y at which the demand for money equals the supply. Figure

14.3 provides a derivation of the LM curve. The left panel shows a money demand curve labeled M^d and a money supply curve labeled M^s. The horizontal axis measures the quantity of money and the vertical axis measures the interest rate. Note that the M^s curve is vertical. This is because the central bank can choose any money supply it wants, independent of the interest rate. The actual value of the money supply chosen is M_0. The money demand curve slopes downward, indicating that the higher the interest rate, the lower the quantity of money demanded.

The inverse relationship between the interest rate and quantity of money demanded is a result of the role of interest as the opportunity cost of holding money. Since money earns no interest, the higher the interest rate, the more you must give up to hold money, so less money is held.

The initial money market equilibrium occurs at point A with interest rate i_A. The initial money demand curve (M^d) is drawn for a given level of income. If income increased, then the demand for money would increase, as seen in the shift from (M^d) to $M^{d'}$. Money

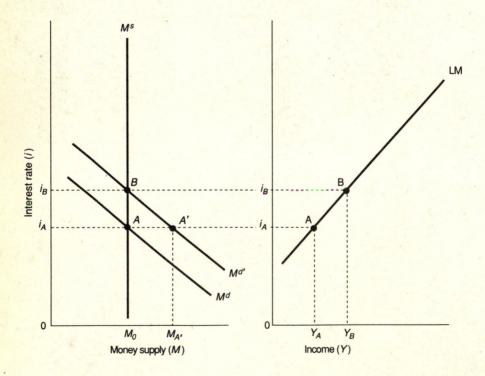

FIGURE 14.3 Derivation of the LM curve.

demand increases because, at the higher level of income, people want to hold more money to support the increased spending on transactions.

Now let's consider why the LM curve has a positive slope. Suppose initially there is equilibrium at point A with the interest rate at i_A and income at Y_A in Figure 14.3. If income increases from Y_A to Y_B, money demand increases from M^d to $M^{d'}$. If the interest rate remains at i_A, there will be an excess demand for money. This is shown in the left panel of Figure 14.3, as the quantity of money demanded is now $M_{A'}$. With the higher income, money demand is given by $M^{d'}$. At i_A, point A' on the money demand curve is consistent with the higher quantity of money demanded $M_{A'}$. Since the money supply remains constant at M_0, there will be an excess demand for money given by $M_{A'} - M_0$. The attempt to increase money balances above the quantity of money outstanding will cause the interest rate to rise until a new equilibrium is established at point B. This new equilibrium is consistent with a higher interest rate i_B and a higher income Y_B. Points A and B are both indicated on the LM curve in the right panel of Figure 14.3. The rest of the LM curve reflects similar combinations of equilibrium interest rates and income.

The LM curve is drawn for a specific money supply. If the supply of money increases, then money demand will have to increase to restore equilibrium. This requires a higher Y or lower i, or both, so the LM curve will shift right. Similarly, a decrease in the money supply will tend to raise i and lower Y, and the LM curve will shift to the left.

THE BP CURVE

The final curve portrayed in Figure 14.1 is the BP curve. The *BP curve* gives the combinations of i and Y that yield balance-of-payments equilibrium. The BP curve is drawn for a given domestic price level, a given exchange rate, and a given net foreign debt. Equilibrium occurs when the current account surplus is equal to the capital account deficit. Figure 14.4 illustrates the derivation of the BP curve. The lower panel of the figure shows a CS line representing the current account surplus and a CD line representing the capital account deficit. Realistically, the current account surplus may be negative, which would indicate a deficit. Similarly, the capital account deficit may be negative, indicating a surplus. The CS line is

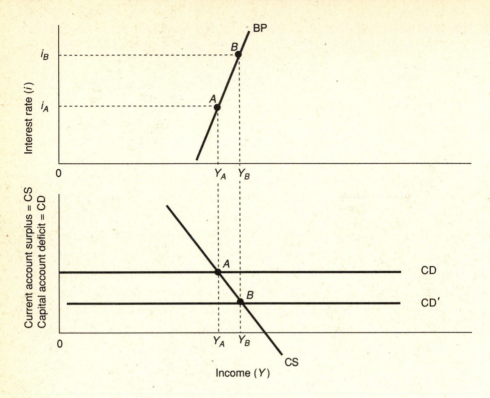

FIGURE 14.4 Derivation of the BP curve.

downward sloping because, as income increases, domestic imports increase and the current account surplus falls. The capital account is assumed to be a function of the interest rate and is, therefore, independent of income and a horizontal line. Equilibrium occurs when the current account surplus equals the capital account deficit, so that the official settlements balance of payments is zero. Initially, equilibrium occurs at point A with income level Y_A and interest rate i_A. If the interest rate increases, then domestic financial assets are more attractive to foreign buyers and the capital account deficit falls to CD'. At the old income level Y_A, the current account surplus will exceed the capital account deficit, and income must increase to Y_B to provide a new equilibrium at point B. Points A and B on the BP curve in Figure 14.4 illustrate that, as i increases, Y must also increase to maintain equilibrium. Only an upward-sloping BP curve will provide combinations of i and Y consistent with equilibrium.

EQUILIBRIUM

Equilibrium for the economy requires that all three markets—the goods market, the money market, and the balance of payments—be in equilibrium. This occurs when the IS, LM, and BP curves intersect at a common equilibrium level of the interest rate and income. In Figure 14.1, point e is the equilibrium point that occurs at the equilibrium interest rate i_e and the equilibrium income level Y_e. Until some change occurs that shifts one of the curves, the IS-LM-BP equilibrium will be consistent with all goods produced being sold, money demand equal to money supply, and a current account surplus equal to a capital account deficit that yields a zero balance on the official settlements account.

MONETARY POLICY UNDER FIXED EXCHANGE RATES

In deriving the BP curve, we assumed that higher interest rates in the domestic economy would attract foreign investors and decrease the capital account deficit. With fixed exchange rates, the domestic central bank is not free to conduct monetary policy independent of the rest of the world. In the discussion of sterilization in Chapter 10, it was argued that, in the short run, the central bank could exercise some control over the money supply if domestic and foreign financial assets were imperfect substitutes. If assets are perfect substitutes, then they must yield the same return to investors. With fixed exchange rates, this means that the domestic interest rate will equal the foreign interest rate. If capital is perfectly mobile, then any deviation of the domestic interest rate from the foreign rate would cause investors to attempt to hold only the high return assets. Clearly, in this case there is no room for central banks to conduct an independent monetary policy under fixed exchange rates.

Figure 14.5 illustrates this situation. With perfect asset substitutability, the BP curve is a horizontal line at the domestic interest rate i, which equals the foreign interest rate i_F. Any rate higher than i_F results in large (infinite) capital inflows, while any lower rate yields large capital outflows. Only at i_F is the balance-of-payments equilibrium obtained.

Suppose the central bank increases the money supply so that the LM curve shifts from LM to LM'. The IS-LM equilibrium is now shifted from e to e'. While e' results in equilibrium in the

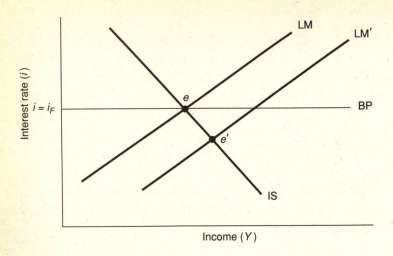

FIGURE 14.5 Monetary expansion with fixed exchange rates.

money and goods market, there will be a large capital outflow and large official settlements balance deficit. This will pressure the domestic currency to depreciate on the foreign exchange market. To maintain the fixed exchange rate, the central bank must intervene and sell foreign exchange to buy domestic currency. The foreign exchange market intervention will decrease the domestic money supply and shift the LM curve back to LM to restore the initial equilibrium at e. With perfect capital mobility, this would all happen instantaneously, so that no movement away from point e is ever observed. Any attempt to lower the money supply and shift the LM curve left would have just the reverse effect on the interest rate and intervention activity.

With less than perfect capital mobility, the central bank has some opportunity to vary the money supply. Still, the maintenance of the fixed exchange rate will require an ultimate reversal of policy in the face of a constant foreign interest rate. The process is essentially just drawn out over time rather than occurring instantly.

FISCAL POLICY UNDER FIXED EXCHANGE RATES

A change in government spending or taxes will shift the IS curve. Suppose an expansionary fiscal policy is desired. Figure 14.6 illustrates the effects. With fixed exchange rates, perfect asset substitutability, and perfect capital mobility, the BP curve is a horizontal line at $i = i_F$. An increase in government spending shifts the IS

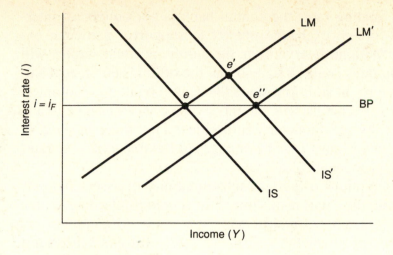

FIGURE 14.6 Fiscal expansion with fixed exchange rates.

curve right to IS'. The domestic equilibrium shifts from point e to e', which would mean a higher interest rate and higher income. Since point e' is above the BP curve, the official settlements balance of payments moves to a surplus because of a reduced capital account deficit associated with the higher domestic interest rate. To stop the domestic currency from appreciating, the central bank must increase the money supply and buy foreign exchange with domestic money. The increase in the money supply shifts the LM curve right. When the money supply has increased enough to move the LM curve to LM' in Figure 14.6, equilibrium is restored at point e''. Point e'' has the interest rate back at $i = i_F$, and yet income has increased.

This result is a significant difference from the monetary policy expansion considered in the last section. With fixed exchange rates and perfect capital mobility, monetary policy was seen to be ineffective in changing the level of income. This was because there was no room for independent monetary policy with a fixed exchange rate. In contrast, fiscal policy will have an effect on income and can be used to stimulate the domestic economy.

MONETARY POLICY UNDER FLOATING EXCHANGE RATES

We now consider a world of flexible exchange rates and perfect capital mobility. The notable difference between the analysis of this section and the fixed exchange rate stories of the last two sections

is that with floating rates the central bank is not obliged to intervene in the foreign exchange market to support a particular exchange rate. With no intervention, the current account surplus will equal the capital account deficit so that the official settlements balance equals zero. In addition, since the central bank does not intervene to fix the exchange rate, the money supply can change to any level desired by the monetary authorities. This independence of monetary policy is one of the advantages of flexible exchange rates according to proponents of a float.

The assumptions of perfect substitutability of assets and perfect capital mobility will result in $i = i_F$ as before. Once again, the BP curve will be a horizontal line at $i = i_F$. Only now, equilibrium in the balance of payments will mean a zero official settlements balance.

Changes in the exchange rate will cause shifts in the IS curve. With fixed domestic and foreign goods prices, depreciation of the domestic currency will make domestic goods relatively cheaper and will stimulate domestic exports. Since net exports are part of total spending, the IS curve will shift right. A domestic currency appreciation will decrease domestic net exports and cause the IS curve to shift left.

Figure 14.7 illustrates the effects of an expansionary monetary policy. The increase in the money supply shifts the LM curve to the right to LM′. The interest rate and income existing at point e' would yield equilibrium in the money and goods markets, but would

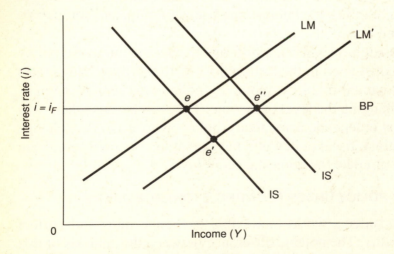

FIGURE 14.7 Monetary expansion with floating exchange rates.

cause a larger capital account deficit (and official settlements deficit) since the domestic interest rate would be less than i_F. Since this is a flexible exchange rate system, the official settlements deficit is avoided by the adjustment of the exchange rate to a level that restores equilibrium. Specifically, the pressure of the official settlements deficit will cause the domestic currency to depreciate. This depreciation is associated with a rightward shift of the IS curve as domestic exports increase. When the IS curve shifts to IS', the new equilibrium is obtained at e''. At e'', income has increased and the domestic interest rate equals the foreign rate.

Had there been a monetary contraction instead of an expansion, the story would have been reversed. A temporarily higher interest rate would decrease the capital account deficit, causing pressure for the domestic currency to appreciate. As domestic net exports are decreased, the IS curve would shift left until a new equilibrium is established at a lower level of income and the original $i = i_F$ is restored.

In contrast to the fixed exchange rate world, monetary policy can change the level of income with floating exchange rates. Since the exchange rate adjusts to yield balance-of-payments equilibrium, the central bank can choose its monetary policy independent of other countries' policies. This world of flexible exchange rates and perfect capital mobility is often called the *Mundell-Fleming model* of the open economy. (Robert Mundell and Marcus Fleming were two early researchers who developed models along the lines of those presented here.)

FISCAL POLICY UNDER FLOATING EXCHANGE RATES

An expansionary fiscal policy caused by a tax cut or increased government spending will shift the IS curve to the right. Earlier it was shown that with fixed exchange rates, such a policy would result in a higher domestic income level. With flexible exchange rates we will see that the story is much different.

In Figure 14.8, the expansionary fiscal policy shifts the IS curve right, from IS to IS'. This shift would result in an intermediate equilibrium at point e'. At e', the goods market and money market will be in equilibrium, but there will be an official settlements surplus because of the lower capital account deficit induced by the higher interest rate at e'. Since the exchange rate is free to adjust to

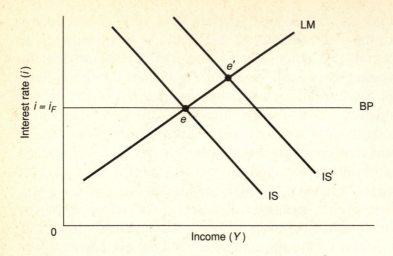

FIGURE 14.8 Fiscal expansion with floating exchange rates.

eliminate the balance-of-payments surplus, the intersection of the IS and LM curves cannot remain above the BP curve.

The official settlements surplus causes the domestic currency to appreciate. This appreciation will reduce domestic exports and increase imports. As net exports fall, the IS curve shifts left. When the IS curve has returned to the initial equilibrium position that passes through point *e*, equilibrium is restored in all markets. Note that the final equilibrium occurs at the initial level of *i* and *Y*. With floating exchange rates, fiscal policy is ineffective in shifting the level of income. When an expansionary fiscal policy has no effect on income, complete *crowding out* has occurred. This crowding out occurs because the currency appreciation induced by the expansionary fiscal policy reduces net exports to a level that just offsets the fiscal policy effects on income.

INTERNATIONAL POLICY COORDINATION

This chapter has so far demonstrated the effects of fiscal and monetary policy under fixed and floating exchange rates. From the early 1970s on, the major developed nations have generally operated with floating exchange rates. In this framework, fiscal and monetary policy can generate large swings in exchange rates. The high degree of capital mobility existing among the developed countries suggests that fiscal actions that lead to a divergence of the domestic

interest rate from the given foreign interest rate will quickly be un-done by the influence of exchange rate changes on net exports, as was illustrated in Figure 14.8. Many economists argue that the sharp reduction in U.S. net exports in the mid-1980s was due to the expansionary fiscal policy followed by the U.S. government.

How could such a reduction in net exports be minimized? If all nations coordinated their domestic policies and simultaneously stimulated their economies, the world interest rate would rise and the pressure for exchange rate change and net export adjustment would fall. The problem illustrated in Figure 14.8 was that of a single country attempting to follow an expansionary policy while the rest of the world retained unchanged policies so that i_F remains constant. If i_F increased at the same time that i increased, the BP curve would shift upward so that balance-of-payments equilibrium would be consistent with a higher interest rate.

Similarly, changes in exchange rates and net exports induced by monetary policy can be lessened if central banks coordinate policy so that i_F shifts with i. There have been instances of coordinated foreign exchange market intervention when a group of central banks jointly followed policies aimed at a depreciation or appreciation of the dollar. These coordinated interventions, intended to achieve a target value of the dollar, also work to bring domestic monetary policies more in line with each other. If the United States has been following an expansionary monetary policy relative to Japan and Germany, U.S. interest rates may fall relative to the other countries' rates so that a larger capital account deficit is induced and pressure for a dollar depreciation results. If the central banks decide to work together to stop the dollar depreciation, the Japanese and Germans will buy dollars on the foreign exchange market with their domestic currencies, while the Federal Reserve must sell foreign exchange to buy dollars. This will result in higher money supplies in Japan and Germany and a lower money supply in the United States. The coordinated intervention works toward a convergence of monetary policy in each country.

The basic argument in favor of international policy coordination is that such coordination would stabilize exchange rates. Whether exchange rate stability offers any substantial benefits over freely floating rates with independent policies is a matter of much debate. Some experts argue that coordinated monetary policy to achieve fixed exchange rates or to reduce exchange rate fluctua-

tions to within narrow "target zones" would reduce the destabilizing aspects of international trade in goods and financial assets when currencies become "overvalued" or "undervalued." This view emphasizes that, in an increasingly integrated world economy, it seems desirable to conduct national economic policy in an international context rather than simply focusing on domestic policy goals without a view of the international implications.

An alternative view is that most changes in exchange rates result from real economic shocks and should be considered permanent changes. In this view, there is no such thing as an overvalued or undervalued currency because exchange rates always are in equilibrium given current economic conditions. Furthermore, governments cannot change the real relative prices of goods internationally by driving the nominal exchange rate to some particular level through foreign exchange market intervention, because price levels will adjust to the new nominal exchange rate. This view, then, argues that government policy is best aimed at lowering inflation and achieving governmental goals that contribute to a stable domestic economy.

The debate over the appropriate level and form of international policy coordination has been one of the livelier areas of international finance in recent years. Many leading economists have participated, but a problem at the practical level is that different governments emphasize different goals and may view the current economic situation differently. Ours is a more complex world in which to formulate international policy agreements than is typically viewed in scholarly debate, where it is presumed that governments agree on the current problems and on the impact of alternative policies on those problems. Nevertheless, the research of international financial scholars offers much promise in contributing toward a greater understanding of the real-world complexities government officials must address.

SUMMARY

1. Internal balance is a domestic rate of growth consistent with a low unemployment rate.
2. External balance is a desired level of trade or capital flows.
3. Macroeconomic equilibrium requires equilibrium in the goods market, money market, and balance of payments.

4. The IS curve presents combinations of i and Y that yield goods market equilibrium.

5. The LM curve presents combinations of i and Y that yield money market equilibrium.

6. The BP curve presents combinations of i and Y that yield balance-of-payments equilibrium.

7. With perfect asset substitutability and perfect capital mobility, the domestic interest rate is equal to the foreign interest rate.

8. With fixed exchange rates, a country cannot conduct an independent monetary policy to shift domestic income.

9. Fiscal policy is effective in changing domestic income with fixed exchange rates.

10. With floating exchange rates, monetary policy is effective in changing domestic income.

11. With floating exchange rates, fiscal policy changes tend to be offset by the balance of payments, so that crowding out occurs and income is unaffected.

12. International policy coordination is viewed as a way to stabilize exchange rates.

EXERCISES

1. How would the pursuit of internal balance be different in a closed economy, where there is no concern over external balance, than in an open economy?

2. Derive the IS, LM, and BP curves. Carefully label and explain each diagram you use.

3. If a nation has a surplus balance of payments, what is the appropriate government policy to induce balance-of-payments equilibrium? What effects might this have on income and employment?

4. Why will central banks have to formulate monetary policy differently under fixed exchange rates than under floating exchange rates?

5. Draw an initial IS-LM-BP equilibrium. Now put four additional points on the graph: one is directly above equilibrium, one is to the right of the equilibrium, one is directly below the equilibrium, and one is directly to the left of the equilibrium. Label these points A, B, C, and D. For each point, explain the nature of the disequilibrium that would exist if income and the interest rate were at levels consistent with each point rather than their equilibrium levels.

6. Why would macroeconomic policy coordination help stabilize exchange rates?

REFERENCES

Bryant, Ralph, Dale Henderson, Gerald Haltham, Peter Hooper, and Steven Symansky, eds., *Empirical Macroeconomics for Interdependent Economies.* Washington, D.C.: Brookings Institution, 1987.

Dornbusch, Rudiger, *Open Economy Macroeconomics.* New York: Basic Books, 1980.

Fleming, Marcus, "Domestic Financial Policies Under Fixed and Under Floating Exchange Rates," *IMF Staff Papers,* November 1962.

Frankel, Jeffrey A., and Katharine E. Rockett, "International Macroeconomic Policy Coordination When Policy-Makers Disagree on the Model," *American Economic Review,* June 1988.

Frenkel, Jacob A., and Michael L. Mussa, "Asset Markets, Exchange Rates, and the Balance of Payments," in Ronald W. Jones and Peter B. Kenen, eds., *Handbook of International Economics,* vol. 1. Amsterdam: North-Holland, 1985.

Ghosh, Atish, "International Policy Coordination in an Uncertain World," *Economics Letters,* 3, 1986.

McKinnon, Ronald I., *An International Standard for Monetary Stabilization.* Washington, D.C.: Institute for International Economics, 1984.

Mundell, Robert A., "Capital Mobility and Stabilization Policy Under Fixed and Flexible Exchange Rates," *Canadian Journal of Economics,* November 1963.

Stockman, Alan C., "The Equilibrium Approach to Exchange Rates," *Federal Reserve Bank of Richmond Economic Review,* April 1987.

Glossary

absorption approach to the balance of trade A theory based on domestic spending for domestic goods (absorption) relative to domestic output.

adjustable peg A system of fixed exchange rates with periodic devaluations allowed when conditions warrant.

adjustment mechanism The method by which the international economy reacts to remove a disequilibrium.

airbill A bill of lading for goods shipped by air.

American depositary receipts (ADRs) Negotiable instruments certifying shares of a foreign stock held by a foreign custodian.

arbitrage Buying in a market where the price is low and then selling in a market with a higher price.

arm's-length pricing Prices that an unrelated buyer and seller would willingly pay.

autocorrelation The errors from a regression equation are related over time.

balance of payments A balance sheet recording a nation's international transactions.

balance of trade Merchandise exports minus merchandise imports.

bank notes Actual paper currency.

bankers' acceptance A time draft drawn on and accepted by a particular bank, to be paid at maturity.

base money Currency plus commercial bank reserves held against deposits.

basic balance The sum of the balances on merchandise, services, unilateral transfers, and long-term capital accounts.

basis point One-hundredth of a percent, or 0.0001.

basket pegger A country that maintains a fixed exchange rate with a composite or weighted average of foreign currencies rather than a single foreign currency.

beta A measure of the portfolio risk associated with an individual asset.

bill of lading Agreement issued by a shipping company to carry goods to a destination port.

bimetallism Two metals, like gold and silver, serving as backing for the money supply.

black market An illegal market in foreign exchange.

broker An intermediary in the foreign exchange market.

call option The right to buy currency on or before a future date.

capital account That part of a balance of payments recording trade in financial assets.

capital budgeting Evaluating prospective investment alternatives in order to fund preferred projects.

capital controls Restrictions on international capital flows like taxes or quotas.

central bank The official bank of a government, like the Federal Reserve in the United States.

closed economy An economy with little or no economic activity involving the rest of the world.

comparative advantage A determinant of the pattern of world trade in terms of which country exports which goods.

compensating balances Bank deposits that must be held as a form of compensation to the bank.

country risk analysis An evaluation of the potential for default or rescheduling on loans made to a particular country.

covariance A measure of the degree to which two variables move together.

covered interest arbitrage Buying or selling assets internationally and using the forward market to eliminate exchange risk, in order to take advantage of return differentials.

crawling peg A system in which the exchange rate is held fixed in the short run but is adjusted at regular intervals to reflect supply and demand pressures.

cross rate The implied third exchange rate, given two exchange rates involving three currencies.

currency contract period The period immediately following a devaluation when contracts negotiated prior to the devaluation come due.

currency union A region within which exchange rates are fixed.

current account The sum of the balances on merchandise, services, and unilateral transfers accounts.

debt-equity swaps An exchange of debt for the debtor's domestic currency, which is then used to buy equity positions in the debtor country.

deep market A market with a large number of buyers and sellers and assets traded, so that trading occurs at all times.

depreciation A decrease in a currency's value.

destabilizing speculation Speculation causing exchange rates to fluctuate more than they would in the absence of such speculation.

direct foreign investment Expenditures related to the establishment of foreign operating units.

discount The forward pricing of a currency at less than the spot price.

dock receipt A document issued by a shipping company listing the quantity and quality of the goods delivered to the dock.

domestic credit The domestic component of base money.

durable goods Goods with useful lives of more than 1 year.

economic exposure The exposure of the value of the firm to changes in exchange rates.

effective return The foreign interest rate of a foreign investment plus the forward premium or discount.

efficient market A market in which prices reflect all available information.

elasticities approach to the balance of trade An analysis that addresses the conditions necessary for a devaluation to improve the trade balance.

elasticity The responsiveness of quantity to changes in price.

endogenous Determined by other factors in a model.

equation of exchange An equation stating that the money supply times the velocity of money is equal to the price level times the quantity of transactions.

Eurobank A bank that accepts deposits and makes loans in foreign currencies.

Eurobond market The market engaging in direct offshore borrowing and lending through the sale of bonds denominated in one currency yet sold in many countries.

Eurocurrency market The offshore banking market where commercial banks accept deposits and make loans in foreign currencies.

European Monetary System (EMS) A monetary union within which exchange rates are fixed, since the countries involved float jointly against the rest of the world.

exchange rate The price of one nation's currency in terms of another nation's currency.

exchange rate index A measure of the average value of a currency.

exchange risk The risk arising from uncertainty regarding future exchange rates.

exogenous Determined by factors given to a model, independent of other variables in the model.

external balance A desired trade balance or desired international capital flows.

factors Firms that buy accounts receivable and assume responsibility for collection.

Fisher effect The expected effect of inflation on the nominal interest rate.

Fisher equation An equation stating that the nominal interest rate is equal to the real rate plus expected inflation.

foreign exchange Bank deposits and currency denominated in foreign monetary units.

foreign exchange market A market mostly comprising large commercial banks buying and selling foreign exchange from and to each other.

forward discount A forward rate at less than the spot rate.

forward exchange rate The price of a currency to be delivered sometime in the future.

forward premium A forward rate in excess of the spot rate.

futures Contracts to buy and sell currency for future delivery that are traded on organized exchanges.

gold exchange standard A standard whereby a currency is valued in terms of a gold equivalent and every other currency is to maintain fixed exchange rates against that currency.

Gresham's law A law stating that cheap money drives out good money.

hedging Taking a position to reduce risk.

IBFs International banking facilities—units of banks located in the United States that conduct Eurocurrency business.

IMF conditionality Economic adjustments imposed on a country by the IMF (International Monetary Fund) before loans will be made.

inflation-adjusted exchange rate The exchange rate minus the inflation differential between two countries.

interest rate parity The equivalence of the interest differential between two currencies to the forward premium or discount.

internal balance Domestic economic growth consistent with a low unemployment rate.

International Monetary Fund (IMF) An international organization that provides loans to countries experiencing balance-of-payments problems.

international reserves The international component of base money, primarily foreign exchange.

intervention The buying and selling of currencies by central banks to affect the exchange rate.

J-curve effect Following a devaluation, an initial decrease in the trade balance followed by an increase.

law of one price A law stating that all goods sell for the same price worldwide when converted to a common currency.

letter of credit A letter issued by a bank that obligates the bank to pay a specific amount of money to an exporter.

LIBOR London interbank offer rate—the interest rate on interbank deposits among the large London banks.

liquidity balance A measure of the change in liquid international assets and liabilities in the balance of payments.

long position Buying a currency to be delivered in the future.

managed float The floating of exchange rates with central bank intervention.

margin Money deposited with a broker to finance futures trading.

marginal propensity to import The change in imports given a change in income.

Marshall-Lerner condition The necessary international demand elasticities that will ensure an improvement in the trade balance following a devaluation.

monetary approach to the balance of payments and exchange rates (MABP, MAER) An analysis emphasizing money demand and money supply as determinants of the balance of payments under fixed exchange rates and of the exchange rate under floating rates.

money multiplier The ratio of the money supply to base money.

multinational firm A business firm operating in more than one country.

Mundell-Fleming model A model of an economy with flexible exchange rates and perfect capital mobility.

netting Consolidating payables and receivables in a currency so that only the difference must be bought or sold.

nominal interest rate The interest rate actually observed in the market.

nonsystematic risk Risk unique to an individual asset, which can be diversified away.

official settlements balance The balance-of-payments account measuring the change in short-term capital held by foreign monetary authorities and official reserve asset transactions.

offshore banking Accepting deposits and making loans in foreign currency—the Eurocurrency market.

open economy An economy actively involved in international trade.

opportunity cost The next-best alternative when undertaking some activity.

optimum currency area The best area within which exchange rates are fixed and between which exchange rates are flexible.

options Contracts that give the right to buy or sell a certain amount of currency on or before a future date.

parallel market A legal free foreign exchange market that exists as an alternative to a regulated official market.

Paris Club An arrangement whereby creditor governments meet with debtor nations in Paris to restructure debts.

pass-through The effects of a devaluation on prices—the devaluing country has its import prices rise while export prices fall to foreign buyers.

percent per annum The percentage return on a 12-month basis.

perfect capital mobility The free flow of capital between nations because there are no significant transactions costs or capital controls.

petrodollars Dollars earned by the export of oil, generally the earnings of the Organization of Petroleum Exporting Countries (OPEC).

portfolio-balance approach A theory of exchange rate determination including relative bond supplies and demands.

premium The forward pricing of a currency at more than the spot price.

present value The value today of some amount to be received in the future.

pricing to market Adjusting domestic currency prices in response to exchange rate changes in order to maintain market share.

purchasing power parity *Absolute:* the equivalence of the exchange rate to the ratio of the foreign and domestic price levels. *Relative:* the equivalence of the percentage change in the exchange rate to the inflation differential between two nations.

put option The right to sell currency on or before a future date.

real exchange rate The nominal exchange rate for two currencies divided by the ratio of their price levels.

real interest rate The nominal interest rate minus the rate of inflation.

regression analysis A statistical technique for estimating the relationship between a dependent variable and one or more independent variables.

relative price The price of one good relative to the price of another good.

risk aversion The degree to which people wish to avoid risk.

risk premium The difference between the forward exchange rate and the expected future spot rate.

seigniorage The difference between the cost of issuing money and the real resources acquired by the money issuer.

short position Selling a currency forward for future delivery.

Smithsonian agreement A December 1971 proclamation that the dollar was officially devalued and that currencies would now be allowed to fluctuate within ±2.25 percent of the new parity values.

special drawing right (SDR) An international reserve asset created by the IMF.

spot exchange rate The price of a currency for current delivery.

spot market Buying and selling currency for immediate delivery.

spread The difference between the buying and selling price of a currency or the differential between the interest rate on loans and deposits.

stable-valued money A currency with a stable and low inflation rate.

statistical significance A concept that allows one to relate estimated values to a hypothesized true value.

sterilization The offsetting of international reserve flows with domestic credit.

striking price The price at which currency may be bought or sold in an option contract.

swap The trade of one currency for another currency to combine a spot and forward transaction (or two forwards) in one deal.

systematic risk The risk common to all assets.

term structure of interest rates The return on an asset over different maturity dates.

thin market A market with a small number of buyers and sellers and assets traded.

tiered exchange rates Different exchange rates applied to different classes of transactions.

transaction costs The costs associated with buying and selling activity.

transaction exposure The foreign exchange risk associated with a particular transaction to be completed sometime in the future.

transfer price The price charged to a subsidiary for internal goods transfers.

translation The conversion of monetary values from one currency to another.

translation exposure The difference between a firm's foreign-currency-denominated assets and its foreign-currency-denominated liabilities.

unbiased The property of being correct on average.

variance A measure of how a variable changes in value about its mean.

Index